FRANS GREENWOOD

F. G. A. M. Smit

•

FRANS GREENWOOD

1680 - 1763

Dutch Poet & Glass Engraver

•

PRODROMUS

•

PUBLISHED PRIVATELY

by

F. G. A. M. Smit

PETERBOROUGH PE3 6PQ

ENGLAND

1988

Printed in England

by

WHITE CRESCENT PRESS Ltd

Luton

C O N T E N T S

I
B I O G R A P H Y

*   *   *

*   *   *

*   *   *

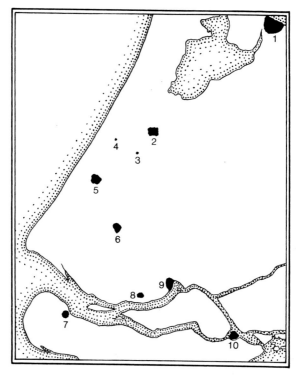

Fig. 1. The main Greenwood-associated localities in Holland (based on a map of ca. 1700). 1 Amsterdam, 2 Leiden, 3 Voorschoten, 4 Wassenaar, 5 's-Gravenhage (Den Haag), 6 Delft, 7 Brielle, 8 Schiedam, 9 Rotterdam, 10 Dordrecht.

* * *

n o t a   b e n e

Five of the 'dramatis personae' have a like-sounding name:

Frans (François) Greenwood	- the main character
Frans (François) Greenwood	- his cousin
Francis Greenwood	- his nephew
Francis (François) Greenewood	- his father
Ffransis Greenewood	- an old namesake

* * *

Numbers in square brackets occurring in the text are those of titles in the list of Literature References (pp. 100 - 107); numbers preceded by "A" relate to Archival References (pp. 108 - 110).

INTRODUCTION

F r a n s   G r e e n w o o d
- nationally once well known as a writer of Dutch poetry
- internationally still renowned as an engraver of glass

Yet, not only is the history of his life and that of his family and relatives virtually unknown but Greenwood's role as poet has never been properly evaluated. Moreover, nearly sixty years have elapsed since Wilfred Buckley published a modest treatise on the glass engravings by Frans Greenwood known at the time.

This dearth of information induced me ten years ago to try and discover - within severe limitations imposed by purse, time and distance - as many facts as possible with the intention of making them readily available in a straightforward manner. This is therefore merely meant to be a prodromal data-book in plain prose rather than a flowery story-book for the coffee-table - it is a chronicle which presents in an unpretentious and cost-effective way the results of my research (never quite finished) concerning Greenwood's life and works.

Whereas many peripheral particulars published here may not directly relate to Frans Greenwood himself, they assist in providing an insight in his entourage and the kind of world he lived in. A diversity of facts, figures and names should at this stage be preferable to a more or less strict selection. Seemingly irrelevant data may yet turn out to be pertinent ones.

Although born and bred in The Netherlands, I am not a neerlandicus and therefore could not assess the quality of Greenwood's poetical output; instead, I merely present some general information. It seems to me, though, that his versification is on the whole absolutely typical of the style and sentiment of good contemporary Dutch poetry. Greenwood's writings being entirely in Dutch, his poetry can only be savoured and appreciated nationally.

I am not quite unfamiliar with glass engraving and I trust that the particulars offered in the third part of this book will constitute a reasonably sound foundation for further studies. In the international domain of glass Frans Greenwood is highly esteemed and valued as he was the first to apply in a truly masterly fashion the technique and art of stipple engraving on glass.

Anyone wishing to proceed with elucidating life and works of Frans Greenwood must be able to read and understand Dutch perfectly well and be conversant with Dutch palaeography of the 17th and 18th centuries because without those indispensable facilities the archivalia will remain closed books. I believe, however, that I have examined Dutch archival documents to a reasonable extent although by no means completely. Archives in Yorkshire have not been searched for ancestorial particulars.

May this preliminary communication stimulate additional facts as well as concealed engraved goblets to emerge which, in turn, might eventually lead to the production of a book which would do Frans Greenwood really proud.

Frans Smit

Peterborough, U. K.

7 June 1988

A C K N O W L E D G M E N T S

Having located potential depositories of materials for the study of a chosen subject, a researcher is subsequently usually entirely dependent on the courteous open-sesame services of custodial depositaries. Virtually all biographical data offered in this publication were dormant in archival documents and I am therefore particularly grateful to the harassed archivists who with unfailing readiness made hundreds of mostly very bulky archive-volumes available to me. Numerous intensely happy hours were thus spent in the reading-rooms of Municipal Archives (Gemeente Archieven) of Rotterdam, Dordrecht, Leiden, 's-Gravenhage, Delft, Amsterdam and Schiedam as well as in the State Archives (Algemeen Rijksarchief), 's-Gravenhage. I also recall with pleasure and gratitude the highly enjoyable perusal of numerous literary sources handed to me over the years by staff of libraries of the Victoria and Albert Museum, London; British Library, London; Koninklijke Bibliotheek, 's-Gravenhage; Rijksbureau voor Kunsthistorische Documentatie, 's-Gravenhage; Rijksmuseum, Amsterdam; Museum Boymans - van Beuningen, Rotterdam; Rijks-Universiteit, Leiden.

As far as glass engravings are concerned, I am greatly indebted to certain private collectors and dealers as well as to staff of the Rijksmuseum, Amsterdam; Museum Boymans - van Beuningen, Rotterdam; Gemeentemuseum, 's-Gravenhage; Historisch Museum, Rotterdam; Gemeentemuseum, Arnhem; Museum Mr Simon van Gijn, Dordrecht; Victoria and Albert Museum, London; British Museum, London; Fitzwilliam Museum, Cambridge; Kunstgewerbemuseum, West Berlin; Museum für Kunst und Gewerbe, Hamburg; The Art Institute, Chicago. In this connection I would like to express my gratitude to Mr A. C. R. Dreesmann, Prof. F.-A. Dreier, Prof. H. E. Henkes, Miss M.-A. Heukensfeldt Jansen, Mr M. Hudig, Dr B. Jansen, Mr F. Laméris, Miss C. Polydoris, Mr P. C. Ritsema van Eck, Mr G. H. Tait, Mr C. Thiels, Miss M. A. J. Thunder, Mr J. Vecht, the late Mr J. Vriesendorp van Renesse and Jhr H. van de Wall Repelaer.

Mr A. F. Schepel kindly provided several baptismal data.

My sister Mrs Ann Wijs generously extended unstinted hospitality to me in The Netherlands - truly, a conditio sine qua non !

Finally, I owe Miss Rachel Russell (Christie's, London) sincere thanks for her continuous interest and encouragement.

* * *

Y O R K S H I R E   A N C E S T R Y

'Greenwood' is an old English name for a deciduous wood when in leaf. For many centuries much of England was covered with such 'grene wodes', 'greene woods' - green woods. They were environmentally ideally suited for outlaw life as is still evident from the expression "to go to the greenwood" (as Robin Hood did), meaning 'to become an outlaw'. Perhaps because wooded areas were such a common feature in the landscape, only one small populated place ever became known as Greenwood (or Greenwood-Lee) - a hamlet once situated 3 KM northwest of Hebden Bridge which is west of Halifax in what used to be called the West Riding of Yorkshire [53]. Both hamlet and name have long since disappeared from the map and gazetteer of the British Isles while 'West Riding', a very old name, was abolished by the Local Government Act of 1974, the region around Halifax now being in the county of West Yorkshire.

As a surname, Greenwood may have first appeared in its oldest form in the Halifax and Wakefield regions of West Riding in 1275 when reference was made to a John del Grenewode - John, dweller by the green wood [95, 96]. Ramification brought the number of Greenwood families in that area of Yorkshire to 7 in 1379, 26 in 1545, 148 in 1641 and 719 in 1965. Greenwood is apparently still the commonest surname in and around Leeds, Halifax and Bradford; in 1965 there were thrice as many Greenwoods in that region than in the whole of Greater London [96]. If indeed Yorkshire is the original home of the Greenwood kin, it should not come as a surprise to learn that the forebears of Frans Greenwood also hailed from that county.

*   *   *

P A T E R N A L   G R A N D P A R E N T S
and   their   children

Judging from his signature (Fig. 2), it was an old "ffransis Greenewood" who was in Rotterdam on business in 1668 [A126, A127, A128]. It is not inconceivable that he was a brother of grandfather James Greenewood, nobleman, Lord of Stapleton (a village at 54.30N 1.35W on river Tees, 3 KM southwest of Darlington) in North Yorkshire [101], whose marriage (to Miss Billis ? - Francis Billis was an uncle of his children [A139]) resulted in at least six sons (order of seniority not known):

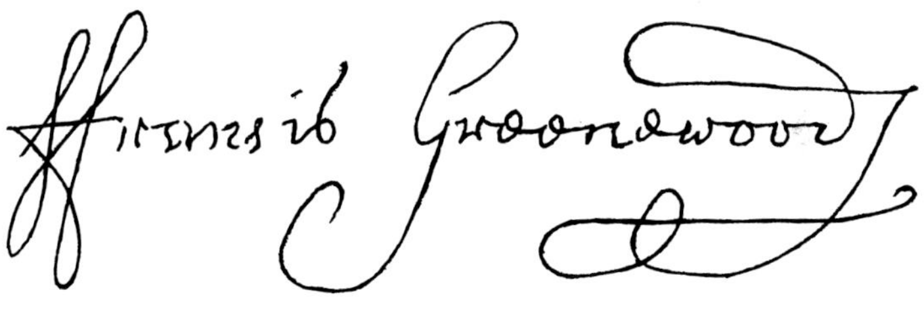

Fig. 2.   Signature of ffransis Greenewood, dated 1668 [A126].

J a m e s - a squire at Stapleton around 1690 [A46].

F r a n c i s - before emigrating to Holland in the 1660s, the father-to-be of Frans Greenwood was living at New Leeds, Yorkshire.

C h a r l e s - of Stapleton. Like his brother Francis, he left the native Yorkshire soil for Rotterdam where, in February 1669, we find him involved in a process between his brother Francis and merchant Jacobus Casteleijn [A134] whose assistant he actually became in 1670 [A151]. Charles must have been an enterprising man as in 1680 he was referred to as planter in Surinam [80]. On May 6th, 1680, after the death of governor Johannes Heinsius, Charles - in his function as police-commissioner - was one of the signatories of the proposals for the establishment of a new government in Surinam [56]. In 1688 he was in Holland, presumably on furlough, as in May of that year Charles purchased country-house 'Vinckenburg' at Wassenaar while in December he drew up a testament in which he bequeathed his estate, on equal share terms, to his five brothers James, Francoys, Henry, John and William [A46]. Charles died in 1690. In July 1693 brother Francis sent Johannes Veen to Surinam to succeed Arnoldus van Pamel who had been appointed by Charles to be his manager on the plantation; at the same time Francis appointed his son James, already on the plantation, to act as managing director [A144].

H e n r y - is mentioned in 1692 as a merchant living at Stapleton, Yorkshire [A45].

J o h n - died prior to 1717. Owned property around Stapleton (Manfield, Cleasby, Barton, Skeeby) which was inherited by his son Charles who, in 1717, was living at Brise-Norton, Oxfordshire. Charles had one sister, Mary, who was entitled to income derived from property in Oxfordshire [11].

W i l l i a m - no data found.

There were some other Greenwoods in Rotterdam during the seventeenth century. For instance mariner James Greenwood, master of a ship, who was there in 1667 - 1669; he came from Yarmouth in Norfolk [A123, A124, A125, A129, A130]. Another was Thomas "Greenewout" who in June 1688 sold eight 'stoop' (= $\frac{1}{2}$ anker = about 16 litres) of wine for 4 guilders 16 stuyvers on the occasion of the funeral of Frans Duyvendyck in Rotterdam [A210].

* * *

M A T E R N A L   G R A N D P A R E N T S
a n d   t h e i r   c h i l d r e n

Johan (John) Glover, the father-in-law of Francis Greenewood, was - as early as 1644 - referred to as an English merchant in Rotterdam [A100, A101], importing tobacco from Virginia [A104 - A108]. In 1647, still importing tobacco [A103, A109], he was living at Nieuwe Haven, Rotterdam; in 1650 he was in partnership with "Franssois" [Francis] Mansell, a merchant of Chichester [A122]. Glover, the merchant, is further mentioned in various notarial protocols [A113 - A121]. The year of his death is not known but it was 1665 at the latest.

Fig. 3. Signature of Johan (John) Glover, dated 1646 [A107a].

Dutch mother-in-law Anna Colenprys (also spelled Colepreys, Colenprijs or Kolenprijs), of Rotterdam, was born in 1621. A certificate of baptismal registration has not been found. We owe a disclosure of the year of birth of Frans Greenwood's maternal grandmother, as well as a confirmation of that of his mother, to the gross misbehaviour of young Floris Adriaensz. Lamshoek towards his mother Leentge Jans, widow of Adriaen Florisz. Lamshoek, residing in Rotterdam. On December 8th, 1665, "Juffr. Anna Colenprijs, weduwe van wijlen Mr Johan Glover, out xliiii, ende Anna Glover, out xvii jaren" [Mrs Anna Colenprijs, widow of the late Mr Johan Glover, aged xliiii (44), and (her daughter) Anna Glover, aged xvii (17) years], together with 63-year old spinster Jacobmijntge Jans, attested a declaration of having witnessed the dreadful behaviour of young Floris Lamshoek by calling his mother a whore, a cadaver, a swine, a devil, a barking dog, &c., by hitting his sister Maria and pulling the coif off her head and by throwing a chafing-dish of burning coal through the house. Little could the highly distressed mother have known that her bitter complaint to Notary Public Adriaen van Aller [A135] would supply us, well over three centuries later, with the year of birth of the witnesses mother and daughter Glover, as well as with their signatures (Figs. 4[1], 6[1]).

Johan Glover and Anna Colenpreys had seven children who were all baptised in the Reformed Church, Rotterdam, on the dates given [A87]:

J o h a n n i s - 23.II.1642. Witnesses: Richard Glover, Joannis White, Maria Harris. Must have died before March 1647.

A n n a - 11.VI.1643. Witnesses: Richard Glover, Maria Adriaens, Peternelle. Died young, probably 26.V.1647.

C a t e r i j n a - 20.IX.1644. Witnesses: Michael Coleprijs, Ruth Smeton [Smeaton], Bridget Glover. Must have died before November 1650.

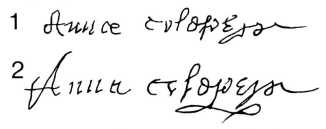

Fig. 4. Signatures of Anna Colepreys, 1 - dated 1665 [A135], 2 - dated 1669 [A142].

J o h a n n u s - 3.III.1647. Witnesses: Phylippus de Ritu, Thomas Dostelwijt [Postlethwaite], Maria Stermont. Died 16.VI.1647 [A89].

A n n a - 26 (born 9).XI.1648 [101]. Witnesses: Michiel Coleprijs, Thomas Postlewaight [Postlethwaite] and his wife Bridget Glover. The mother-to-be of Frans Greenwood; died 20.II.1712.

C a t h a r i j n a - 10.XI.1650. Witnesses: Nyclaes Harris, Ruth Smaetton [Smeaton], Marya de Graven.

B e n j a m i n - 11.VIII.1652. Emigrated to North America; was in Boston, New England, in 1670 [A133].

Richard Glover, who witnessed the baptism of the first two children, was very likely a brother of John Glover (the father). On 23.V.1632 "Ritchert" [Richard] Glover gave notice of his impending marriage to Maria Jans [A56]; both were living in 's-Gravenhage. They had at least two daughters, both baptised in the Groote Kerk, 's-Gravenhage: Maria 27.II.1633; Dorote 5.XI.1634 [A56].

On 8 August, 1646, Anna's bachelor step-brother Michiel Coleprijs, being ill, drew up his testament before Notary Public Balthasar Basius in which he appointed as heirs the children of his brother-in-law Johan Glover and his step-sister Anna Colenpreys, as well as Sara and Johannes Colenpreys.

After the death of Johan Glover, his wife Anna apparently took over his business. For instance, in August 1667 she acknowledged to owe Gideon Deutz of Amsterdam 300 Caroli guilders [A137] while in June 1668 she owed him no less than 1,500 [A138]. The Deutz family became well-known during the 18th century as financiers lending large sums to planters in Surinam, thereby eventually sustaining great losses [124]. In January 1669 Anna Colenpreys rented from Adrianus Kool and Hendrik Slager a house situated at the end of the Hooftstraat near the Roode Brug [a bridge] in Rotterdam [A141] while on Christmas Eve 1669 she rented from Catharina Cock, widow of Ulrich van Zoelen, a house and warehouse called "Den Witten Eenhoorn" [The White Unicorn] situated on the north side of Nieuwe Haven, Rotterdam [A142].

It is not known when grandmother Anna Glover née Colenpreys died.

*   *   *

DESCENT OF THE PARENTS OF FRANS GREENWOOD

P a t e r n a l	M a t e r n a l
James GREENEWOOD	John GLOVER
x	x (±1641)
(?) Billis	Anna Colenpreys 1621- ?
= James	= Johannis 1642-?1647
= **Francis** 1634-1731	= Anna 1643-?1647
= Chârles	= Caterijna 1644-?1650
= Henry	= Johannus 1647-1647
= John	= **Anna** 1648-1712
= William	= Catharijna 1650- ?
	= Benjamin 1652- ?

*   *   *

PARENTS

Francis Greenewood, one of the six sons of James Greenewood, was apparently born at New-Leeds, Yorkshire, on 5.X.1634 [101]. Presumably at some time in the 1660s he emigrated to Holland, settling in Rotterdam. In May 1669 "franscois Greenwout engels coopman alhier" [Francis Greenewood English merchant in Rotterdam] confirmed that he had had and was still having business connections with Adriaen van Linden in Rotterdam and was offering as surety his person and all his landed estates in Yorkshire [A139]. In January and March 1670 he is likewise referred to as Mr fransis Greenewood English merchant in Rotterdam [A131, A132]. Although rather variable, his signature on numerous Dutch notarial documents confirms his identity throughout his years.

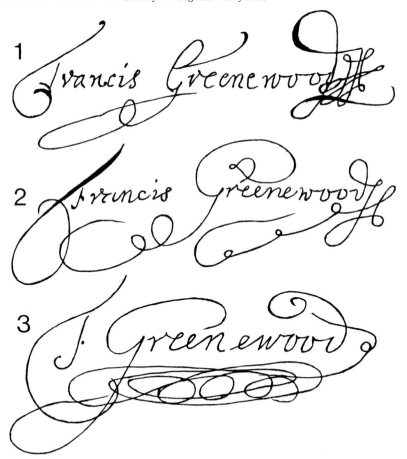

Fig. 5. Signatures of Francis Greenewood, 1 - dated 1669 [A139], 2 - dated 1670 [A131], 3 - dated 1709 [A230].

On Sunday 21 December, 1670, the first banns were read in the English Church - situated on the north side of the Haringvliet canal in Rotterdam [29] - announcing the forthcoming marriage in that church on Wednesday 7 January, 1671, of François Greenwood, a bachelor from "New Laeds" [New-Leeds, at the time (but no longer) a village in Yorkshire] residing at Houttuyn, Rotterdam, to Miss Anna Glover of Nieuwe Haven (which backed on to Houttuyn) in Rotterdam [A88; 134]. The bride was the 22-year old daughter of Johan (John) Glover, an English merchant in Rotterdam, and Anna Colenpreys.

Fig. 6. Signatures of Anna Glover: 1 - daughter, dated 1665 [A135], 2 - mother, dated 1670 [A133].

The Christian name of the groom was Francis but in official Dutch documents is always given as Francois. His son Frans (or François) referred to his father as Francis. Interestingly, the father invariably signed his surname as Greenewood; it is usually written as Greenwood in the text of documents. Clerical variation in spelling was common at the time and one comes across Ffrancis, Ffransis, Francoes, Francoijs, Franscois, Franchois, Franssos - Greenwoot, Greenwoodt, Greenwoud, Greendwoud, Greenwout, Greenewout, Grenwood, Greijnwout, Grienwout, Grijnwout, Groenwout, Groenewout. Prior to the establishment of Register Offices in The Netherlands in 1811, such variation in the spelling of names was quite common. - Greenewood is actually very similar to the Dutch form of the name: Groenewoud.

After their marriage, Francis Greenewood and Anna Glover moved from Houttuyn to the more fashionable Nieuwe Haven which was to become the parental home for their children, a home where Frans Jr presumably continued to live after his marriage until his departure for Dordrecht in 1726. Nieuwe Haven, being a quay, was an ideal location for a businessman with shipping interests; quite a number of English merchants resided there as well as along nearby Haringvliet. After the destruction of the heart of Rotterdam on 14 May, 1940, the Nieuwe Haven was filled up with rubble and has quite disappeared, name and all; the canal was in an area between Groenendaal and the Haringvliet canal.

Having decided to invest some money in property, in October 1677 Francis bought for Hfl. 700 from Pieter Coddaeus a house, garden and summerhouse on the north side of the Goutse rywegh [Gouda carriageway], adjacent to the residence of Mr Nicolaes Reve on the east side and to that of Mr Rombout van Maastrigt on the west side [A93]. Houses did not appreciate in those years. When he sold the property at Goutse rywegh to Samuel Greene, a merchant and burgher of Rotterdam, in May 1692, Francis received only Hfl. 630 for it [A95]. Similarly, in May 1689 Francis purchased from Hendrik Penn a house and garden on east side of Jaep Quakersteeg [85] for Hfl. 1017 and sold it for Hfl. 740 in 1711 [A97].

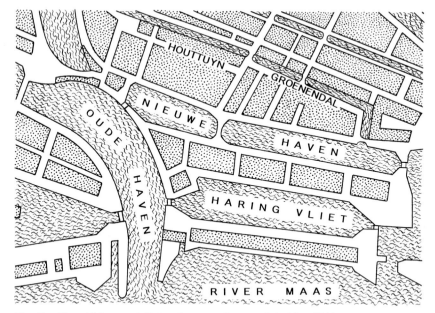

Fig. 7. The old heart of Rotterdam - destroyed in May 1940.
The Greenwoods resided in this area for a number of years.

Brother Charles died in Surinam presumably in 1690. In his testament of
11 December 1688 he had bequeathed his valuable possessions to his five surviving brothers who therefore inherited his estate 'Vinckenburg' at Wassenaar,
north of 's-Gravenhage. In July 1692 two of the brothers, Henry and James,
each sold their 1/5th part for Hfl. 440 to Francis [A45] who then owned 3/5th
of Vinckenburg - eventually he became sole proprietor.

A few words about the history of Vinckenburg. - As long ago as 1625 some
land at Oostdorp, Wassenaar, southeast of Middelweg, was administered by
IJsbrandt van Vinckenburg. It was presumably he who first built a house there
which then became known as Vinckenburg (later on often spelled Vinkenburg).
In March 1687 mention is made of homestead Vinckenburg with a farmhouse and
21 'morgen' land [= 21 x 2¼ = 47¼ acres] owned by Thomas More of Yorkshire
who, with his wife Jacoba van de Braak, agreed to sell the property to another
Englishman, namely Thomas Moony, a merchant living in 's-Gravenhage (where
he resided already in 1685 - and was still present in 1700). However, no sooner
than the following year, in May 1688, Moony sold the estate to Charles Greenewood. - For the next owner, Francis Greenewood, Vinkenburg may in the long
run have been too large to manage: in October 1702 he sold some of the land to
Cornelis van Ellemeet for Hfl. 225 [A48] and again, in July 1703, for no less
than Hfl. 3,000 worth [A49].

It must have been a pleasant country house; two of the rooms were actually
hung with wallpaper (presumably painted), there was a dovecot and there were
nets for fishing and for trapping finches (a popular pastime/'sport' in those days).

It is not known when Francis left Nieuwe Haven to live permanently at Vinkenburg. In 1711 he and his wife Anna drew up their testament there [A77]. It is certain, though, that from 1713 till his death in 1731, Vinkenburg was Francis Greenewood's permanent address [A78]. His daughter Sara, a spinster, looked after him (a widower since 1712) at Vinkenburg. Sara was able to buy the estate from her father for Hfl. 3,200 cash on 18 July 1719 [A50]. After her father's death in 1731, Sara sold Vinkenburg on 4 September 1732 to Nicolaas André Weenix who renamed the homestead 'Oostdorp'. Weenix sold Oostdorp in March 1754 to Pieter Pielat who renamed the property 'Lindenhof' but permitted Weenix to continue living in the house. In May 1767 Pielat sold Lindenhof to Sam Gilles, a counsellor at the Court of Holland. The property then consisted of a homestead, stables, gardener's lodge, summerhouse, well-stocked fish ponds, alleys, beautiful fences with exquisite fruit trees, orchards. Gilles died the same year he bought Lindenhof but his widow continued to live there until 1768. Next, the estate was sold for Hfl. 8,000 to Mr Crommelin, former Governor of Surinam, in 1771. Crommelin sold Lindenhof in November 1775 to Debora Stoel, widow of Pieter van Swieten of Rotterdam. In April 1782 Mrs Stoel sold the estate to Hermanus van Bork of 's-Gravenhage, Hendrik van Bork and Gerrit van der Aa both of Haarlem. These new owners demolished homestead Lindenhof in 1783 after having sold the gardener's lodge with three 'morgen' of land in March of that year. - During ground work at the site of former Vinckenburg / Oostdorp / Lindenhof in 1943 - when the name Lindenhof was still known in Oostdorp, Wassenaar - numerous large bricks as well as traces of a pond were discovered.

*　　*　　*

On the death of Charles, the Greenewood brothers also inherited his sugar plantation 'The Black Creek' in Surinam (Fig. 8). However, it was Francis who somehow eventually became sole proprietor [A144]. It appears that neither Francis, nor later on his son Frans, ever went to the sugar plantation in Surinam. They can therefore not have had first-hand experience of, for instance, the treatment meted out to their slaves. Considering that a plantation the size of Black Creek may have employed at least two hundred slaves, wastage cannot have been too high; from 1711 onwards no more than six slaves were to be purchased annually. Earlier on that number was higher - for instance in April 1700 Francis had ten new slaves delivered to The Black Creek; they had arrived in the Gideon, master Dirk Willemszoon Cock [A188].

Some European personnel also had to be appointed. For instance, on 6 December, 1700, Francis signed a contract with spinster Maria de Bruyn to go to Surinam aboard 'De drie goede vrienden' [The three good friends], captain Cornelis Klinkert, in order to act as governess on the plantation and as housekeeper for his nephew Frans Greenewood [A207]. The contract was for five years @ Hfl. 100 a year with the proviso that if she did not like the job and wanted to return to Holland she would have to pay the return fare herself. After having drawn up her testament on 5 December, 1700, Maria de Bruyn sailed forth, arriving in Surinam in the spring of 1701. The same year she died and was buried in Paramaribo. Her possessions were subsequently shipped back to Rotterdam by nephew Frans [A208]. Various problems had to be solved before the case with personal effects of the deceased could finally be opened in the warehouse of Francis on 25 September, 1702 [A209].

*　　*　　*

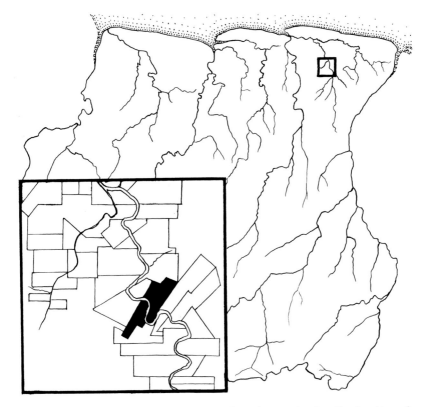

Fig. 8. Map of Surinam with as inset an enlarged area showing the location of The Black Creek sugar plantation (in black).

Protocols of various Notaries Public often dealt with aspects, not seldom of a problematic nature, concerning business activities of father Greenewood. The following selection may provide some idea of Francis Greenewood's professional worries and headaches.

In 1679 Francis is mentioned as a merchant and burgher of Rotterdam, a co-owner of a pinnace-ship which, sailing from Hull, England, laden with seed, lead, butter and several casks of red-lead, was caught in a heavy gale which stranded her on the island of Goeree, province of Zeeland, on Wednesday 15 November 1679 [A98].

On 1 June, 1682, Francis set up company with merchant Jasper van Zoelen, also of Rotterdam. That business association was to last until the end of 1700 [A63, A140, A145, A146, A148, A161, A219] after which Francis and Jasper still occasionally joined in trading [A172]. In 1686 the two companions drew up a contract with the captain and commander of Fort Frederik Hendrik in Surinam for the transport of goods to Rotterdam and vice versa [A58]. They also recruited staff for plantations in Surinam and, e.g., arranged for Jacob Dirksz Valbrugh, of Amsterdam, to work as carpenter on the plantation of Arnold van Pamel during two years for free board and lodging and wages of Hfl. 32 a month. Taking his tools with him, Valbrugh sailed on ship Juffrouw Maria, master Bastiaen Reyne [A1]. - Jasper van Zoelen was also an alderman of Schieland (a district adjoining Rotterdam) for some time; he died before 1708 [A152, A180].

Shipping produce home from Surinam was not without risk. Late in 1690 vessel De Erasmus, captain J. de Lange, navigator P. A. Crans, after having been tossed about in heavy seas for some eight days, finally went down at 39.30N 36.32W, i.e., in mid North Atlantic Ocean. She was laden with 50 hogshead of sugar from The Black Creek. Master and navigator somehow managed to reach Plymouth where they boarded the Goude Leeuw bound for Vlissingen [Flushing]. Shortly after leaving Plymouth harbour, the Goude Leeuw went down and with her the documents which de Lange and Crans had managed to salvage from De Erasmus [A153] - a good story.

In February, 1691, Francis bought for Hfl. 250 a 1/16th share in fluyt-ship De Christina, master Pieter Maertensz. de Wit [A154]. As ever, there were crooks about in those days. Gerrit Gesmel, a cooper, arrived in Amsterdam in July 1692 on board that fluyt-ship which was laden with sugar from Surinam. At the instigation of Francis Greenewood - having a financial interest in the vessel - Gesmel formally complained that de Wit had also employed him as secretary and bookkeeper. Gesmel told of de Wit's swindling practices, e.g., selling an oxhead of nails in Surinam so that eventually he was forced to buy some for use by the cooper. De Wit also sold by auction shares and other documents of value below their actual worth; this took place in the Surinam tavern 'De schoone waerdin' [The beautiful hostess - named after Margriet den Eijsch]. By the time he sailed from Surinam in April 1692, de Wit was again short of money so he borrowed the meagre sum of 28 stuyvers from the boy Jan Tobiasz who had received it from his father as pocket money for the trip [A143].

On 9 October, 1693, Eduard Towse, skipper of the "InDijffer" [Endeavour] which was anchored at Brielle but bound for London, signed a contract of bottomry whereby Francis Greenewood lent him Hfl. 1,500 at a premium of 8% [A147].

On 10 June, 1695, Francis was in Delft where, with Judith van Son (wife of burgomaster Teeckman of Amersfoort), he was a witness at the baptism in the Oude Kerk of Wouter Jan van Eenhoorn, a son of the illustrious Delft-ware potter Lambert van Eenhoorn and his wife Margaretha Teeckman [68; A14].

In January 1696 Francis and his partner van Zoelen were claiming no less than Hfl. 15,000 from Elisabeth van Lanen, widow of William Hartley who had been a merchant in Rotterdam. This is another example of the presence of a fair number of English immigrants in Rotterdam in those days; the town was even referred to as "Little London". Greenewood also had dealings with Dudley Irish who resided in Dordrecht [A149, A169, A171].

By 1698 Francis was affluent enough to consent to acting as a guarantor for Jan de Graeff for Hfl. 12,000 [A149, A150]. Until that year Francis Greenewood was usually referred to in notarial protocols as being an English merchant. From 1699 onwards he is invariably "a merchant", so presumably he had acquired Dutch citizenship by that time.

Trade with England was apparently brisk. For example, in June, 1701, Francis, together with two other English merchants in Rotterdam, chartered the vessel 'Nicolas & Francis', master George Woodhouse, to sail to Stockton-on-Tees where she was to take in "such quantity of lead, butter or paks of stokkings as the freighters shall ship him, but in all to his full and convenient lading, wherewith the master is to part from whence with all speed wind and weather serveing, and to returne directly to this port, where haveing delivered his loading in good order and wel conditioned to the order of the freighters, the danger of the sea always excepted, they are to pay him for freight eight stivers for every pig of small lead, six stivers for every ferkin of butter, and three guilders for every pak of stokkings, which he shall have delivered out, and moreover two stivers per guilder for primage and portcharges avaridge grosse according to the custome of the sea." [A190].

In September, 1701, Francis, William Spencer and John Firth, city merchant freighters of Rotterdam, chartered the 'John', master Thomas Brett, to sail to Stockton "where he is to report to Mssrs James Cook Sr & Jr of whom he is to receive orders for loading of goods and merchandise" and then to return to Rotterdam [A211].

On 19 October, 1701, Francis agreed to stand surety for Hendrick Dircksz. Boon of Ylpendam [A165].

In June, 1702, Greenewood was importing "Engelse saayen" (English serge] [A216].

Several English merchants in Rotterdam were in contact with Greenewood, e.g. in September, 1702: Michael Watson, Joseph Lindall, Ralph Southeran, Robert Hunter and Robert Atkinson [A189].

In January, 1703, it was stated that Francis owned 3/8th, Pieter Pedij ½ and Patrick Harper 1/8th part of the fluyt 'De drie goede vrienden' - this reveals who the three good friends were [A192]. That ship, of 140 'last' (280 tons), master Cornelis Klinkert, was sold by them on 12 April, 1708 [A206].

Weather was rough in April, 1703, when the 'Providence', master William Godfrey, from Hull, stranded on entering river Maas; it had merchandise on board for Francis [A193]. Furthermore, on 30 April, 1703, Greenewood and Nicolaes Reve, both merchants in Rotterdam, granted burgomaster Cornelis Karrebroeck of Brouwershaven the right to salvage goods from the wrecked 'd'Amitié', master Thomas "Tomlijn" [A170].

During 1703 Greenewood entered into various shipping contracts [A194, A195].

In October, 1705, Greenewood appointed his nephew Francis (François, Frans) Greenwood and Ferdinandus van Overschelde, both residing in Surinam, to be his administrators and managers - in fact directors - of his plantation The Black Creek, large 1322 'akkers' (568 hectares) [A199]. Meanwhile, in 1704 or earlier, Francis had formed a new company with his son Frans: "Francis Greenewood en Soon" [A198, A223]. In December, 1705, they appointed Geleyn de Keyser, residing in Surinam, to be a director of The Black Creek on the understanding that he was to succeed nephew/cousin Frans Greenwood or van Overschelde if one of them either left or died [A200]. A year later Francis Greenewood en Soon seem to have changed their opinion a little about de Keyser because in November, 1706, they instructed nephew/cousin Frans and van Overschelde to dismiss de Keyser as director should he prove to be unsuitable for the post [A202].

A company which Francis had formed with Cornelis de Niet of Rotterdam was dissolved in 1706 [A91].

Textiles from England were also imported; in April, 1706, such goods arrived via Thomas Nodes, a son-in-law of Francis.

Lead was another common commodity to be imported from England. In 1707 John Firth and Thomas Hold, merchants in Rotterdam, as well as Francis declared that several times they had warehoused quantities of lead unloaded from English ships; sometimes some of it went missing which the first two merchants suspected Greenewood to have mislaid in his warehouse [A204, A205].

In 1709 Charles, another son of Francis, joined 'Francis Greenewood en Soon' and in December of that year the threesome empowered nephew/cousin Frans Greenewood, director of The Black Creek plantation in Surinam, to prosecute debtors [A230].

In 1711 Francis, John Firth and William Spencer signed a business contract, Charles Greenwood and William Wilberforce acting as witnesses.

Troubled Francis stated under oath in November, 1711, that sugar destined for Hamburg which he had insured for Hfl. 950, had not been loaded into the 'Isabella', captain Willem de Goyer [A244].

*　　*　　*

Francis Greenewood and his wife Anna drew up a new testament on 24 May, 1709; they were then both described as being physically and mentally hale and healthy. However, Anna's health deteriorated in 1711. Now residing at Vinkenburg, Wassenaar, Francis and Anna drew up yet another new testament, this time before Notary Public Pieter Kerkhooven of Leiden, on 5 September, 1711 [A77]. This testament provides very useful data as it gives the names of their children in order of seniority, enabling an estimate for the year of birth of the two children for whom no record of baptism has been found. The seven then living children (James had died) were each to receive one-seventh part of their parents' estate after the death of both parents. Sara being the only unmarried child, she would first receive an eighth part in her father's plantation in Surinam as well as 4,000 guilders while she was to retain all her personal jewelry, gold, silver and clothing, these being gifts which the married children had already received as dowry. Elisabeth, married to a spendthrift, was to keep all inherited money herself, to be used only for herself or her children - her husband being strictly excluded from any profit. Charles, the youngest son, who was about to depart for Surinam, would have first refusal to purchase plantation The Black Creek. All friends, maids and orphanages were excluded from the testament. As executors were appointed Hendrik Grimes and Johannes van der Heyden, both of Rotterdam, while Thomas Nodes (a son-in-law) and Hendrik Grel, of Rotterdam, were to act as guardians over minors.

Anna Greenewood née Glover died on 20 February, 1712, and was buried at Wassenaar on the 24th following at Hfl. 15 impost [A54]. The poet Jacob Zeeus wrote a poem "To Mr Frans Greenwood on the death of his mother Mrs Anna Glover, wife of Mr Francis Greenwood" [52, 139] and Frans Greenwood himself composed a moving poem "On the death of my dear mother Anna Glover. To my father Francis Greenwood" [44] - both poems in Dutch.

Now a widower of advancing years, Francis nevertheless continued business activities. This is obvious from a statement made on 23 July, 1712, indicating that in previous March Francis had insured for transport to Hamburg ten hogshead of sugar @ Hfl. 50 a hogshead each in 'De Stad Limburgh', captain Arie Dobber, as well as in a ship of Michiel Joost van Eyk. However, each vessel had actually loaded only five hogshead [A249]. - On 3 September, 1712, he declared to have received nothing at all from six named ships which during that year arrived from Surinam [A250]. Similarly, on 3 October, 1713, he declared to have received nothing at all from three vessels arriving from Surinam (Cornelia, master Jacques Girodet; Christina, master Pieter Carstens; De Stad Paramaribo, master Hendrik Kleyn) while from the Isabella (master Willem de Goyer) and the Sr Jan (master Cornelis Carstens) he only received ten hogshead of sugar each [A251].

On 17 June, 1713, Francis Greenewood altered his testament apparently because of a special affection for his daughter Sara who, after his death, now was to profit specially from the sale of Vinkenburg and the farm house [A78].

From about 1719 onwards Francis - who was then already 85 years old - seems to have retired from active business life although he retained an interest in it [A269]. His daughter Sara, a spinster, continued to look after him at Vinkenburg.

On 10 September, 1722, some financial matters were settled concerning Jeronimus Clifford, a merchant in London. He was a son of Andreas Clifford who already owned a plantation in Surinam when the colony was acquired by the Dutch in 1667. Through his marriage to Dorothea Watson, Jeronimus became the owner of the Corcabo plantation along the Cottica river [56].

On 9 March, 1724, Francis affirmed that the executors of his will should be Hendrik Grimes, a former alderman of Rotterdam, and Johannes van der Heyden, a merchant in Rotterdam, while as guardians over minors were to be appointed his son-in-law Thomas Nodes and Hendrik Grel, a grain-broker in Rotterdam; he now also added his son François (Frans) as executor and guardian [A79]. On the same day [A80], Francis - who was said to be healthy and in full possession of his mental faculties - altered his 1711 testament by bequeathing to daughter Sara, looking after him at Vinkenburg, all furniture, horses, carriages, harnasses, garden implements but not the bed- and other linen nor all silver. Of the silver objects Sara was to be allowed to keep twelve spoons and forks. In case of opposition by other heirs, or of disappearance of the goods mentioned, Sara would be entitled to receive 4,000 Caroli guilders from the estate.

On 27 November, 1727, Francis empowered his grandson Frans Schas, counsellor at the Court of Justice and Police in Surinam, to replace Klaas Hendrik Timmerling (who had expressed the wish to be relieved from his post) as director of The Black Creek together with Anthonij Segijn [lapsus for Saffin ?], already working for the plantation, at least if the latter would be suitable for the job [A81].

By 1 October, 1728, Thomas Nodes and Johannes van der Heyden are both "recently deceased" while Hendrik Grel was suffering from an imbalance of mind since 1726. These three were therefore replaced as executors of the testament of Francis by his son François (Frans) and his grandson Jacques Saffin [A82].

On Saturday 5 May, 1731, Francis Greenewood died at his homestead Vinkenburg, Wassenaar, at the then truly great age of 96 years [A264]. He was buried at Wassenaar on Friday 11 May, 1731 [101]; the impost was Hfl. 15 [A55].

On 17 May, 1731, Hendrik Grimes asked to be exempted from acting as executor of Francis' testament because of his "great age" (72), his ailing wife and the "great distance" between Rotterdam and Wassenaar (±30 KM) [A264]. It was therefore left to the two remaining executors, Frans Greenwood and Jacques Saffin, to sell by auction, on 13 December 1731, some of the late Francis Greenewood's property in Oostdorp, Wassenaar, namely a farmhouse, sheds, barns, orchard, kitchen-garden, 17 'morgen drie hant' of land for Hfl. 2,000 to Leendert Jansz Ruijgrock [A52]. As mentioned earlier, Vinkenburg itself was sold by Sara Greenewood to Nicolaas André Weenix on 4 September, 1732.

THE FAMILY OF

FRANCIS GREENEWOOD 1634 - 1731
x (1671)
ANNA GLOVER 1648 - 1712

(Note: Anna and most of the children spelled the surname as Greenwood)

M a r i a   1671-1711
   x [I] (1695 ?) Adriaen FANNIUS ? -1699
     = Adriaen
   x [II] (1701) Thomas NODES ? -±1728 *
     = Elizabeth Anna Maria 1709- ?
     = one other child
       * x [II] (1712) Johanna HOSTEIJN 1685- ?
         = Elisabeth 1712- ?
         = Sara Maria 1714-±1717
         = Sara 1717- ?

J a m e s   1674-1698
   bachelor

A n n a   1676-1736
   x [I] (1695) Hendrik SCHAS 1662-1704
     = Maria 1696-1778
       x Jacques SAFFIN
     = Francois (Frans) 1698-1761
       x [I] Geertruyda VAN VHEELEN
       x [II] Sara PICHOT
     = Helena Antonia 1699-1764
       x Dithmurus HACKMAN
     = Hendrik Roeland 1701-1730
       bachelor
   x [II] (1710) Paul DIERS DE RAS

F r a n ç o i s   (Frans)   1680-1763
   x (1706) Maria VAN DEN HOLAERT 1683-1711
     = Anna 1707-1794
       spinster
     = Kornelis 1708-1736
       bachelor

S a r a   ±1684-after 1740
   spinster

C a t h a r i n a   1686- ?
   x (1707) Robert BARTON ? -1711

C h a r l e s   (Carolus)   ±1688-1711
   x (1708) Maria HOSTEIJN 1685-1711
     = Francis 1709-1711
     = Charles 1710-1711

E l i s a b e t h   1690-1764
   x (1707) George August VAN DER HECK 1688- ?
     = Fredrik August 1707- ?
     = François Johannis 1709- ?
     = Melchior Ernest 1711- ?

FRANS GREENWOOD

In olden days a birth was not registered, only a baptism. Francois Greenwood (always named so in official documents, the c always lacking a cedilla) was apparently baptised in the English Church, Rotterdam, on Sunday 21 April, 1680. As for the actual date of birth: Frans Greenwood's good friend Aart Schouman painted a portrait miniature of him on 30 April, 1740, and wrote on verso "Frans Greenwood Gebooren den 17 April 1680". This date of birth was confirmed by Frans himself in the title of a poem "Heilbede op myn 63ste verjaardag, verschenen den XVII. April 1743" (A prayer for bliss on my 63rd birthday, issued 17 April 1743) [50]. So we can accept Wednesday 17 April, 1680, as the day of birth of Frans Greenwood.

A great friend of Frans Greenwood, from childhood onwards, was Kornelis Boon who later became known as Cornelis Boon van Engelant - there was no British connection but Cornelis had inherited the title 'Heer van Engelant' [Seignior of Engelant], this Engelant being the name of certain polders near Heenvliet (where eventually he lived) on the island of Putten, southwest of Rotterdam. Frans and Kornelis were born in the same year, 1680, (the latter on 18 June) [A87], both presumably went to the same school and both developed a great interest in poetry and actually became equally well-known in their life-time through published works.

Poets in those days felt an urge to write eulogies for friends and we owe a glimpse into the life of the young Greenwood to Boon's lengthy poem written for one of Frans's birthdays [24]. In the first part of that undated poem, published in 1724, Boon referred to the blissful cessation of bellicose events, the disastrous effects of rinderpest and floods. This seems to allude to the Peace of Utrecht in 1713, the rinderpest of 1715 and the floods of December 1717. The poem could therefore have been written at the earliest in 1718, for Greenwood's 38th birthday. In it, Boon van Engelant indirectly named the place of birth of his friend and himself: ". . . De Rotte, aen welkers stroomen / Wy beiden woonden, en ter weerelt zyn gekomen, . . ." [The Rotte, on the banks of which we both lived and came into this world . . .] (Fig. 9). - Indeed, Frans Greenwood was born and lived for a number of years in Rotterdam -- the town on river Rotte.

Van kintsbeen af, dat wy noch naer de vruchten fprongen
Die aen het laegfte lot in onzen boomgaert hongen,
Gong ik, gelyk ge weet, gemeenzaem met hem om.
Wy quamen overeen zoo wel in ouderdom
Als in genegentheit. De Rotte, aen welkers ftroomen
Wy beiden woonden, en ter weerelt zyn gekomen,
Hoorde onder ons noit twift. 't Is waer, het geen ik zeg.
Wy hadden eenen zin, en liepen eenen weg.
Had Bofchert luft om eens met allerhande netten
In eene klare beek de vifchen te bezetten,
Of te bedriegen met een' kromme hengelroe,
Of met een fleur of ftrik, ik had ook luft daer toe.
Had hy vermaek om 't wilt in zyne legerftede
Te gaen betrappen wyt en zyt, ik had het mede.

Fig. 9. Part of a poem on a birthday of Frans Greenwood by C. Boon van Engelant (1724: 104) ["Boschert" = Greenwood].

Frans and Kornelis were boys as most others, so we learn from the poem. They used to pinch apples from an orchard, they snared hares and fished in streams with net and rod; they never quarreled, said Boon. As a young man, in 1698, Kornelis was sent to "the Rhine" - possibly denoting the University in Leiden - for further education. Boon spoke of that separation not having had an affect on their friendship, which confirms that Frans Greenwood continued to live in Rotterdam.

From 1702 until his marriage in 1706 Frans Greenwood was a Standard-bearer in the Civic Guard of Rotterdam [120]. There used to be twelve Companies of Civic Guards each with a captain, a lieutenant and a standard-bearer.

In another poem, Boon van Engelant [24] revealed that when on a visit to "the town of Mr Goverts" (a reference to Godevaart, Duke of Lotharingia, one of the founders of Delft in the 11th century), Frans at once succumbed to the irresistible fire radiating from the eyes of Maria van den Holaert. He obviously measured up to Maria's expectations of a good husband and eventually on Saturday 29 May, 1706, "Francois Greenwood, bachelor living at Nieuwe Haven, Rotterdam, and Maria van den Holaert, spinster of Delft" had the banns put up in both the Oude Kerk (Old Church) [A16] and Nieuwe Kerk (New Church) [A15] in Delft, while the banns were read in the Reformed Church, Rotterdam, on Sunday 30 May [A88]. The final banns were read on Sunday 13 June, 1706, in the Dutch Reformed Church, Rotterdam.

Because the bride hailed from Delft, Frans and Maria were married in that town, notably in the Gasthuyskerck (the church of an adjoining hospital), on Monday 14 June, 1706 [A17]; the impost amounted to 15 guilders (Fig. 10).

The Gasthuyskerck (Fig. 11), situated opposite the Koorenmarkt, was a small church in Delft favoured for weddings by patricians [76]. Every Sunday two sermons used to be given by a preacher of the Dutch Reformed Church as well as two in English. However, after the death of the 'last' English clergyman, some time in the 1720s, no more sermons were preached in English because by that time the English community in Delft had dwindled [5].

Fig. 10.   An excerpt from the Register of Marriages, Delft.   "Den 29. Mey 1706 / francois Greenwood J: M. [jonge man] tot Rotterdam / Maria van de Hoolaert J: d. [jonge dochter] alhier / Rotterd[am]. / 15 gl [gulden; impost] / Getrouwt in den / gasthuyskerck den / 14. juny 1706"   (29 May 1706 / francois Greenwood bachelor of Rotterdam / Maria van de Hoolaert spinster of Delft / Rotterdam Hfl. 15 impost / married in the / Gasthuyskerck on / 14 June 1706. [A17].

Fig. 11. Gasthuyskerck, Delft.

On 9 January, 1707, Frans and Maria made a testament before Notary Public Gerard Blockerus in Rotterdam [A226]. This specified that the surviving partner would become the universal heir(ess) and be obliged to bring up the procreated child(ren) until the 25th year or earlier in case of marriage, teaching the child or children to read, write, a craft or any other honest exercise enabling them to earn their own living; moreover, the child or children should receive as generous a dowry as could be afforded.

Frans and Maria (who had signed her name on the testament as Maria van den hoolart - Fig. 12) lived at Nieuwe Haven, Rotterdam [125] where two children were born:

A n n a - on 6.III.1707

C o r n e l i s - on 2.IX.1708

Alas, Maria died already in December, 1711, and was buried on the 14th of that month in the Nieuwe Kerk, Rotterdam; the impost was Hfl. 6 [A89].

She left a heartbroken Frans, a daughter of four and a son of three years old. Frans Greenwood wrote a tender poem "On the death of my dear wife Marie van den Holaart" [44]. Jacob Zeus wrote one "On the death of Mrs Maria vanden Holaert, wife of Mr Frans Greenwood" [139]. Cornelis Boon van Engelant composed a poem [24] "On the funeral of Mrs Maria van den Holaert, dedicated to her husband, Mr Frans Greenwood." All poems are in Dutch.

On 30 December, 1711, "Francois Greenwood junior" accepted guardianship over his children [A91a].

Bereaved Frans Greenwood never remarried.

*   *   *

Fig. 12. Signature of Maria van den Hoolart [Holaert, Holaart], dated 1707. [A226].

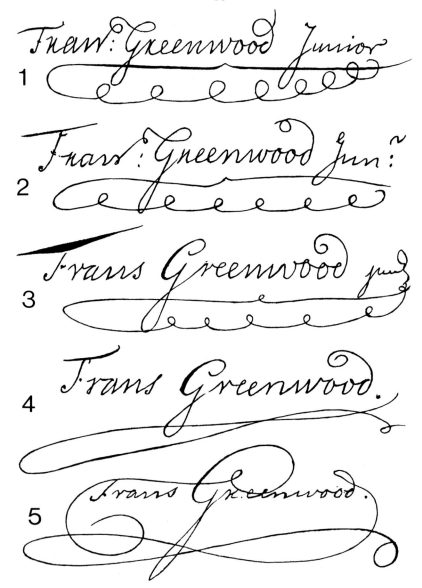

Fig. 13. Signatures of Frans Greenwood, 1 - dated 1707 [A226], 2 - dated 1709 [A230], 3 - dated 1714 [A252], 4 - dated 1721 [A274], 5 - dated 1743 [MS of poems on the sword which beheaded Johan van Oldenbarnevelt].

Living at or near his parental home, there was very likely always one of his sisters, or a maid, available to look after his two young children. Frans could therefore still enjoy an occasional evening out, one example of which has been recorded [A253]. It was on Saturday 9 February, 1715, that he whiled time away between 9 p.m. and midnight by leisurely chatting with Hendrik Huijsbergen in the tavern Het Swyns Hooft [The Boar's Head] on the Groote Markt, Rotterdam. On leaving they witnessed two men outside the tavern fighting with swords. After an honest fight the men went back inside the pub; Greenwood had noticed that one of the duellists was a son of the Secretary of the Noble College of Admiralty on the Maas.

*   *   *

Early in 1726 Frans and his two children Anna (aged 18) and Kornelis (aged 17) went to live in Dordrecht, staple-town for Rhine-wines and English wool; an old town which in 1732 counted 3950 houses with 18,000 inhabitants.

By 1745 Frans Greenwood was living at Schrijversstraat (the street is still there) but he finally moved to Steegoversloot (Fig. 14). The street "Het Steeg-oversloot", already named so in 1399 and still existing, originally belonged to the six principal streets; at first there were houses on one side only: over sloot [on the other side of the canal] [131]. It was, and still is, a respectable area of Dordrecht where the well-to-do used to live, for instance Gillis Hoolaart, father

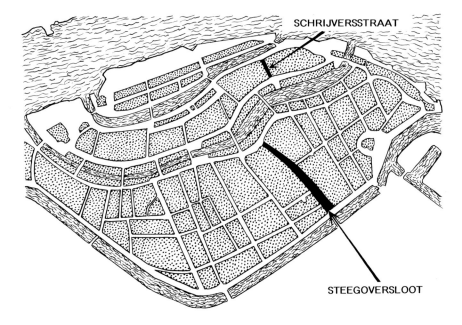

SCHRIJVERSSTRAAT

STEEGOVERSLOOT

Fig. 14. Map of Dordrecht in the 18th century, showing the two streets (in black) where Frans Greenwood used to live.

of painter Jacob (1713-1789) and his half-brother the glass-engraver Gillis Hendrik (1731-1816) [62], Vriesendorp [127], painter Adriaen van der Burgh (1693-1733) who taught Cornelis Greenwood and Aart Schouman. The St Joris Doelen (Stadsdoelen), where Cornelis and Aart used to practise painting, was also situated in that street. In 1793 daughter Anna was still living at the Greenwood residence, Steegoversloot, where her neighbours were: verger R. Abdorf / ex-councillor Jacob Boon / Anna Greenwood / mason Van der Voren.

Frans Greenwood did not lack entertainment in his advancing years. On 14 November, 1733, he was guest of honour at one of the dinners organised from time to time by the executors and members of the Water Board of the Driemanspolder (near Zoetermeer and Leidschendam) to finish off in a congenial manner a day devoted to business matters. Inviting one or a few guests for these copious wine-and-dine parties was an old-established custom in the Driemanspolder [21, 28, A86], as indeed it was in other Water Boards. Frans had presumably been invited to the dinner by his friend Willem Snellen, a member of the Driemanspolder Board who in fact was also present at that gathering. Earlier that year, 1733, Greenwood had presented Snellen - being the dedicatee - with a copy of a luxury edition of his new publication 'Boere-Pinxtervreugt' [Peasants' Whitsun Revelling]. Not having suitable premises of their own, the diners used to meet at De Swaan [The Swan], a tavern at Leidschendam (just north-east of 's-Gravenhage).

The guest was supposed to drink a toast, to mutual friendship and the prosperity of the polder, from a so-called hensbeaker and to write a poem or adage, with his or her name and date, in the Minute-Book of the meetings. Among the 74 jottings written in the Minute-Book (covering 1713 - 1749) between 1721 and 1742 is one by Frans Greenwood with the above-mentioned date. It is a six-line poem panegyrizing the Driemanspolder:

De wakkre Heemraat leve in eenigheit en trou.
De Deugt en Wysheit blyve aan zyne zy gebonden.
Nooit worde 't heil van beemd en akkren hier geschonden;
Maar Driemanspolder bloeije in weelde en akkerbou.
Dees zegening en al wat menschen wenschen mogen
Dale op haar' Dykgraaf en den Heemraat uit den hoogen.

$17\frac{11M}{14d}33$.   F: *Greenwood*

The hensbeaker (Fig. 15) from which he then drank - it usually had to be ad fundum - is of interest. In 1721 the landholders of the polder expressed the wish to own a brotherhood goblet which could be used during their dinners. They then commissioned Claude Robert, a "master glassdriller" (whose name has fallen into oblivion) to engrave a goblet with a polder scene, including six windmills, and the inscription "Sex rapido cursu vigiles tres ordine servant". The bill for the large (32 cm high) goblet and the excellent wheel-engraving amounted to Hfl. 54.50. This brotherhood goblet, or hensbeaker, was first used at a meeting on 11 October, 1721 [28].

Greenwood's poem of 1733 is not included in the 1760 volume of his poetry which, on the other hand, contains eulogies on several other Water Boards, namely those of Overwaart, Putten and Voorne. Maximiliaan van Berchem, who had married niece Francina Greenwood, was alderman and councillor of the Admiralty in Rotterdam. He was also an important member of Heemraadschap [Water Board] Voorne and in that capacity van Berchem may have invited Frans Greenwood to attend one of the meetings as guest of honour.

*   *   *

Fig. 15. Contour of hensbeaker
of Driemanspolder, 1721

One may conclude that Frans used to be a welcome partaker of dinner parties who must have enjoyed quaffing a large hensbeaker. It is friend Boon van Engelant who considered it worth remarking that Frans Greenwood was indeed a popular figure at social gatherings because of his "benevolence, cheerfulness, generosity, wit, humour and noble character"; he just always greatly entertained a company. "When he left a party of merrymakers, merriment went out with him."

The Greenwoods were of a tough constitution and Frans and his daughter Anna were in their eighties when they died - not quite as old, though, as Francis Greenewood who lived to be 96. However, at least once Frans had been quite ill. Boon van Engelant [24] in the poem on Greenwood's birthday warned him not to go out too early in the morning lest the morning chill would harm him and he wondered whether Frans had already forgotten that a great fever had laid him up recently. Perhaps this was the same serious illness to which Frans devoted an undated poem as a token of gratitude for recovery [50].

*   *   *

Frans Greenwood died in October 1763 and was buried on Saturday the 29th of that month in the Groote Kerk, Dordrecht. The entry in the Register of Burials reads: "29 October 1763 / den comies Francous Greenwooud / in Het Steeg Over Sloot / met drie Koetzen Extra [with three extra carriages] / Laet kinder na. [leaves a child] / s morg. ½ uur / s midd. 1 uur / luyen [bells tolled for half an hour in the morning, for a full hour in the afternoon]" [A21]. The impost was Hfl. 6 [A20].   - Van Dalen [30] published a list of tombstones in the Groote Kerk but Greenwood is not included; however, by that time (1927) many stones had been defaced.

The Dutch branch of Greenwoods died with Frans.

*   *   *

FRANS   GREENWOOD

a name now greatly revered in the small world

populated by connoisseurs of the art of engraved glass

hardly remembered, if not quite forgotten,

as a poet in the small world of his own country

*   *   *

FRANS GREENWOOD
PROFESSIONAL LIFE

Not until August, 1704, can one find mention of Frans Greenwood in his capacity of businessman. At 24 years of age, he was then referred to as being a merchant in company with his father. Not always quite successfully, so it seems. In July, 1706, the two partners owed Jeronimus Clifford Hfl. 3,750 - fortunately, three colleagues in Rotterdam were prepared to stand surety for them [A225]. The two were still in partnership - Francis Greenewood en Soon - in June, 1707 [A203].

We do not know what exactly their business entailed but probably they were importers and exporters, also acting as insurance brokers. Only an insignificant incident has been recorded [A227]. It happened that around noon on Friday 17th June, 1707, Frans Jr wanted a large parcel, which had been unloaded from a ship in Rotterdam harbour, to be sledged to the ferry for Dordrecht. He approached a sledger who was struggling to reload his sled with timber that had fallen off and therefore was not willing to oblige. So Frans simply ordered him to fetch another sled from the Groote Wijnbrug, paid him 10 cents extra and thus managed to get his parcel in time on to the ferry. - Evidently the young Greenwood was quite a resolute character.

Some time after September, 1707, when the Company was still that of Francis Greenewood & Son, the other son, Charles, joined them - on 16 October, 1709, the three are referred as "merchants in company" [A229]. On that day the three signed before Notary Public Gerard Blockerus, in Rotterdam, a contract with Johannes Kruijff (who signed his name as Johannis Cruijf), "Mr. Chirurgijn" [a medical doctor] of Amsterdam which stipulated that the latter:
(a) shall depart, on the first ship sailing, for plantation The Black Creek on the Comawina River in Surinam, the property of the Greenwood Company;
(b) for a service period of three years as doctor @ Hfl. 200 a year plus half of what he may earn for medical services outside the plantation;
(c) the doctor must also serve the director (at that time François Greenwood, a cousin of the two younger Greenwoods) of the plantation by acting as messenger and collector of debts, by communicating with the military fort, going out into the fields to observe the working negroes and to ascertain that they were working in a manner most profitable to the Greenwoods;
(d) he must sleep in the boiler house at times of sugar-boiling so as to keep an eye on the procedure;
(e) he will be given a negro assistant whom he must teach the art of medicine up to examination standard;
(f) if the present director wanted to repatriate after three years, Kruijff should be able to step in as acting director during 7/8th of the following year @ Hfl. 600 a year;
(g) the fare to Surinam will be paid for;
(h) among the tasks of the director are: proper management of the plantation, shipping sugar, keeping books in order, keeping in contact with the proprietors in Holland, annually making an inventory of all slaves, horses and other animals, kettles and other tools, house, financial matters;
(i) he is not to sell any property unless authorised thereto, or in case of emergency;
(j) a directorship would last for seven years;
(k) a director may only go to the military fort in utmost emergency and he is not to stay there longer than three or four days if it can be helped, not spending more than Hfl. 4 a day;
(l) he may not carry out any business for himself;
(m) he will get proper accommodation and 3 ankers [120 litres] of wine a year.

On 18 September, 1711, brothers Frans and Charles Greenwood dissolved their special business partnership in view of the latter's imminent departure for Surinam.

On 4 April, 1712, after the death of Charles, Francis Greenewood granted Frans (his only surviving son) full ownership of an eighth part of The Black Creek including slaves, horses, &c.; he had already received the income from that part since his wedding day [A247]. Frans gratefully acknowledged that gift.

In May, 1714, Frans appointed his trusted friend William Crowse of Hull to be his attorney in that town for settling matters of finance [A252]. In July, 1715, he signed himself "Frans Greenwoods zoon" and empowered Paul Diers de Ras to settle financial matters in Frankfurt [A254]. Frans was also for some time a dealer in textiles; in November, 1717, he was one of the Regents of the Laken-koopers Gilde [Cloth Merchants Guild] in Rotterdam, a function which he relin-quished in March, 1719 [A99].

Financially, Frans had his ups and downs. For instance, his old father agreed to stand surety for him in February, 1719, while from an inventory, made in April, 1719, of the estate of Mattheus and Maria Verwey, of Rotterdam, it is clear that he had pawned them a ring set with one large and twelve smaller dia-monds which, in a letter of 30 October, 1719, he declared to be buying back for Hfl. 130 and 7 stuyvers within two weeks [A91].

*   *   *

The year 1720 was a disastrous one commercially because of the financial crisis in the European money-markets due to the collapse of John Law's Bank of Issue in Paris. Moreover, the economic problems worsened as a result of a plague epidemic in Europe. - In two poems about a genuine and a false Golden Age, Frans Greenwood [50] greatly bemoaned the deplorable state of commercial affairs. Obviously he saw little hope for improvement in the immediate future [in another ten years commerce would be quite healthy again] which may well be a reason why he said farewell to commercial activities. - Frans started work as 'commies ter recherche' [customs and excise officer] for the Noble College of the Admiralty on the Maas, housed in the 'Admiraliteitshof' (later renamed 'Zee-kantoor') which since 1644 was situated on the corner of the Spaanschekade and Haringvliet. The building was demolished in 1882 (a model of it can be seen in Museum De Dubbelde Palmboom, Rotterdam). The task of that office was to provide protection to the fishing fleet and to impose import duties as one of its customs and excise functions. According to Nicolaes Versteeg [121], this profes-sion was a poorly paid one (Hfl. 50 per annum at Hellevoetsluis in 1746) - at least if the officer was an honest and incorruptible man. Moreover, the job called for a robust constitution as in all weathers a 'commies' had to be rowed in the harbour to various ships which he then had to clamber for inspection. In that new function Greenwood - whose main income must have been the pro-ceeds from The Black Creek plantation - acknowledged on 18 January, 1724, a debt of Hfl. 3,000 which he promised to repay at Hfl. 500 annually @ 4% interest [A259, A278]. On 27 December, 1724, Greenwood also admitted to owe Adriaen van Schuylenburgh, Heere van Duckenburg, Hfl. 3,786 for rent of a house, ware-house and yard, situated on the north side of Nieuwe Haven, Rotterdam, where he was still living [A289]. He promised to repay at least Hfl. 250 during each of the next three years, thereafter Hfl. 350 a year @ 3½% interest a year. Next, on 9 January, 1725, 'commies ter recherche Frans Greenwood' appointed Johan van Gelder, procurator at the Court of Justice in Rotterdam, to be his commis-sioner [290]. In July, 1725, Greenwood still owed the estate of deceased skipper Thomas Cock Hfl. 350 [A265, A266].

*   *   *

For reasons which cannot be fathomed - perhaps the bad luck which he had experienced privately and professionally at Nieuwe Haven was a contributing factor - Frans left Rotterdam early in 1726 and with his two children went to live in Dordrecht where at once he continued working as 'commies ter recherche' (he was known as such until his death). From a complaint to a Notary Public in April, 1726, about an importer of ten bales of linen with a total length of 30,200 ell and a value of Hfl. 17,500, having arrived from London, not paying import duty [A29], we know that Greenwood had at least three colleagues in Dordrecht.

Of course, The Black Creek continued to be a good source of income. After his father's death, in 1731, it took several years before the sale of the plantation was settled. In 1736, Jan Bout, a merchant of Dordrecht, was temporarily in charge of The Black Creek to the satisfaction of Frans Greenwood [A272]. The plantation was finally sold on 16 January, 1738, for Hfl. 27,000 [A10 - A12]. For Frans and the few of his sisters still alive this was a very welcome windfall.

In February, 1755, and March, 1757, when he was respectively 74 and 76 years old, Greenwood was still called a 'commies ter recherche in Dordrecht'. Most likely he was no longer active in that function.

*   *   *

FRANS   GREENWOOD
PARENTAGE   OF   HIS   WIFE

The father-in-law of Frans Greenwood was Cornelis Willemsz. van den Holaert, one of the noted Delft-ware potters [68]. A pottery named "De Wildemanspoort" was started in 1661 by Sebastiaen Maertensz. van Kuyck, a master potter who owned the works until his death in 1678 when his widow Catarina, née Van Steenhuysen, took over till her death in 1681. Cornelis Willemsz. van den Holaert then became manager/owner of the pottery, renaming it "De twee Wildemannen". His father was Cornelis Cornelisz. van den Holaert who had owned the pottery "De vier Helden van Roome" from 1656 - 1668 [63].

The first wife of Cornelis van den Holaert was Quirina, or Krijntje, van Kuyck, a daughter of Sebastiaen Maertensz. van Kuyck and Catarina van Steenhuysen whose seven children were all baptised in the Nieuwe Kerk, Delft [A13]:

C a t e r i n a   -   2.X.1652. Died before XI.1661

M a r t i n u s   -   6.XI.1653. Died before VII.1665

Quirina (Krijntje)   -   18.X.1657. Died 1716. Future mother-in-law of Frans
Greenwood.

J a n n e t j e   -   14.IX.1659

C a t a r i n a   -   17.XI.1661

M a r t i n u s   -   17.VII.1665

E l i s a b e t   -   9.XII.1674

Interestingly, one of the witnesses at Quirina's baptism on 18 October, 1657, was Huijg Leeuwenhoeck, an uncle of the now world-famous Antonie van Leeuwenhoek the naturalist, father of bacteriology, of protozoology, &c.

The children of Cornelis and Quirina were also all baptised in the Nieuwe Kerk, Delft [A13]. They were:

M a r i y a - 23.XII.1683. Witnesses: Frans Goversz. van den Backer and Geertrui van Cuyck. Future wife of Frans Greenwood. Died XII.1711.

W i l l e m - 29.I.1688. Witnesses: Adrijaan Leeuwenhoek and Geertruit Bastiaensdr van Cuijck. Died before 1720.

C a t h a r i n a - 2.XI.1692. Witnesses: Hendrik van Heden and Anna van Rees. Married Jacob in de Betou.

H e l e n a - 1.I.1694. Died before V.1697.

H e l e n a - 14.V.1697. Witnesses: Martinus Ravestein and Geertrui Bastiaensdr van Cuick.

Mother-in-law Quirina (Krijntje), of De Twee Wildemannen at Broerhuyslaan, Delft, died in October, 1716, and was buried on the 13th of that month in the Nieuwe Kerk, Delft, in the choir of the church vault [A18]. She left one child of age and two grandchildren under age [the two children of Frans Greenwood]. There were 14 coffin bearers.

Widower Cornelis van den Holaert remarried in Delft in March, 1719, taking as wife Geertruid Pothoven née van Leuven who previously, in May 1690, had married Gerrit Pothoven [A17]. - Cornelis drew up a testament before Notary Public Cornelis van der Heyden in Delft on 15 August, 1719. When living at Turfmarkt, Delft, Cornelis van den Holaert died on 15 February, 1720, and was buried in the afternoon of the 20th of that month in the same church vault as his first wife; there were 14 coffin bearers [A18].

The house, garden and pottery 'De Twee Wildemannen', situated at the south-side of Broerhuyslaan and adjoined to the east by the house of Joris Bleijswijk, to the west by that of Jan Jansz. Montrans, were sold for Hfl. 4,950 to Mattheus van den Boogaert in 1720 [A270].

On 10 May, 1721, a notarial protocol declared the only and universal heirs of Cornelis van den Holaert to be: Geertruy Pothoven (his widow), Catharina van den Holaert (widow of Jacob in de Betou), Adriaen van Besoyen (guardian of the children of Frans Greenwood) and Frans Greenwood [A257], the latter already profiting from the sale of shares in June, 1721 [A274].

In November, 1721, Geertruy Pothoven remarried, this time Joannes Ulhorn (or Ulhoorn), an organist living in Rotterdam.

When Adriaen van Bezooyen (or Besoyen), a baker in Rotterdam, died in 1719, he left nett Hfl. 21,731. About half that sum (Hfl. 10,965) went to Geertruy Pothoven, the remainder was divided into three sums of Hfl. 3,621 each which were inherited by Catharina van den Holaert and Anna and Cornelis, the two children of Frans Greenwood [A270].

*   *   *

CHILDREN OF FRANS GREENWOOD

Anna Greenwood

Anna was baptised in the Dutch Reformed Church, Rotterdam, on Tuesday 8 March, 1707 [A87]; it is possible, therefore, that she was born the previous Sunday, 6 March. Witnesses at the baptism were the parents of the father, Francis Greenewood and Anna Glover.

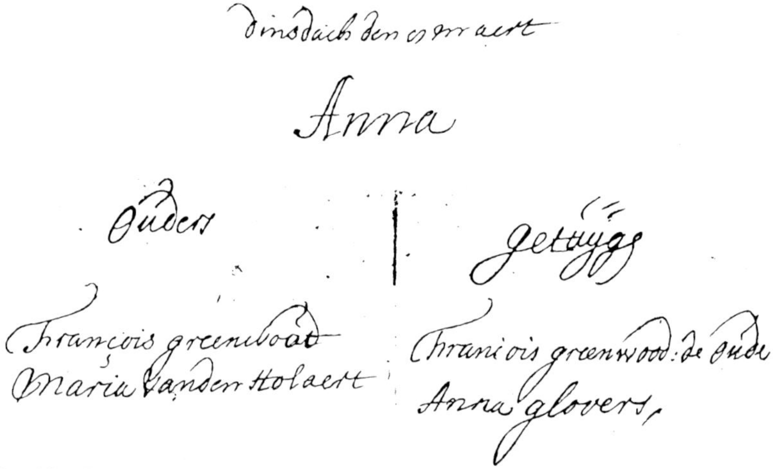

Fig. 16. Extract from the Register of Baptisms, Dutch Reformed Church, Rotterdam: "dinsdach den 8 maert (1707) [Tuesday 8 March, 1707] / Anna / Ouders [parents] / François greenwout (corrected to Greenwood) / Maria van den Holaert // getuijgen [witnesses] / François greenwood : de oude [Sr] / Anna glovers. [A87].

Anna never married and it appears that as a devoted daughter she spent much of her life looking after her father Frans Greenwood until his death in 1763. A friendly and cheerful woman no doubt, Anna was mentioned in and benefited from several testaments, a few examples of which are mentioned here.

She received a legacy (Hfl. 3,621) of Adriaen van Bezooyen, master bread baker in Rotterdam, on 8 May, 1724.

On 8 March, 1732, Anna empowered her father to claim from the heirs of deceased Petrus van Abcoude, Dordrecht, her heirloom according to a bequest of 15.VII.1720, namely the two rings and a gold brooch which his late wife used to wear [A27].

When on 23 January, 1753, Pauls Schepers made his testament, he directed that Anna Greenwood should receive Hfl. 2,500 [A279]. Pauls Schepers, an affluent high-ranking official in the Dutch United East India Company in Rotterdam, made a new testament on 7 February, 1755 [A280] and again on 31 July, 1755 [A281] - Anna was now to receive Hfl. 3,000 cash. Yet another new testament followed, on 7 March, 1757, but with much the same provisions [A282]. Pauls Schepers died 13 April, 1757. On 5 June, 1758, Anna received three shares of Hfl. 1,000 each, presumably the Schepers inheritance [A294].

Fig. 17. Signature of Anna Greenwood, dated 1735 [A31].

Together with her brother Kornelis, Anna drew up a joint testament on 13 July, 1735 [A30].

On 21 November, 1763, soon after her father's death, spinster Anna appointed John Edwards, a London merchant, to be "my True and Lawfull Attornij" . . . . "to contract for purchase & Buy, & to take & accept Assignments or Transfers at anij Time or times of Anij Intrest or Share in the Capital or joint Stock of 4pct Ann/s Erected by an Acte of Parliament of the third year of the reign of his Majesty King George the third, Entitled an Act for Granting to his Majesty several Additional duties upon wines Imported into this Kingdom et certain duties upon all Cyder et Perry et for raissing the sum of £3,500,000 by waij off Ann/s & Lotteries to be charged on the said duties Transferable at the Bank of England, etc." [A35]. These instructions were renewed on 14 January, 1768 [A33]. - On 15 December, 1763, Anna appointed Mr Paulus Gevaerts, a former burgomaster of Dordrecht, to be her executor as regards shares &c. which she had in England [A36]. On the same day she made a testament [A37] in which her property is stated to be worth not more than Hfl. 20,000. Apart from donations to her maid Sebilla Gips, the universal heirs were to be Mr Paulus Gevaerts and his wife Susanna Adriana Beelaards [Beelaerts].

On 4 June, 1767, Anna revoked her testament [A32] and made a new one in which the following are now mentioned as new universal heirs: Miss Erckenraadt, Misses Maria and Adriana Cornelia Vrolijkhardt. Alterations to that testament were made on 13 November, 1772 [A34].

Steven Hoogendijk, a wealthy horologist in Rotterdam, made a testament on 3 June, 1769, in which Anna is mentioned to receive Hfl. 75 annually [A283]. She cannot have profited much, because Hoogendijk was still alive and confirming his will in May, 1784 [A293].

Apart from English financial interests, Anna had some French ones as well - in December 1782 she appointed bankers van den IJver, Sr & Jr, to look after her French monetary affairs [A38].

On 26 January, 1789, Anna once again revoked her previous testaments and - still living at Steegoversloot - made a new, final, one before Notary Public Anthony de Fockert in Dordrecht [A39]. Her maid Sebilla Gips was now to inherit (apart from some money) the drawer-table and the cabinet standing in the back-room complete with everything on or in it; universal heirs: med. dr Jacob Kort-hals and Notary Public Abraham Adrianus van den Oever, both of Dordrecht. The house and garden at Steegoversloot were left to Abraham Smak of Dordrecht [A39] which was confirmed on 16.VII.1799 [A26].

Anna Greenwood died on Thursday 15 May, 1794, and was buried in the Nieuwe Kerk, Dordrecht, on 16 May, 1794; the impost was Hfl. 30 [A20]. The Register of Burials simply records: "Juffrouw Anna Greenwood in het Steeg Over Sloot / Ongehuwt met drie koetsen Extra [unmarried, three extra carriages]. Out 88 Jaaren Verval van kragten en koortsen [loss of strength and fevers]. 1 Uur Luye [tolling of bells for one hour]."

K o r n e l i s   G r e e n w o o d

Born on Sunday 2 September, 1708, at Nieuwe Haven, Rotterdam, the son was baptised as Cornelis [after his maternal grandfather; Anna was named after her paternal grandmother] in the Dutch Reformed Church, Rotterdam, on Tuesday 4 September, 1708. Witnesses were the parents of the mother: Cornelis van den Holaert and Quirina van Kuyck [A87].

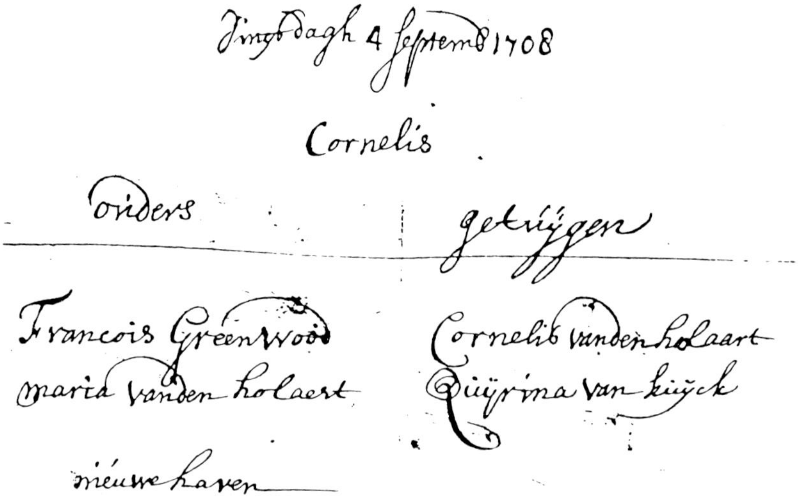

Fig. 18. Extract from the Register of Baptisms, Dutch Reformed Church, Rotterdam: "dingsdagh 4 septemb 1708 [Tuesday 4 September 1708] / Cornelis / Ouders [parents] / Francois Greenwood / Maria van den holaert / Nieuwe Haven / getuijgen [witnesses] Cornelis van den holaart / Quijrina van kuijck [A87].

Kornelis was taught the art of drawing by Arent Vygh who had been a pupil of Adriaen van der Werff, the famous painter. The untimely death of Vygh was said to have affected Kornelis so much that he temporarily interrupted his studies [40].

Frans Greenwood and his two children went to live in Dordrecht early in 1726. At that time Adriaen van der Burgh (1693-1733) was a popular painter in that town and Kornelis, through meeting him, rekindled his zest for art [40]. With his father's permission he became a pupil of van der Burgh and after three or four years training, Kornelis was considered a good enough draughtsman to start painting at which he made good progress, much to the satisfaction of his father and the teacher. After a few more years - which must have been in the early 1730s - Kornelis was able to paint from life. Fine examples of his work were to be seen at his father's home and at other collectors' residences in town; they were genre pieces as well as portraits which were all cleverly executed. One wonders whether any of these drawings or paintings are still extant.

Meanwhile Kornelis had befriended Aart Schouman who was a co-pupil of van der Burgh. They stimulated each other to better the quality of their work.

Winter evenings were spent at Greenwood's house where drawings were made from plaster casts. Kornelis, Aart and some of their enthusiastic friends became eager to try their hand at life models, so they rented a room in the Stadtsdoelen (probably St Jorisdoelen in Steegoversloot) and also managed to hire a real model; the cost was shared by the members of this informal art club.

In 1735, a cousin of Kornelis - this must have been Frans Schas - who owned several plantations in Surinam, invited him to come to Surinam to become manager of one of the plantations [40]. Kornelis assumed that such work would be more lucrative than painting, so he wrote the 'art club' a letter of resignation - such was the blow that the club disbanded.

Fig. 19. Signature of Kornelis Greenwood, dated 1735 [A31].

On 13 July, 1735, Kornelis together with his sister Anna made a joint testament, the one to be heir of the other, and in case of the death of both, their father to be heir [A30]. On the same day Anna and Kornelis offered thanks to baker Adriaen van Bezooyen for his guardianship arising from the will of their maternal grandfather Cornelis van den Holaert [A31].

*　　*　　*

Rather hurriedly Kornelis left for Surinam in the autumn of 1735. After some four months in the promised land he fell ill and died from a "hot fever" (very likely malaria tropica [Plasmodium falciparum] transmitted especially by the mosquito Anopheles darlingi) [27], on 3 April, 1736, aged 27 years 7 months.

Frans Greenwood [50] composed a moving poem on the passing of his son: "Lykklagt over myn zeer lieven zoon, Kornelis Greenwood, overleden in Surinamen den 3 April 1736. in den ouderdom van 27 jaren 7 maanden en 1 dag."

Particulars about the burial of Kornelis Greenwood have not come to light. In Surinam Europeans were buried, since 1685, in Paramaribo in the 'Oude Oranjetuin' [Old Orange Garden] so called after the orange trees planted there [88]. Since 1694 tombs and graves had to be paid for in sugar. A family tomb in the Reformed Church, Paramaribo, cost 20,000 pounds of sugar (@ 1 stuyver a pound = Hfl. 1,000); a single tomb in that church required a payment of 10,000 pounds of sugar (Hfl. 500) while for a burial in a cemetery or on a plantation the cost was only 400 pounds of sugar (Hfl. 20).

*　　*　　*

PORTRAITS OF FRANS GREENWOOD

Portrait A

Jacob Zeeus, who died in November 1718, referred in an undated poem [139] to a portrait of his friend Frans Greenwood "on a panel" which therefore indicates an oil-painting. This is the earliest reference to a portrait of Greenwood which must have been painted well before the end of 1718, i.e., when Frans was at most 38 years old. Could it have been executed by their mutual friend Arnold Houbraken in Dordrecht, whom Greenwood had assisted with a portrait he made of Zeeus ? The painting (very likely not a miniature) is perhaps still extant but unrecognised. - Zeeus wrote:

> *Op de afbeeldinge*
> *van den Heere*
> *Frans Greenwood.*

> *Dus toont zich GREENWOOD op 't paneel,*
> * Wiens zuivere inborst en geweten*
> *Van Valscheit nimmer wiert bezeten.*
> * De Dichtkunst is het lustpriëel*
> *Van zyn verhevene gedachten.*
> * Lang zweef zyn geest, van onlust vry,*
> *Waer van wy zoo veel vrugts verwachten,*
> * Op wieken van de Poëzy;*
> *Terwyl wy op zyn vrientschap bogen*
> *Zoo lang 'er licht straelt uit onze oogen.*

[On the portrait of Mr Frans Greenwood. / The panel shows the effigy of Greenwood, / Whose noble character and spirit / Were always free from insincerity. / Poetry is the abode of delight / For his exalted thoughts. / May his untroubled great mind / From which we expect many fruits, / Long hover on the wings of poetry - / While we glory in his friendship / As long as light radiates from our eyes.]

The same painting may also have inspired Cornelis Boon van Engelant (1680-1746) whose eulogy was first published in 1724 [24]:

> *Op de afbeelding*
> *van den Heere*
> *Frans Greenwood.*

> *Dit 's Greenwood, die alleen geen' aerdschen schat,*
> * zoo ras*
> *Vaek ebbende als die vloeit, vergâert door koopmanschappen;*
> * Maer ook, op eer belust, den Hollantschen Parnas*
> *Gelukkiglyk beklimt met mannelyke stappen.*
> * Noit spant hy zyne lier, of Rotte en Maes, noit môe*
> * Van luistren, juicht om stryt met hantgeklap hem toe.*

[On the portrait of Mr Frans Greenwood. / This is Greenwood, who not only gathers commercially / A worldly fortune which often ebbs and flows, / But who also ambitiously, with virile strides, / Fortunately ascends the Dutch Parnassus. / He never plays his lyre without Rotte and Maas / - never tired of listening - / Rivalling in applauding him.]

It is noteworthy that neither poem refers to Greenwood as glass engraver. Zeeus died well before his friend's first dated engraving (1720) and Boon van Engelant had perhaps also composed his lines prior to that year.

PORTRAITS MADE FOR THE PANPOETICON BATAVUM

Arnoud van Halen (1673-1732), a wealthy bachelor who lived and worked in Amsterdam, dabbled in painting, mezzotint engraving, sculpturing, ivory carving and writing poetry. In common with other rich burghers of his day, van Halen delighted in forming a collection to be proud of; unlike others, he created part of the collection himself [58]. In fact, he painted - with rather sparse use of colour - portraits of well-known Dutch poets on small (ca. 9 x 11 cm) oval metal plates. In 1719 he had a splendid walnut cabinet made to house his collection. That cabinet, now lost, had 82 removable trays on each of which up to eleven miniatures were mounted [19]. This 'Cabinet of illustrious Dutch poets' became known as the 'Panpoëticon Batavum". The latter is also the title of Lambert Bidloo's lengthy and long-winded encomium of 1720 [22]. Bidloo made no mention of Frans Greenwood, who in fact was not included among his brethren during van Halen's lifetime.

After van Halen's death in 1732 the Panpoëticon Batavum was bought by Michiel de Roode (1685-1771), a broker in Amsterdam, who replaced 22 portraits with improved versions while in the course of time he also added no fewer than 113 new miniatures. These additions had been assigned to various painters, among them Aart Schouman - who contributed seven portraits including one of Frans Greenwood - and Kornelis Greenwood who was commissioned to paint one portrait, namely that of his father Frans.

In 1771 the cabinet came into the hands of Arnoud de Jongh and subsequently, upon his death in 1772, it became the property of the Leiden literary society 'Kunst wordt door arbeid verkreegen' (K.W.D.A.V.) [Art is acquired through work] and was kept in the Society's premises on Langebrug [19, 58]. Already the next year the Society published a volume of collected essays [9] exalting the cabinet and the poets represented. That book contains a eulogy by Frans Greenwood (pp. 116-117) "Op het / Pan Poëticon Batavûm, / aangelegd door den heere / Arnoud van Halen, / en na deszelfs overlyden vervolgd / door den Heere / Michiel de Roode." [On the Pan Poëticon Batavum, formed by Mr Arnoud van Halen and continued after his death by Mr Michiel de Roode], signed and dated: "Frans Greenwood, Den 28den. van Wynmaand 1735" [28 October, 1735]. Apparently Greenwood visited Amsterdam in the autumn of 1735 - at which time his son Kornelis departed for Surinam.

When, on 12 January, 1807, an area around Rapenburg, Leiden, was devastated by an exploding gunpowder barge, the cabinet suffered damage but not the miniatures it contained.

The cabinet with its 350 portraits was auctioned in Amsterdam on 9 April, 1818, by Roos, de Vries & Brondgeest [15] and bought for Hfl. 605 by Anthonie Kluijtenaar in whose family it remained until 16 October 1849, when it was sold at auction by de Vries, Roos & Brondgeest, Amsterdam [18] and purchased for Hfl. 725 by Samson, a dealer, who soon disposed of the collection piecemeal.

Fortunately, the Rijksmuseum in Amsterdam now owns 78 of the portraits, among them one of Frans Greenwood by Aart Schouman [58, 118].

*   *   *

The Panpoëticon Batavum may have contained the following three portraits of Frans Greenwood:

P o r t r a i t   B

The first portrait miniature must have been the one commissioned by de Roode from Kornelis Greenwood. This can be dated between 1732 (when Michiel de Roode acquired the cabinet) and 1735 (when Kornelis Greenwood left Holland for Surinam).

There is no trace of this portrait; the chances are slim that it is the miniature from the collection of van der Willigen sold in 1874 [14].

Anonymous 1773: xx. Moes 1897: 350 (No. 2925:1 - erroneously stated to be in the Rijksmuseum, Amsterdam). Van Thiel et al. 1976: 725 (wrongly attributed the Schouman pen-and-wash ink portrait of Greenwood in the 23.II.1909 de Vries auction, Amsterdam, [lot 2812] to Kornelis Greenwood).

P o r t r a i t   C

In 1739 Joan Vermeulen, a friend of both Greenwood and Schouman, wrote two poems "Op de / afbeelding / van den Heere / Frans Greenwood" [On the portrait of Mr Frans Greenwood] which were published in 1773 [9]:

I

Dit 's GREENWOOD, door 't penseel van Schouman afgemaalt;
Wiens geest in Poëzij en Schilderkunst ervaaren;
Gelijk een Kunstlicht aan de Maaze en Merwe straalt.
Apollo leerde hem het handlen van de snaaren:
Minerva onderwees zijn' geest, vol eedle drift,
Op 't glas te teiknen, met een diamanten stift.

II

Dus ziet men 't aangezicht van Greenwood afgebeelt,
Beschaafde geestigheit is hem als aangeboren.
Al wat Natuur en Kunst heeft uit dit brein geteelt;
't Zij Dicht, of Schilderkunst, kan oog en oor bekoren.
Minerva leerde hem, bezielt van kunst en drift,
Op glazen teiknen, met een diamanten stift.

1739   *Joan Vermeulen.*

[I: This is Greenwood, painted by Schouman's brush; / Whose spirit - experienced in poetry and painting - / Radiates like an artificial light along Maas and Merwede. / Apollo taught him to play the lyre (i.e., poetry): / Minerva inspired his spirit, full of enthusiasm, / To draw on glass with a diamond point.
II: Thus one sees Greenwood's face depicted, / With an innate cultured mind. / All that Nature and Art brought forth from his brain / Can enchant eye and ear, whether in painting or poetry. / Inspired by art and eagerness, Minerva taught him / To draw on glasses with a diamond point.]

From the first poem the conclusion may be drawn that Aart Schouman had painted a miniature [untraced] in or before 1739 (see Portrait D).

Did Vermeulen write two different poems for one and the same portrait or had he intended the second poem to be a eulogy for the portrait by the late Kornelis Greenwood ?

Anonymous 1773: xx (attributed to J. M. Quinkhard), 186. Moes 1897: 351 (No. 2925:2 - with the remark that the painting is not by J. M. Quinkhard as stated in Anonymous 1773: xx). Heeren 1919: 239.

Fig. 20. Portrait D.

Portrait D (Fig. 20)

A miniature portrait in colour by Aart Schouman, signed AS, inscribed on verso: "Frans Greenwood Gebooren den 17 April 1680 / 1740 30/4." On an oval copper sheet, 9½ x 11 cm. In the Rijksmuseum, Amsterdam (inv. A 1968; previously inv. 1081).

If this is indeed different from the above mentioned Schouman portrait (C), one might ask why he painted two miniatures within so short a time. Did the former meet with an accident or did de Roode have the Kornelis Greenwood portrait replaced by this one ? There is no telling.

Anonymous 1773: 186. Auction catalogue Roos 1902 (No. 1081 - erroneously attributed to Arnoud van Halen who died in 1732). Van Riemsdijk 1903: No. 1081 (likewise wrongly ascribed to van Halen). Heeren 1919: 239 (overlooked the fact that Vermeulen's poems are dated 1739 while this Schouman portrait bears as date 30.IV.1740). Van Hall 1963: 118 (No. 757:1 - also wrongly ascribed to A. van Halen), 119 (No. 757:3). Van Thiel et al. 1976: 725, 734, fig. A 1968. Liefkes 1987: fig. p. 56.

Portrait B, C or D

In 1752 Nikolaes Teyssen also wrote a poem on Greenwood's portrait in the Panpoëticon Batavum but it cannot be ascertained which portrait was referred to.

> Op de beeltenisse
> van den heere
> Frans Greenwood.

Dit 's Greenwoods beeltenis, voor wien d'aloutheit bukt,
Wiens diamanten stift op glaezen drinkbokaelen.
Wiens dicht- en schilderkunst haer, schaemrood, houd verrukt:
Die kunst en wetenschap doet op een' eertroon praelen.
Zij hoort in hem Apol, als hij de snaeren drukt,
En ziet Apelles geest door zijn tafrelen straelen.

1752   *Nikolaes Teyssen*
                                    J. U. Stud.
                      [Juris Utriusque Studiosus = lawyer]

[On the portrait of Mr Frans Greenwood. / This is the effigy of Greenwood, for whom antiquity stoops, / whose diamond point on glass goblets, / Whose poetry and painting blushingly enchants antiquity: / Who induces art and science to be displayed on a throne of honour. / Antiquity hears Apollo in him when he touches strings, / And sees the spirit of Apelles radiating from his pictures.]

Anonymous 1773: 223.

*   *   *

PEN / BRUSH-AND-WASH [INK] PORTRAITS BY AART SCHOUMAN

Portrait E

A drawing on paper "en grisaille" showing a half-length portrait of Frans Greenwood, wearing a long wig, on an oval panel held by an emblematical figure (supposedly Thalia) and surrounded by embellishments; inscribed on a blank rectangular panel below: "Frans Greenwood oud 58 jaren." and to one side of the drawing "1738" [74]. This short description points to a design similar to the pen-and-wash drawing by Aart Schouman of 1748 (Portrait F) and this drawing may be assumed to be by the same hand; indeed, it is ascribed to Schouman in the Auction Catalogue of de Vries, 1909. It is noteworthy that a very similar portrait design was drawn by Schouman (and etched by J. Houbraken) of the poet Jakob Spex (1704-1755) for the title-page of his collected poems published in 1755 [116].

Kramm [74], who in the middle of the nineteenth century owned this drawing, remarked that Greenwood looked younger than 58 on this portrait. According to the 1875 Auction Catalogue (Beijers) of the Kramm collection (p. 279, No. 3640), Schouman's mezzotint portrait differs from the drawing by the face being of an older appearance, with a different wig, &c. - but this was to be expected as the mezzotint is based on a drawing made ten years later than the 1738 drawing.

Fig. 21. Portrait F.

Subsequently the drawing passed into the collection of A. J. Nijland, Utrecht, and was sold by auction (together with a Schouman mezzotint portrait of Greenwood) in 1909 to Mayer for Hfl. 6. Its present whereabouts are not known.

Kramm 1858: 602; 1861: 1495. Auction catalogue (Beijers) 11.XII.1875: 279 (lot 3640 part - erroneously attributed to "A. v. d. Werff (?)", who died in 1722). Auction catalogue (de Vries) 23.II.1909: 180 (lot 2812 part). Van Hall 1963: 119 (No. 757:5). Van Thiel et al. 1976: 725 (erroneously attributed to Cornelis Greenwood).

P o r t r a i t   F   (Fig. 21)

A pen / brush-and-wash half-length portrait on an oval panel held by an emblematical figure (Thalia), signed: "A Schouman ad viv. Delin:". Size 146 x 180 mm.
On verso, in browned ink: "F. Greenwood 1748 out 68 jaren" and "F. Greenwood /
was in 1748 oud 68 jaren". Below the drawing, within a rectangular panel, a poem
by Dirk Smits (1702-1752), dated 1751, apparently in Greenwood's handwriting.
According to the poem, this is the design for a copperplate (mezzotint) engraving
(by Schouman). The original remained in Schouman's possession until his death in
1792; it was included in the sale of the contents of his house at Beestenmarkt,
's-Gravenhage, on Monday 10 December, 1792 (lot 653 - "Pourtrait van F. Greenwood, in 't grauw met olieverwe" - grey in oil-paint [sic]) [16]. In 1817 the drawing was in the collection of Dr A. van der Willigen, Haarlem; subsequently in
that of A. G. O. Visser and, presumably since 1881, is now in the Department of
Prints and Drawings of the Museum Boymans - van Beuningen, Rotterdam (inv.
A. Schouman 1).

Dirk Smits' poem was published in 1753:

Op de / afbeelding / van / den Heer / Frans Greenwood.

Aldus leeft GREENWOOD, met zyn Zangheldinn' en Lier',
Door 't stael in 't koper, en door 't koper op 't papier;
Doch schooner weet zyn Geest zichzelven af te malen,
Door 't diamanten stift op glazen drinkbokalen.
Maer 't glas is bros ! 't papier; ja 't koper slyt de tydt !
Geen noodt ! zyn lier heeft hem aen de eeuwigheit gewyd.
1751.   *D. SMITS*

[On the portrait of Mr Frans Greenwood. / Thus lives Greenwood, with his muse
and lyre, / By a steel graver into copper, via copperplate on to paper; / But his
spirit knows how to project itself better / On glass goblets with a diamond
point. / But glass is fragile ! paper, yes, even copper, eventually / perishes !
Not to worry ! / His lyre has made him immortal.]

As we now know, just the opposite has turned out to be the case: Greenwood
is famed for his fragile glasses, not for the lyrical products of his quill.

Smits 1753: 254 [misprinted 154]. Auction catalogue (Scheurleer) 10.XII.1792:
22 (lot 653). Van Eijnden & van der Willigen 1817: 67. Kramm 1858: 602.
Van Hall 1963: 118 (No. 757:2).

*   *   *

MEZZOTINT PORTRAITS

P o r t r a i t   G   (Fig. 22)

A copy of a first state pull of Schouman's mezzotint portrait (portrait I), signed:
"A: Schouman, Fecit.", with D. Smits' poem (see Portrait F) written by Schouman
in ink within the rectangular panel below the portrait. Schouman was notoriously
bad at orthography and the spelling of various words in his copy of the poem
differs somewhat (without being incorrect) from the original printed version:
Aldus leeft Greenwood met zyn Zangheldinn' en Lier, / Door 't Staal in 't
Koper, en door 't Koper op Papier; / dog te schoner weet zyn Geest zig zelven
af te malen / door 't Diamanten stift op Glasen Drinkbokalen. / Maer 't Glas
is bros: 't Papier, ja 't Koper slyt de tyd; Geen nood: zyn Lier heeft hem
aan d'eeuwigheid geweyd. / D: SMITS

In Rijksprentenkabinet, Rijksmuseum, Amsterdam (inv. 27998).

Fig. 22. Portrait G.

P o r t r a i t   H   (Fig. 23)

A contra-print (counterproof) taken from a first state pull of Aart Schouman's mezzotint portrait (portrait I), signed at bottom left of blank bottom panel: "A. Schouman. fecit ad viv."

Schouman kept a number of proofs of his graphic work, as is evident from lot 700 in the catalogue of the 1792 auction of his estate: there were in all 81 different prints of his 40 etchings and mezzotints.

This contra-print was subsequently coloured in with a brush, possibly by Schouman himself.

In Rijksprentenkabinet, Rijksmuseum, Amsterdam (inv. A 4545).

Buckley 1930b, c: 9, pl. 1; 1931: 19, pl. 23 (the print erroneously stated to be the original drawing for the mezzotint [portrait I]). Van Hall 1963: 118 (No. 757: sub 2).

Fig. 23. Portrait H.

Portrait I (Fig. 24)

A mezzotint half-length portrait by Aart Schouman, unsigned, within an oval panel held by an emblematical figure (supposedly Thalia [38]), based on Schouman's pen-and-wash drawing (portrait F). In the rectangular panel below the portrait a poem in Roman type by Arnold Hoogvliet (1687-1763). The size is 198 x 155 mm. This mezzotint very likely dates from the early 1750s; several copies exist. - Hoogvliet's poem was published in 1753 [61]:

> Op de / beeltenis / van den Heere / Frans Greenwood.

De wakkre GREENWOOD, d'Eer van 't Nederduitsch gedicht;
De Roém der Teekenkunst, word hier vertoont naar 't leven;
De vriendelyke Deugt, te zien in 't aangezicht,
Strydt met de Kunst, wie Hem den grootsten naam zal geven.
Die met den diamant op myne Drinkbokaal
Aan Vondel 't leven gaf, leeft dus door Schoumans staal.
Arnold Hoogvliet.

Fig. 24. Portrait I.

[On the portrait of Mr Frans Greenwood. / The diligent Greenwood, the Honour of Dutch poetry; / The Fame of Draughtsmanship, is depicted here from life; / The friendly Virtue visible in his face, / Vies with Art to give Him the greatest name, / He who with a diamond on my goblet / Gave life to Vondel, thus lives by Schouman's steel. / Arnold Hoogvliet.]

Hoogvliet 1753: 198. Auction catalogue (Scheurleer) 1792: 24 (lot 700, part).
Van Eijnden & van der Willigen 1817: 67. Muller 1853: 100 (No. 1986). Weigel
1856: 198 (No. 1255 - erroneously stated to be a portrait of "C. Greenwood
Junior"). Kramm 1858: 1495. J. C. K. 1865: 299. Auction catalogue (Beijers)
10.XII.1875: 259 (lot 2993); 11.XII.1875: 279 (lot 3640, part). Overvoorde
1899: 191 (No. 1641; No. 1642 a first state pre-lettering pull). Wurzbach
1906: 615. Van Gijn 1908: 213 (No. 3357). Auction catalogue (de Vries) 23.
II.1909: 180 (lot 2812, part). Moquette 1917: 95 (No. 814). Buckley 1930b,
c: 9, pl. 2. Bol 1960: 86 (No. 161). Breman & Rijken 1983: fig. p. 14.

Portrait J

A mezzotint bust portrait, to sinister, with face rather different from Schouman's
mezzotint (portrait I), on an oval panel with surrounding embellishments, a palette
and brushes in front of effigy. Because of its great similarity to a mezzotint
portrait by R. Jelgerhuis, dated 1767, of poet J. Buma (1694-1756), Muller (1853:
52, No. 804) implied that this [untraced] mezzotint was made by R. Jelgerhuis.

Muller 1853: 100 (No. 1987 - a pull without name). Kramm 1858: 602; 1861:
1495. Wurzbach 1906: 615. Van Hall 1963: 119 (No. 757:4).

Fig. 25. Portrait K.

PORTRAIT STIPPLE-ENGRAVED ON GLASS

P o r t r a i t   K   (Fig. 25)

A stipple engraving on the bowl of an eighteenth-century goblet, unsigned (but perhaps by L. Adams), based on Schouman's mezzotint (portrait I). In very faint stipple: "Ce portrait y est introduit au pointillé et d'une finesse tellement extrême qu'on ne s'en aperçoit pas à primavista." (Auction catalogue Muller 1913b). Height of goblet 192 mm. Bowl round funnel, ⌀ 80 mm. Stem with an angular knop over a knop on a ball knop with a double row of tears, above an inverted baluster on a base knop. Foot conical, pontil mark unpolished, ⌀ 84 mm.

Ownership: H. A. Steengracht van Duivenvoorde, 's-Gravenhage / auction Muller, Amsterdam, 8.V.1913 (Hfl. 300) / auction Muller, Amsterdam, 28.XI.1913 / private collection in England.

Auction catalogue (Muller) 8.V.1913: 65 (lot 872); 28.XI.1913: 101 (lot 1587). Buckley 1930 b, c: 9, pl. 4; 1931: 19 (No. 7), pl. 14. Honey 1946: 134.

*   *   *

P O R T R A I T S   O F   K O R N E L I S   G R E E N W O O D

P o r t r a i t   L   (Fig. 26)

An etched bust portrait, face ¾ to sinister, by Aart Schouman who drew and etched it while P. Tanjé, prior to publication in Van Gool [40] retouched the plate with engraving in 1751.

Van Gool 1751: pl. H, part (facing p. 212). Van Someren 1890: 293 (No. 2101). Moquette 1917: 95 (No. 813). Van Hall 1963: 118 (No. 756).

P o r t r a i t   M

A mezzotint bust portrait within a medallion, with surrounding embellishments, signed "W. Pether sc.". William Pether was born in Carlisle in 1731 and died in London in 1795. His mezzotint [untraced] can presumably therefore only be based on the Schouman etching (portrait L) in Van Gool.

Weigel 1856: 197 (No. 1254). Kramm 1858: 602. Wurzbach 1906: 615.

*   *   *

Fig. 26. Portrait L.

*　　*　　*

BROTHERS AND SISTERS

Francis Greenewood and Anna Greenewood née Glover had eight children in all, three sons and five daughters: Maria 1671-1711, James 1674-1698, Anna 1676-1736, François 1680-1763, Sara ±1684-after 1740, Catharina 1686- ? , Charles ±1688-1711 and Elisabeth 1690-1764.

Maria

The first child was baptised as Mariya in the Dutch Reformed Church, Rotterdam, on 18 October, 1671. Witnesses were Anna Colenpreys (maternal grandmother), Michiel Colenpreys and a certain Mariya [A87]. - As is the case with the other children, nothing is known about her adolescence.

Maria married, in Rotterdam on 17 April, 1695, widower Adriaen Fannius (whose first wife had been a Van Bueren, apparently from Amsterdam), who was a bailiff and a dike-reeve of the High Seigniory of Hagesteyn near Vianen which at the time was situated in the province of Utrecht. Fannius is an old family - in the 13th century known as Fannin, later as Fanneau; it was Pierre Fanneau, a professor in Leuven [Louvain], who had changed the name to Fannius [108]. Adriaen died in early 1699; on 21 May, 1699, Daniël Fannius was appointed to act as procurator on Maria's behalf [A60]. On June the 1st of that year Maria Greenwood was indeed mentioned as widow and heiress of Adriaen Fannius [A61]. She then had a young son, Adriaen Fannius Jr.

Maria, living at Nieuwe Haven (where her parents also resided), subsequently married English bachelor merchant Thomas Nodes (also from Nieuwe Haven) in the Reformed Church of Rotterdam on 1 June, 1701 [A88]. Thomas Nodes was born at Shephalbury, 51.53N 0.11W, a hamlet in Hertfordshire (3 KM south of Stevenage) but he eventually settled in Rotterdam [92]. On 12 May, 1701, prior to their wedding, they had agreed to certain marital conditions [A162]: if Thomas were to die first, Maria would receive Hfl. 12,000 from the estate; if she were to die first, he would receive Hfl. 10,000. On 28 May, 1701, Maria appointed her father to act as legal executive [A163, A164]. Thomas and Maria Nodes drew up a testament on 6 November, 1701 [A166]. In that month the conditions concerning Maria's finances were modified [A179]. - On 10 August, 1706, Thomas Nodes acquired citizenship of Rotterdam; he was then said to have in marriage the daughter of a burgher, namely of Francis Greenewood [92].

The couple had two children but particulars could be traced for only one, namely Elizabeth Anna Maria, baptised 10 February, 1709, in the Dutch Reformed Church of Schiedam, with witnesses Francis Greenewood and his wife Anna Glover, Charles Greenwood and his wife Maria Hosteijn [A295].

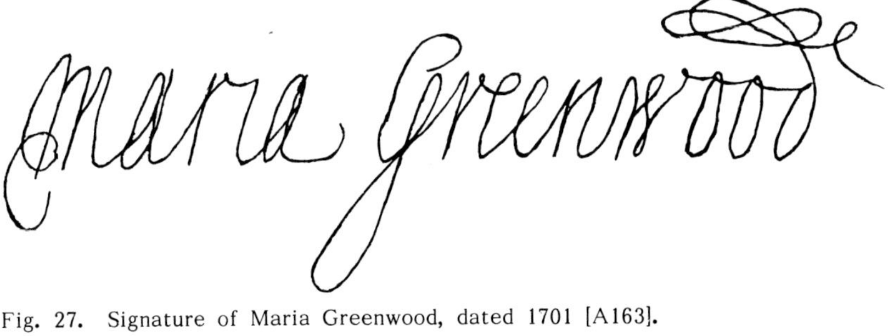

Fig. 27. Signature of Maria Greenwood, dated 1701 [A163].

Thomas Nodes apparently spent some time in London. In December, 1704, he was mentioned by Francis Greenewood as his son-in-law and merchant in London whom he required to settle financial matters in London on his behalf [A224]. In April, 1706, Nodes was still referred to as a merchant in London [A235 - A237] but from July, 1706, onwards he again was a merchant in Rotterdam [A178].

Perhaps to set her up in business, Francis Greenewood presented his daughter Maria on 7 April, 1708, with a house and garden with a long rope-walk behind it, as well as a proper stove, tar-kettle, twining-alley and all implements, situated on the north side of Gooystraat with Baanstraat to the east, in Schiedam (just west of Rotterdam) [A181]. Maria officially acknowledged receipt of the gift and agreed to thank her father in a proper manner [A296].

Two years later, on 1 February, 1710, Maria "housewife of Thomas Nodes, living in Rotterdam" bought a small property at Noordvest, Schiedam, from Cornelis Bood for Hfl. 85 [A297] which, after her death, was sold by Thomas Nodes for Hfl. 100 in April, 1712 [A298].

On 27 May, 1711, Maria was again mentioned as wife of Thomas Nodes, living in Rotterdam [A184]. By that time she was physically of poor health but mentally alert. On that day in 1711 Maria confirmed the validity of the testament which she and Thomas had made on 6 November, 1701; their property was now valued to be in excess of Hfl. 4,000.

Maria Nodes née Greenwood died on 22 June, 1711. Strangely enough, her parents were apparently not aware of her departure from life when on 5 September, 1711, they drew up a testament in which Maria was referred to as being married to Thomas Nodes [A77]. On 10 August, 1711, Nodes accepted guardianship over his children but on 15 December, 1711, he appointed Maria's father Francis Greenewood to act as guardian over his infant (presumably Elizabeth Anna Maria) in case he himself would come to die [A185].

Widower Thomas Nodes, still residing at Nieuwe Haven, Rotterdam, quite soon found himself another spouse. On 14 January, 1712, marital conditions were drawn up between him and spinster Johanna Hosteyn, daughter of Olivier Hosteyn, born in Leiden in September 1685 and also living at Nieuwe Haven [A186]. Johanna was a twin-sister of the late Maria Hosteyn whom Charles Greenwood (brother of Maria) had married in 1708. The wedding took place in Rotterdam on 26 January, 1712 [A88]. Their three children were all baptised in the Reformed Church, Rotterdam [A87]: Elisabeth on 10.XI.1712, Sara Maria on 29.III.1714 and Sara on 29.IV.1717. While the first two children were born at Nieuwe Haven, the third child was born at Kipstraat.

In October, 1715, Thomas Nodes was living at Schiedam, owing his former father-in-law Hfl. 1,000 and still owning the inherited rope-walk [A299] which, on 24 October, 1718, he sold for Hfl. 2,500 for the benefit of the two children (still under age) from his marriage to Maria Greenwood [A300].

Thomas Nodes died in or before 1728.

* * *

J a m e s

Baptised in the English Church, Rotterdam, on 18 November, 1674. When still a young bachelor, James was already working on The Black Creek plantation in Surinam in 1693; on 9 July, 1693, his father Francis Greenewood appointed him to be a co-manager and director.

James died in Surinam on 23 December, 1698. The Governor and Councillors of Surinam notified the relatives in Holland and appointed Johannes Veen to act as temporary supervisor [134]. In May, 1699, Francis appointed another director to take the place of his deceased son [A159].

*   *   *

Anna

This daughter was baptised in the English Church, supposedly in Dordrecht, on 28 July, 1676 [69, 101, 103]. Although there was an English/Scottish church community in that town since 1623 (until 1839), there are no records of the parents having resided there; it would seem more likely that the baptism, like that of the other Greenwood children, took place in Rotterdam.

On 17 April, 1695, when still living at the parental home at Nieuwe Haven, Anna married - in the nearby English Church on the north side of Haringvliet, Rotterdam - widower Hendrik Schas from Utrecht who was a prebendary of the Oud-Munster church in Utrecht. The second son of Laurens Schas and Maria van Leeuwen, Hendrik was baptised in the Kloosterkerk, 's-Gravenhage on April 10th, 1662. His first wife had been Bartha van Steenbergh (Utrecht 23.IV.1663-26.III.1693) [101, 103, A88] from 's-Gravenhage whom he had married in Utrecht (St Anthony Gasthuis) on 23.X.1688; three sons born unto them all died young [103].

Fig. 28.   Signature of Anna Greenwood, dated 1703 [A173].

In 1703 the couple were living in 's-Gravenhage. Meanwhile, in 1699, Hendrik Schas had purchased some land at Wassenaar-Zuidwijk, west of Vinkenburg, for Hfl. 3,350 [A47, A157]; he bought some more land there in May, 1703. It appears that Schas was commercially in some degree associated with Anna's father [A168].

Hendrik and Anna Schas had four children:

(1) M a r i a - baptised in the Reformed Church, Rotterdam, 14.VI.1696. Witnesses: maternal grandfather Francis Greenewood and paternal grandmother Maria van Leeuwen [A87]. - At Wassenaar, on 1 December, 1722, Maria married Jacques Saffin, born in Bordeaux, alderman of Schieland [102]. Presumably after the death of Francis Greenewood in 1731 (Saffin was an executor of his will), the Saffins emigrated to Surinam where Jacques died on 8 July, 1759. Maria Saffin at some time returned to Holland. In her testament, made at Voorburg on 23 January, 1770, she stipulated that the family portraits should not be sold after her death but instead go to her eldest son [A66]. Six children are mentioned in that testament: (a) Jacobus Hendrik - a councillor of Civil Justice in Surinam (at least from 1770 till 1796), married 27.I.1759 Maria Philippina van Steenbergh (two children: Francina Susanna Henrietta and Maria Jacoba Hendrina); (b) Frans - a councillor of Justice in Surinam; (c) Paulus - ibidem; (d) Samuel Constantijn, emigrated to the Dutch East Indies; (e) Volkert - in Surinam; (f) Francina Lucretia - deceased wife of Estienne Ferrand (two children: Maria Jacoba and Francina Lucretia who married van den Santheuvel [102]).

Residing at Vasteland, a street near Leuve Haven, Rotterdam [A89], Maria died on 6 March, 1778, and was buried in the Kloosterkerk, 's-Gravenhage, on 10 March, 1778 [102, 103]. A portrait of Maria Saffin née Schas is said to be in the Frans Halsmuseum, Haarlem [103].

(2) F r a n ç o i s (Frans) - baptised at Wassenaar, 9.III.1698 [103]. Emigrated to Surinam where he was a Judge at the Court of Civil Justice, also functioning as church warden. - On 21 January, 1722, he married Geertruyda van Vheelen (10.X.1677 - 8.VIII.1731). The bride, at 44 too old to conceive, was perhaps a daughter of C. K. van Vheelen [32] or of J. B. van Vheelen who owned the sugar plantation 'Meulwijk' (called "Van Veeri" by the negroes) along the Perica Creek and which abutted the Nieuw-Belair plantation which in turn adjoined nephew / cousin Frans Greenwood's sugar plantation 'Kortenduur'.

Together with Jean David Lafreté and Theodore Passalaique, Frans Schas bought at public auction in Amsterdam on 13 January, 1738, from executors Frans Greenwood and Jacques Saffin the plantation The Black Creek for the sum of Hfl. 27,000 [A12]. Gerard Lemmers was appointed to supervise the take-over in Surinam. Frans Schas also owned plantations Schassenburg, Ostage and Goudmijn (the latter called "Schassi" by the negroes) - according to the map of Lavaux, he owned the last two already in the mid 1730s.

Frans Schas, a widower since 1731, returned to Holland and remarried in 's-Gravenhage on 3 February, 1743, the bride being Sara Pichot (Paramaribo 7.X. 1717 - 's-Gravenhage 18.VII.1754) [101]. Several members of the Pichot family owned plantations in Surinam such as the Penoribo, Siparipabo, Rac-à-Rac, La Paix, Patience, Zorg-en-Hoop and De Hoop [78, 79]. - Sara gave birth to a son, François Willem, on 23.II.1744 in 's-Gravenhage; a witness at the baptism was her mother Catharina Marcus, widow of Daniël Pichot [A56].

François Schas Sr died on 20 February, 1761, and was buried on the 26th of that month in the Kloosterkerk, 's-Gravenhage [101, 103]. A quartered shield put up by his son François Willem Schas used to hang in that Kloosterkerk until 1795 when French occupiers ordered it to be taken down and no doubt destroyed. According to a copy which the caring verger P. Moccaud had made of it, the quarters were those of Schas, van Leeuwen, van Hoogstraten, van de Poll, Greenwood, Glover, van der Eem and Kolenprijs [12].

(3) H e l e n a A n t o n i a - baptised at Wassenaar, 13.IX.1699. She married Dithmurus Hackman (1707-1778), a preacher at Wassenaar, on 4 July, 1743. Lived apparently at Wassenaar all her life because it was in that village where she died on 7 June, 1764 [103].

(4) H e n d r i k R o e l a n d - baptised at Wassenaar, 30.X.1701. Emigrated to Surinam where he died, a bachelor, on 2 March, 1730 [103].

Hendrik Schas died on 16 March, 1704, and was buried in 's-Gravenhage on the 20th of that month [101].

Six years later Anna, now living in Leiden, remarried, her second husband being merchant Paul Diers de Ras of Amsterdam (born in Bordeaux). The wedding took place in the Walloon Church, Amsterdam, on 10 May, 1710 [103]. From 29 June, 1710, onwards the couple resided at Oude Vest in Amsterdam [A68]. In March, 1713, Diers de Ras is mentioned as a merchant in Amsterdam who had appointed Frans Greenwood Jr to represent him for business and legal matters in Rotterdam [A262] while in July, 1715, "Frans Greenwoods zoon" asked him to settle financial matters for him in Frankfurt [A254].

Anna Schas née Greenwood died in early 1736 and was buried in the Walenkerk (Walloon Church), Amsterdam, on 11 January, 1736 [101, 103].

* * *

Sara

Date of birth or baptism not known but assumed here to be ca. 1684. Like her father, Sara at times signed her surname as Greenewood (Fig. 29). She never married but spent a good deal of her adult life looking after her ageing father who died in 1731 - perhaps atoning for domestic trouble she had caused in her younger days.

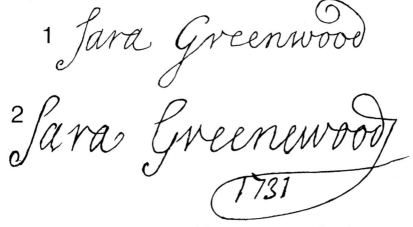

Fig. 29. Signatures of Sara Green[e]wood, 1 - dated 1703 [A175], 2 - dated 1731 [A84].

The story of some events in Sara's life provides a rare chance of viewing - as if through a peep-hole for a fleeting moment - the household of the Greenewoods at Nieuwe Haven in the late autumn of 1703. The narration of this episode should in no way diminish our distant sympathy and respect for Sara.

Some trusted friends of father Francis Greenewood, namely Thomas Schieman of Hull, medical doctor Paulus van Walwijk and merchant Nicolaas Taverner of Rotterdam, declared at his request on 3 November, 1703, before Notary Public Dirck Vos van Weel, Rotterdam, [A231] that Francis Greenewood had asked them a few days before to read a declaration, dated 31 October, 1703, written on a sheet of unruled paper by the young man Augustyn Reve, son of merchant Nicolaes Reve. In this, young Reve declared that after much verbal conversation with Sara Greenwood about the possibility of marrying her, he had had carnal conversation with her some six months ago and that she was now expecting his child; he still had hopes of marrying Sara, whom he respected, if only he would obtain his father's consent, both being under age.

Schieman added that when visiting Francis Greenewood earlier on, he had witnessed Reve asking Greenewood to return to him the above written statement. Francis did not quite trust the young man and by way of precaution made him first sign a copy of the statement, entrusting the original to Schieman's hands.

After vows of restitution, Reve being assumed to be honest, and persuaded by Sara, mother Anna Glover and Hendrik Schas, Greenewood took the original from Schieman and handed it to Reve who at once messed up his signature on it with a pen and then tore the declaration to pieces, some of which he took home.

A few weeks later, on 24 November, 1703, at about 6 p.m., the doorbell was pulled at the Greenewood Nieuwe Haven residence [A173]. Anna de Biet, a maid, answered the door and saw Augustyn Reve standing there, asking her how Sara was. To this the maid replied "not so well, the women are already with her". Indeed, Sara must have been already in early stages of labour. This much surprised Reve who uttered "how is it possible, is it already that near ?" - so he asked to be allowed to speak to Catharine Greenwood, who was in her 18th year at that time. The maid went upstairs, where the living-quarters were, and called for Catherine who then went downstairs, taking Reve into the office on the ground floor and asked him why he had not turned up before. Well, Augustyn had not dared to, but now he did not want to leave. - Entered Catharine's older sister Anna, wife of Hendrik Schas, who asked Reve why he had come. Had he come to keep his word and to see everything to a good ending ? The reply was: "yes, otherwise I would not have bothered to come." Anna thought this too general a reply so she asked him further whether the affection he had had for her sister Sara was likely to continue and be lasting. Augustyn having confirmed this with an emphatic "yes", Anna advised Reve to go upstairs and see Sara. "Saertje, hoe waert gij"? [Saartje, how are you ?] asked Augustyn on entering the room, then embraced and kissed her and implored her to sit down. He sat down next to her, holding her hand. At that moment Sara's mother Anna Greenwood née Glover entered the room, saying "welcome Mr Reve, I am pleased to see that you want to be an honest man who is keeping his word".

Reve did not want to leave before he had received permission for marriage from his father - so he calmly undressed, donned a chintz dressing-gown, put slippers on and asked for a napkin to serve as night cap. Reve next discussed what the name of the expected child should be: Nicolaes, after his father, when a boy; Maria, after his mother, when a girl.

Paterfamilias Francis Greenewood finally entered the stage and had the last word, making it quite clear that if Reve wanted to stay, he would not kick him out but on the other hand he strongly advised him to go home, inform his father and ask for his consent for marriage. So at long last Augustyn left the Greenwoods at eleven o'clock that evening.

A few hours later, between 1 and 2 a.m. on 25 November, 1703, midwife Maritje Plaetswijck née Pieters was called and also Brigitta Brugman and Anna de Bruyn (the three of them had witnessed the events of the previous evening) in order to assist with the birth [A174]. When about to give birth, the midwife - according to custom - asked Sara who the father was. Sara solemnly declared under oath that "It is Reve, I have never had carnal conversation with any other man." Soon thereafter a girl was born, prematurely - a seven-months baby in the opinion of the attending women. The baby died after three hours.

Curtain.

On 13 December, 1703, Francis Greenewood and Sara empowered Abraham Selkart van Wouw, procurator at the High Court in 's-Gravenhage, to sue Nicolaes Reve and his son Augustyn for damages [A175]. The following year, on 23 September, 1704, the Rotterdam merchants Willem Tierens, Nicolaes Taverner, Caspar Hudig and William Spencer, as well as the English skippers Thomas Staman and Ralph Southeran, declared on behalf of Francis Greenewood and Sara before Notary Public Johan van den Pavort [A177] that Francis Greenewood and Nicolaes Reve had been very good friends who used to visit one another for a chat or dinner, but that this friendship and familiarity was discontinued since the affair between Sara and Augustyn Reve. - The relationship between the former friends did not improve. On the contrary, in May, 1706, Nicolaes Reve retaliated by inducing Claesje van Tiel, living at the house of Caspar Hudig (who had witnessed the 1704 statement) and Elisabet van den Broek, seamstress in Rotterdam, to declare that they were told by a certain Willemijntje, who had been a maid of Mr Graswinkel in the domicile of the West India Company on the Haringvliet canal, Rotterdam, and who often visited the Greenewoods, that Sara Greenwood had had a miscarriage, the result of courtship with a certain Brouwer [A201].

Francis Greenewood and Anna Glover made a new testament in May, 1709. In it Sara is mentioned as still being under age, i.e., not yet 25 years old. The stipulation was made that in case Sara was still unmarried when her parents had died, she should receive the same legacy as the other children while she also ought to keep all her clothes of silk, linen, wool, as well as gold, silver and all jewellery received or still to receive from her parents [A183].

When her parents moved to live permanently at Vinkenburg, Wassenaar, Sara joined them and it was there where she herself drew up a testament in 1715. On 18 July, 1719, Sara was able to purchase from her father (a widower) the homestead Vinkenburg complete with orchards, gardens, lanes (in all two 'morgen' three 'hant' of land) for Hfl. 3,200 cash. - On 9 March, 1724, Francis Greenewood, still in good health physically and mentally and living at Vinkenburg, made some changes in his testament: after his death Sara was to get full ownership of all furniture and pieces of decoration, also the horses and carriages with gear and the garden tools, a dozen silver forks and spoons - this arrangement not to be opposed by any of the other children.

Among Sara's friends was Joost Apourceaux, born in 1687, a merchant in Leiden and a cousin of Maria Hosteyn whom her brother Charles had married (both died in 1711). Joost was mentioned in January, 1711, as vendor of a meadow at Zoeterwoude, just south-east of Leiden [A75]. - On 9 January, 1731, the "spinster living at Wassenaar [Vinkenburg]" was lying sick at the house of Joost Apourceaux in Leiden. Ill enough for Sara to send for a Notary Public in order to amend her testament to the effect that if her father would survive her, he would also receive a legitimate portion of her estate [A84]. In the event, Sara recovered and her very old father died in May, 1731. The following year, on 4 September, 1732, Sara sold Vinkenburg to Nicolaas André Weenix for the sum of Hfl. 2,800 cash [A51].

Sara moved to Leiden where on 3 April, 1733, she consented that her brother Frans Greenwood and Jacques Saffin, executors of her father's will, should sell The Black Creek plantation including her eighth part to the highest bidder [A85].

On 7 November, 1740, Sara - still living in Leiden - acted as executrice of the will of her deceased friend Joost Apourceaux [A277].

It has not been discovered where and when lonely Sara died.

*   *   *

C a t h a r i n a

This daughter was baptised as Biateres Catarina on Monday 15 April, 1686. Witnesses were Jan van Zoelen (a brother of her father's business partner Jasper van Zoelen) and [his wife ?] Beiateres Ricke (daughter of Isaek Ricke and Beiateres Jans, baptised in Rotterdam on 7 September, 1639) [A87].

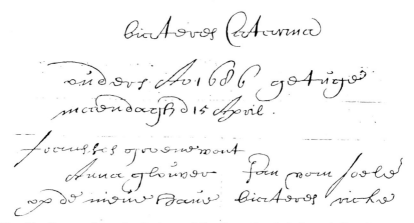

Fig. 30. Extract from the Register of Baptisms, Dutch Reformed Church,
Rotterdam: "biateres Catarina / Ao 1686 / maendagh 15 April / ouders
[parents] franssos groenewout / Anna glouver / op de nieue Haven / getugen
[witnesses] Jan van Soelen / biateres ricke [A87].

The name Beiateres or Biateres appears to be an old form of Beatrijs (Bea-
trice, Beatrix); the girl may not have liked that name because she became known
as plain Catharina.

On Sunday 10 April, 1707, the banns were read in the Reformed Church,
Rotterdam, announcing that Catharina, spinster living at Nieuwe Haven with her
parents, intended to marry - in the English Church, Rotterdam, on Wednesday
13 April, 1707 - Robert Barton from Brigstock, Northamptonshire, a captain in
the Regiment of Colonel Meredyth, being in garrison at Gent (near Nijmegen ?)
[A88]. - The couple were residing in Rotterdam in May, 1709, when they made
their testament [A182] in which Catharina is mentioned as the wife of Robert
Barton, captain of the Company of Infantry in the service of Queen Anne in
the Regiment of Major General Meredyth [A182].

Married bliss did not last long for on 28 November, 1711, Catharina - still
in Rotterdam - is referred to as widow of Robert Barton, a lieutenant-colonel
formerly in the service of Her Majesty the Queen of Great Britain [A245].

Fig. 31. Signatures of Catharina Greenwood, 1 - dated 1703 [A173],
2 - dated 1709 [A182].

Her father promised to pay her the outstanding 1,500 Caroli guilders with 6% interest which was part of her dowry.

Date and place of death of Catharina Barton née Greenwood are not known.

*   *   *

Charles

Date of birth or baptism untraced but the year assumed here to be ca. 1688. Charles "Grynwout" married Maria Hosteyn in the Waalse Kerk [Walloon Church], Leiden, on 13 March, 1708 [A71]. The bride, baptised in Leiden on 12.IX.1685, was a daughter of corn merchant Olivier Hosteijn and Sara Apourceaux.

Olivier Hosteyn's first wife was Marie de Plancqué whom he had married in 1674 and who presented him with two daughters (one surviving). After her death he remarried in 1682, taking as bride Sara Apourceaux (born in Leiden, 1650), widow of Dr Petrus Gesquier and one of eight children of Josse Apourceaux [no biographical data] and Sara Catoir (Leiden 1.IV.1629 - 1.III.1703). Maria Hosteyn had a twin-sister Johanna and two brothers: Johan (born in 1684) and Eleazar (born in 1688) [A69]. - Grandmother Sara Catoir, residing in Leiden, was quite affluent. On 5 January, 1703, when still fit physically and mentally, the old lady drew up her testament [A73]; she died in Leiden on 1 March, 1703 [A74]. It was not until 8 July, 1709, that Charles and Maria received Hfl. 3,000 from the bequest of Sara Catoir.

Fig. 32.   Signature of Charles Greenwood, dated 1708 [A228].

Charles and Maria Greenwood, residing at Nieuwe Haven, Rotterdam, made their testament on 25 May, 1708 [A228]. Their short-lived marriage resulted in two children [A87]:

F r a n c i s - baptised 11.VI.1709. Witnesses: paternal grandparents Francis Greenewood and Anna Glover.

C h a r l e s - baptised 17.VI.1710. Witnesses: maternal grandfather Olivier Hosteyn and his daughter Johanna (twin-sister of Maria, the mother).

Charles had joined his father and brother Frans as a partner. However, the business partnership between Charles and Frans was dissolved on 18 September, 1711, [A241] and that between Charles, Frans and their father on 22 September, 1711, because on the latter date Charles signed a contract with his father which offered him a directorship of The Black Creek plantation in Surinam [A242].

Charles and family were to sail at the first opportunity as he was to take over from nephew / cousin François Greenwood who desired to be relieved of that position. The contract, drawn up in much the same wording as that of Johannes Kruijff [A229] (see p. 28), was likewise for a duration of seven years. Charles was to be allowed to purchase not more than six slaves a year, unless instructed otherwise. Whereas Kruijff was promised a supply of three ankers [120 litres] of wine a year, Charles should have four [160 litres]. The salary was to be: Hfl. 600 a year for the first two years, Hfl. 700 for the next two, and Hfl. 800 for the last three years each. Father Francis empowered Thomas Carruther, a director of the plantation of Jeronimus Clifford in Surinam, to take over the directorship temporarily in case Charles came to die or was to leave.

On 25 September, 1711, Charles together with his wife Maria and their two little boys were about to leave for Surinam [A243]. He appointed his father, respectively his brother Frans (in case of his father's death), to look after his financial affairs during their absence from Holland. Maria stipulated that her brother Eleazar should receive Hfl. 2,173 on attaining his majority; that sum had been deposited in the Orphan's Court in Leiden the previous year. Prior to departure Charles took out cash against a pledge of debenture.

A few weeks after they had sailed for Surinam, disaster struck at sea and Charles, Maria and the two infants were drowned [134].

When the terrible news reached Holland, the question arose whom the heritage should go to and who would be the executors of the testament [134]. Although Charles Greenwood and his wife Maria had lived in Rotterdam as a married couple, they had drawn up their testament before Notary Public Johannes Blocqeau (an uncle of Maria) in Leiden on 25 August, 1711 [A76]. At that time, i.e., shortly before their impending departure for Surinam, they were probably staying in Leiden with one of Maria's relatives. Moreover, Charles and Maria had appointed uncle Blocqeau to be one of the guardians (the others were his father Francis Greenewood, his brother Frans, Maria's brother Eleazar and her uncle Jean Hosteijn). The Orphan's Court (or Court of Chancery) in Leiden being named as executor of the testament, the wardens of the Orphanage prepared themselves to fend for the rights of any minor heirs, should there be any. On the other hand, the wardens of the Rotterdam Orphanage thought it their duty to embark upon the task of executors as they reckoned that logically Rotterdam was the place of death. Correspondence between the two Orphanages ensued while the wardens of Rotterdam also wrote to jurist Andries Hoffland in 's-Gravenhage begging him for his wise counsel. He answered, on 12 September, 1712, that the longest living person was stated to be the heir of the first person to die. In common with old Roman law it was presumed that the children had died first in the calamity, next the woman so that the man, Charles, would have been the last to drown. Consequently his parents, if still alive (they were) would be heirs and executors. More correspondence between Leiden and Rotterdam followed but papers relating to the final outcome have not been found. There seems little doubt that either Francis Greenewood, the father of Charles, or brother Frans, was appointed as executor of the will [A92].

*   *   *

E l i s a b e t h

From the age given on the notification of her death in 1764, we know that she was born in Rotterdam in 1690.

On 17 April, 1707, the impending marriage was announced of George August van der Heck [later on spelled: van der Hek] of 's-Gravenhage to Elisabeth Greenwood of Rotterdam. The actual date of marriage has not been found but it will have been the end of April or early May, 1707. The husband was baptised in the Hoogduitsche Kerk [German Church], 's-Gravenhage, the son of Gillis van der Heck and Alida Brandt [A56]. There was clearly a German connection as George's godparents were the Royal Highnesses George Wilhelm and Rudolff August, Dukes of Brunswick and Lüneburg, and Sophia Duchess of Brunswick and Lüneburg Hannover.

The three children of George and Elisabeth were all baptised in the Groote Kerk, 's-Gravenhage [A56]:

F r e d r i k   A u g u s t   -   baptised 7.XII.1707. Godparents: Frederik Duke of Saxen Gotha and his wife, by proxy of George's parents.

F r a n ç o i s   J o h a n n e s   -   baptised 7.VIII.1709. Godparents: grandparents François Greenewood and Anna Glover.

M e l c h i o r   E r n e s t   -   baptised 4.II.1711. Godparents: grandfather Gillis van der Heck and George's 19-year old sister Maria Anna van der Heck.

On 7 July, 1712, Elisabeth is referred to as being married to George August van der Heck, a captain in the service of His Royal Majesty of Denmark in garrison in the Royal Burgh of Rensburgh in Holsteyn (now Rendsburg, in the middle of Schleswig-Holstein, Germany) [A248]. Her husband had received as dowry from her father one eighth part in the plantation The Black Creek, valued at Hfl. 6,000. Actually, Francis Greenewood had already paid him Hfl. 5,000 of that amount while van der Hek also received the value of the produce of that eighth part, amounting to Hfl. 1,000. Even so, George had the nerve to claim yet another Hfl. 2,000. Van der Hek cannot have been very popular with his father-in-law and no further records of events in the lives of Elisabeth and George have been traced.

Elisabeth van der Heck née Greenwood died of a stroke in 's-Gravenhage on 15 December, 1764. She was 74 years old and impecunious as she was buried Pro Deo [A56].

*   *   *

COUSIN   FRANS   GREENWOOD

Born in Yorkshire in 1679 [23], this Frans [François] Greenwood - a nephew of Francis Greenewood and a cousin of his son Frans Greenwood - went to work on his uncle's sugar plantation The Black Creek in Surinam presumably when he was about 20 years old because he was there already in 1702 (shipping from Paramaribo a case of personal effects of the late Maria de Bruyn). In 1709, cousin François is mentioned as director of The Black Creek, fully authorised by the proprietor to settle all financial matters concerning the plantation. In September, 1711, Francis Greenewood signed up his son Charles to serve as director of his plantation so as to enable nephew / cousin Frans to return to Holland. However, Charles and his family were fatally shipwrecked on the outward journey and it is not known for certain who succeeded François as director. The latter had very likely been director since 1704 as contracts for that post usually covered a seven= year term of service.

*   *   *

Fig. 33. Signature of cousin Frans Greenwood, dated 1719 [A268].

By 1715 cousin Frans was living at the Singel canal, Amsterdam. On 21 November of that year the banns were read announcing the forthcoming marriage of bachelor Frans to Maria Anna de Vaux of Surinam, now also residing at Singel. She was the widow of Gerard [Gerrit] Wobma who, in Surinam, had been a sugar inspector (1677), planter (1680) and a police-commissioner (1684, 1686) [56]. - The parents of François being deceased, the groom was assisted by his nephew Paul Diers de Ras (the second husband of Anna Greenwood). The couple were married on 8 December, 1715, in the Waalse Kerk [Walloon Church], Amsterdam.

These Greenwoods were quite affluent. On 7 May, 1716, Pieter van der Dussen - one of the heirs of deceased Johan de Bye, formerly a burgomaster of Leiden - sold to cousin Frans for Hfl. 13,700 the homestead Bijdorp at Voorschoten (south of Leiden) [A42], consisting of a residence, coach-house, stable, gardener's lodge, two summerhouses, two orchards, &c., as well as '8 morgen 3 hant' of land. The estate was bordering the Orphanage of Leiden on one side, Pieter Reynard Baron van Stepraad Heer van Doddendael on the other side, fronting the Heerweg [now Veurseweg] and backing on the Delffse Vliet stream.

This homestead, situated immediately south of Voorschoten on the east side of the Veurseweg, was probably built by a Meerman family in the middle of the 17th century [71]. In May, 1696, Gerard Franszoon Meerman acknowledged a debt of Hfl. 5,500 to Messrs Adriaen and Nicolaes Ghijs, promising to repay the sum @ $4\frac{1}{2}$% interest, offering the Bijdorp estate as surety [A40]. - G. F. Meerman sold Bijdorp for Hfl. 8,750 cash to Johan de Bye and his second wife Anna Oorthoorn on 2 March, 1697; it then comprised several rooms and apartments, a coach-house, stable, gardener's lodge, orchards, kitchen gardens, a lane, woodlands and meadows [A41]. De Bye, a high-ranking official in the municipality of Leiden, made a number of improvements to the country-house and added two summerhouses. He also had an imposing entrance gate made between 1697 and 1700 (the year his second wife died) [75]. The left gate-wing includes a wrought iron mirror monogram of JB (Johan de Bye), the right wing bears an AO mirror monogram (Anna Oorthoorn, his second wife) [71]. The gate still graces the road [Veurseweg] (Fig. 34).

The marriage of cousin Frans to Maria Anna de Vaux was blessed with the birth of a daughter Frances who was baptised on 20 July, 1717, in the Reformed Church at Voorschoten with as witnesses uncle Francis Greenewood and daughter Sara, and Mrs Maria Wainwright [23]. Although baptised as Frances (an English name), the daughter became known as Francina, a Dutch form of the name.

*   *   *

Fig. 34. Entrance gate of former homestead Bijdorp, Veurseweg, Voorschoten [photograph: F. G. A. M. Smit, 1987].

Cousin Frans was obviously a very successful businessman who retained contacts with England. For instance, in March, 1719, he signed an English contract appointing goldsmiths Nathaniel Pearse and John Matthew, of London, to be his true and lawful attorneys mainly for matters of finance [A268]. In September, 1720, he requested admittance to a Dutch Company of Assurance involving the sum of Hfl. 20,000 [Kon. Bibl. Handschr. 135 D 19 G]. On 16 August, 1724, François was mentioned as one of the owners of the ship Agathe which, on her outward sailing to Surinam, stranded at Calais and burned out [A2]. This setback forced the owners to put their shipping company into liquidation.

At some time or other, cousin Frans became the proprietor of the large plantation Belair (3,427 acres, on the Perica stream) in Surinam. On 13 August, 1727, he hired Franz Heinrich Möller from Hamburg to serve as medical doctor on Belair for four years at a salary of Hfl. 200 for each of the first two years, Hfl. 250 for each of the following years [A7]. Free board and lodging, the meals to be taken together with the white servants; for every illness exceeding 14 days a year he was to make up for lost time after the elapse of the four years.

François and his wife Maria Anna made a testament on 14 August, 1727 [A8].

They were then living at the fashionable Heerengracht near Utrechtschestraat in Amsterdam. As heiress is mentioned their daughter Francina who would receive all goods and moneys in Amsterdam, Surinam and elsewhere. If Francina were to die before her father, then her mother was to become heiress. In turn, Maria Anna Greenwood née de Vaux, widow of Gerard Wobma, would then appoint as heiress daughter Francina Greenwood as well as her three children from her marriage to Gerard Wobma: Gerard François Wobma, Daniël Wobma and Samuel Gideon Wobma. (The Wobmas owned plantations in Surinam such as Nieuw-Belair [adjoining Kortenduur and Meulwijk], Corisana and Contentement). Both Frans and Maria Anna must have been well at that time as on 20 August, 1727, he empowered her to be his deputy whenever he should be out of town [A9]; this shows that they were not constantly living at Bijdorp.

In September, 1727, François appointed Cornelis Sneeuwater of Delft to serve as carpenter on Belair in Surinam or to work there on other plantations in which he had an interest [A3]. The carpenter's task was simply to build houses, mills, ships, to obtain wood from the forest, to oversee the plank sawers and to instruct negroes in the craft of carpentry. Sneeuwater was to take his own tools except for implements used in ship building. The contract was for five years @ Hfl. 240 for each of the first two years, then @ Hfl. 400 for each following year.

Early in March, 1728, Maria Anna Greenwood née de Vaux died and was buried in the Nieuwe Kerk, Amsterdam, on 11 March, 1728. Retiring to Bijdorp must have lost its appeal since the death of his wife: Frans sold the estate at public auction on 7 January, 1730, to Paulus Apourceaux for Hfl. 9,600 [20, A6, A43]. This is another example of how property depreciated in those years. - Further to the history of Bijdorp: Apourceaux sold it on 8 May, 1739, for Hfl. 9,900 to Mattheus Hoeufft van Oyen, colonel of the Regiment of Carabineers [A44]; his brother Leonard (1697-1772) eventually inherited the estate but he sold it on 3 June, 1771, to P. Changuion and his wife A. A. van der Hoeven. Apparently, in 1780, they let at least part of the country-house to Nicolaas Simon van Winter (1718-1795) and his wife Lucretia Wilhelmina van Merken (1722-1789), a couple well-known in the world of Dutch poetry. Lucretia died at Bijdorp in 1789 and her husband in 1795. Because living at Bijdorp was too uncomfortable for them during the winter months, in 1782 the Van Winters also rented a house at Rapenburg, Leiden, from D. Vijgh. - The three daughters of Changuion inherited Bijdorp, the last one of them dying there in October, 1862, was Susanna Arnoldina. F. Fahrensbach then bought the property in 1863 and in 1876 his widow sold it to the Congregation of St Catharina of Siena [?0]. The old house was replaced by a new building [75], a boarding school for girls. In 1965 Huize Bijdorp was known as Pensionaat Onze Lieve Vrouw van Lourdes. Next, a Lucas College had joined Huize Bijdorp which, however, at present is in use as a convent.

Meanwhile François continued his business activities and in July, 1730, had a 1/8th stake in the ship Pickfatt, master Richard Bell, owner Richard Pickfatt, a wealthy merchant in Rotterdam [A288]. At around this time Frans may have given his stepsons Daniël and Samuel Gideon Wobma access to Belair - they are mentioned as proprietors on the map of Lavaux (1737) which shows that they also owned the adjacent Corisana and Contentement, both on the Comawine river. Daniël Wobma was furthermore the owner of Creek Potameca and Societeits Land.

After a widowerhood of three years, François remarried at Voorburg, near 's-Gravenhage, on 17 June, 1731, the bride being Jacoba Elisabet Ghijs of Leiden. This second marriage was blessed with a daughter, Adriana Anna Maria, born 24 (baptised 31) July, 1735. Frans Greenwood of Dordrecht wrote a poem "On the birthday of my very dear niece Adriana Anna Maria Greenwood, published 24 July 1750, old 15 years." - Adriana married Imbertus Ludwig Berseth in the French

Church, 's-Gravenhage, on 19 November, 1752 [A56].

Daughter Francina, from his first marriage, married at Voorburg on 11 December, 1735, Maximiliaan van Berchem, a man who had many official functions, e.g., at the Water Board of Voorne. Francina was his second wife; the first, Adriana Molewater of Brielle whom he had married on 22 December, 1733, died childless and was buried on 27 September, 1734. Maximiliaan and Francina van Berchem had four children:

J a c o b - baptised 11.IX.1736. Witnesses: Jacob van Berchem and Jacoba Elisabeth Ghijs [66].
J a c o b a E l i s a b e t h - baptised 25.VIII.1737 in the Walloon Church, Brielle [65]. Witnesses: Francina's father François and his second wife Jacoba Elisabeth Ghijs [66].
M a r i a A n n a F r a n c i n a - baptised 7.III.1739. Witnesses: Daniël Wobma and his wife Susanna Francina Pichot [66].
F r a n c i s - baptised 5.III.1741 in the Walloon Church, Brielle [65, 66]. Witnesses: Francina's father François and his second wife Jacoba Elisabeth Ghijs.

Although Francina, together with her husband, was well enough to witness the baptism of Maximilien Overgoor on 20 August, 1741 [67], Francina died soon after as a result of a stillbirth on 16 November, 1741. That same year two of her young children had also died: one on 12 June, the other on 16 September. Maximiliaan van Berchem died on 18 November, 1761, and was buried on the 24th.

In 1742 François, the nephew / cousin, is a retired businessman with an annual income of Hfl. 3,000 and living comfortably with his wife Jacoba Elisabeth in 's-Gravenhage on the south side of fashionable Voorhout in a house of Hfl. 400 rent a year; three maids looked after them [1, 10].

"Frans Greenwout" died in July, 1753, aged 74. On the 25th of that month an impost @ Hfl. 30 was paid for the first-class funeral [A56]. His wife and daughter Adriana were the only heiresses, not only to property in Holland but also in Great Britain. The widow was also obliged by a decree from the Prerogative Court of Canterbury to make an inventory of all her late husband's effects including those in Great Britain.

*   *   *

N O T E S   O N   S U R I N A M

The fortunes and misfortunes of the Greenwoods were to a certain extent linked with their activities as sugar planters in Surinam. It is relevant, therefore, to present some notes on the history of that country which is now (since 1975) an independent territory bordered by Guyana to the west, Brazil to the south and French Guiana to the east.

Dutch explorers made their first trade contacts with Guiana in 1578 and they subsequently based several settlements on the coast of Demerara and Essequibo while by 1616 they had also penetrated inland. The Dutch West India Company was founded in 1621 for mercantile purposes which did not exclude piracy. In 1630 the Company occupied parts of Portuguese Brazil but, having failed to root, had to withdraw in 1654. The returning settlers had become acquainted with a revolutionary new agricultural system introduced by the Portuguese: the slave plantation [27]. Soon the English, French and Dutch adopted that system in the West Indies and elsewhere. The trade in slaves also proved to be highly lucrative. In England slaves were sold in Liverpool (metaphorically said to be built on skulls of slaves) and Bristol. The Dutch honoured the principle that all those entering Holland were free persons - therefore, ships from ports in the provinces of Holland and Zeeland sailed to the Gold Coast [Ghana] where slaves were bought and taken to Guiana from whence the vessels brought sugar and other produce back to the Dutch market.

Meanwhile British colonists had entered Surinam and in 1663 Charles II issued Letters Patent granting Lawrence Hyde and Lord Willoughby the region between the Coppename and Maroni rivers because it was ideal for the establishment of sugar plantations. At that time the Dutch owned certain regions on the east coast of North America such as Nieuw Nederland with Nieuw Amsterdam as its capital. Without any provocation these possessions were seized in 1664 by a jealous England and occupied in the name of James, Duke of York - hence the fortress Nieuw Amsterdam was renamed New York. The second Anglo-Dutch war, fought mainly at sea, ensued in 1665 and lasted till 1667 when in June a Dutch fleet, under Michiel Adriaensz de Ruyter and Cornelis de Witt, sailed up the Thames and destroyed much of the English fleet near Chatham, causing veritable panic in London which, in 1665, had already suffered from the Great Plague and in 1666 was gutted by the Great Fire. - The Peace of Breda followed in July, 1667. It was agreed that England could keep the entire Dutch colony of Nieuw Nederland including barren Manhattan with New York, in exchange for much more promising Surinam which Dutchman Abraham Crijnssen had conquered in early 1667. At that time no fewer than 178 plantations were under cultivation, mostly of sugar, and they were mainly situated along rivers upstream [27]. - From 1667 onwards the English were therefore without any possessions in northern South America until 1781 when British privateers - who at times still attacked Surinam - took possession of a region which became known as British Guiana. - In 1671 there were only 60 sugar and 51 tobacco plantations in Surinam, a number of which still in English hands. By 1700 there were some 100 plantations but that number rose to nearly 400 in the 1730s.

In 1674 the Dutch West India Company went bankrupt but at once a new company was formed to govern Surinam on behalf of the Dutch States-General. This eventually led to the formation of the Chartered Society of Surinam with three owners.

When in 1807 the slave traffic was abolished, it struck a hard blow to both sugar and cotton cultures. Slavery itself was abolished in Surinam in 1863. Owners of plantations often safely stayed in Europe, leaving the running of the business to their managers on the spot. Risks were great, but so were profits. Many owners became quite well off - among them the Greenwoods. Their plantation The Black Creek was situated on opposite sides of the Commewijne [Comawina] river, well upstream (Fig. 8). The large 1737 map of Surinam, drawn in the early 1730s by de Lavaux [78], shows "Blakkieeck", owner "Grenowoud d'Oude", to be intersected by the Comawina river and bordered by plantations Klarenbeek to the north, Carrawassibo to the west and Goed-Accoord to the south and east. - ". . . . the river Comawina is divided into two branches - one bears the same name to the south-east for a length of above fifty miles - the other is the Cottica. Into all these rivers, the courses of which are not straight but serpentine, are discharged a number of very large creeks or rivulets, the banks of which are inhabited by Europeans, and cultivated with sugar, cocoa, and indigo plantations, which form the most delightful prospects that can be imagined to those who travel by water, the universal mode of journeying in this country, as the soil is in general ill adapted for the construction of roads. . . " [117].

*   *   *

II

ART AND POETRY

*   *   *

FRANS GREENWOOD AND ART

Frans Greenwood was a man who genuinely appreciated works of artistic merit. Not only did he become a successful collector of artefacts but Frans delighted also in executing his skills as an ardent amateur artist [40]. In a letter in verse [50] to his friend Arnold Willis, Greenwood described that after a day's work he liked nothing better than reading a little or taking up a drawing-quill or a stylus (the latter presumably for engraving glass) - and to feast his eyes upon pictures of de Heem, Potter, Wouwerman and van de Velde which he saw every day (i.e., at home) with undiminishing admiration. Furthermore, when his eyes were fully saturated with paintings, he would let them enjoy drawings or he would, for a change, play some tunes on his fiddle. Frans obviously liked music as well: in his first book [44] he praised the singing and playing of the clavicord by Jacoba van der Wallen while his second book [50] opens with a poem extolling the playing of the violin by Mr J. Quikklenberg [J. F. van Quickelenberg, a well-known violinist at the time]; there is also a similar poem in praise of stringplayer Pieter van Hagen.

Aart Schouman, in his capacity of art dealer, jotted down [99, 109] that on 12 September, 1737, he sold Mr Greenwood a "piece with dead birds and other cattle by J. Fijt" for Hfl. 21 : 10 stuyvers, the price he himself had paid for it; Greenwood, however, topped it with a "verfsteen in een kas" [a sort of mortar and pestle used in the preparation of paints] and a number of drawings. On 2 February, 1738, Schouman sold Mr Greenwood two watercolours for the sum of Hfl. 15 : 15 stuyvers plus a number of drawings. On 23 April, 1738, Schouman had made two watercolours after J. Griffier (Amsterdam 1645 - London 1718) for Mr Greenwood and was paid Hfl. 15 plus two drawings by Rademaker valued at Hfl. 30. Schouman also recorded that on 26 March, 1737, he purchased at the house of Greenwood a "fiool" from "een Duyster" [perhaps a lapsus for 'Duytser', i.e., a German] for Hfl. 9 : 9 stuyvers. The 'fiool' was either a bottle with a long neck, possibly of the shape favoured by the 17th century calligraphic glass engravers or - but at that price less likely - a violin (among the 2,495 lots sold after Schouman's death was "Een Fiool, door N. A. Cremonen, 1632" [16] (A violin by ? Nicolò Amati, Cremona).

*   *   *

In the eighteenth century it was indeed bon ton in Holland for prosperous businessmen to collect important works of art in impressive quantities. Just to mention one example: after the death of merchant Richard Pickfatt - who used to trade with cousin Frans Greenwood - his collection of 108 paintings was sold in Rotterdam on 12 April, 1736 [59]. Among the masters represented were Bril, Castiglione, Titian, Murillo, Poussin, Bassano, Veronese, Brueghel, Steen, Rubens, Netscher, Ruisdael, Both, de Lairesse, van Dyck, Teniers, &c. - Then, as now, one did not always succeed in buying that which had appeal. "Mynheer Grynwout" was eager to buy a cabinet of works of art formed by a certain Vervel Doen of Dordrecht but he was unlucky as the great collector Jan Bisschop, of Rotterdam, managed to purchase it [135].

Greenwood obviously had a good library as is evident from a short [pre-1719] poem by Zeeus "On the library and poetry of Mr Frans Greenwood" [139]. He also collected such curiosities as the sword which was supposed to have been used to decapitate old Johan van Oldenbarnevelt in 's-Gravenhage on 13 May, 1619. Frans obtained this sword from Maximiliaan van Berchem - husband of Francina Greenwood who was a daughter of cousin Frans - living at Brielle. Greenwood having asked him about the provenance of the sword, van Berchem wrote to him from Brielle on 12 September, 1743: "Concerning your enquiry about the sword in question: it came from Colonel Steenhuizen, my grandfather, who - as a collector of antiquities - once bought from the estate of a burgomaster in 's-Gravenhage whose name my father cannot remember, various items including some weaponry among which was this sword. The inclusion of the sword in the sale must have been a mistake, or was based on carelessness, because a few days after my grandfather had bought the goods, the heirs of the deceased burgomaster requested - thereby even offering great sums - the return of the sword in question which, according to them, had been used to behead van Oldenbarnevelt. This is all that I learned today from my father General Major van Berchem. Cousin Greenwood, all evidence points to its genuineness." - The sword is now in the collection of the Rijksmuseum, Amsterdam.

Greenwood is said to have painted miniatures [40] but, as far as could be ascertained, there are no examples extant.

Arnold Willis, in his introduction to the posthumous poems of Jakob Zeeus which he published in 1726 [140], explained that he was issuing in that book a new portrait of Zeeus (a copperplate engraving) because existing ones were of a poor likeness. Willis had an ad vivum portrait drawing made by Arnold Houbraken before 1719 [Zeeus died in 1718]. In order to make the portrait perfect in all respects, Frans Greenwood assisted Houbraken in the task. Afterwards Willis commissioned Jakob Houbraken to make a copperplate engraving of that drawing for use in the 1726 book.

Although Frans was surely a good draughtsman, it is doubtful whether he ever etched or engraved a copperplate. In the 1792 catalogue of the auction of the estate of Aart Schouman [16], lot 703 was of 22 prints (including duplicates) by "Greenwood". These were probably by John Greenwood who in any case was definitely the maker of the mezzotints listed as lots 1978 (Mieris and his wife, by Greenwood, after Mieris) and 1979 (His Royal Highness Willem V, and a girl with a lighted candle, by Greenwood, after Haag and Verkolje). That particular artist was John Inigo Greenwood, born in Boston, North America, 7 December, 1727, a pupil of Th. Johnston of Boston. Commissioned by the Dutch Republic, he went to Surinam in 1752 in order to make drawings of plants and animals. From 1758 - 1761 he was in Amsterdam where he learned engraving from Mr M. Elgersma; in 1761 in Alkmaar where he painted 33 portraits. In 1763 in Paris and London; visited Holland and France in 1771. He died at Margate, England, 15 September, 1792.

Fig. 35. A meeting of the art club Sint Lukas Broederschap, Dordrecht, as recorded by Aart Schouman in 1736: a brush-and-wash drawing (15 x 22 cm) in ink (above) as a preparatory sketch for an etching (below).

TOERBEURTE

VAN HET

SCHILDER COLLEGIE.

1743. en 1744.

1 *November*	KETELANUS.
15 *dito*	VAN OURYCK.
6 *December*	BROUWER.
20 *dito*	BELAERTS.
3 *Januarii*	MEERDERVOORT.
17 *dito*	DE BRUYN.
7 *Februarii*	HALLINCG.
21 *dito*	GEVAERTS.
6 *Maart*	GREENWOOD.
20 *dito*	KETELANUS.
3 *April*	VAN OURYCK.
17 *dito*	BROUWER.

Fig. 36. Schedule of meetings of the Sint Lukas Broederschap, Dordrecht, for the 1743 - 1744 season.

Frans Greenwood was a member of the art society (rather a club) in Dordrecht called "Sint Lukas Broederschap" [Brotherhood of St Luke - the patron saint of painters and physicians] (Fig. 35). That society had originalyy been formed by painters in Dordrecht as long ago as 1641 [60]. Some fifty years later it ceased its activities due to worsening economic conditions. - An enterprising Johan Diederik Pompe van Meerdervoort founded a new Art Circle in 1716, reviving the old title of Sint Lukas; Jakob Zeeus was one of the first members [140].

TOERBEURTE

VAN HET

SCHILDER COLLEGIE.

1745. en 1746.

5 *November*	HALLINCG.
19 *dito*	GEVAERTS.
3 *December*	GREENWOOD.
17 *dito*	KETELANUS.
7 *Januarii*	VAN OURYCK.
21 *dito*	BELAERTS.
4 *Februarii*	MEERDERVOORT.
18 *dito*	DE BRUYN.
4 *Maart*	HALLINCG.
18 *dito*	GEVAERTS.
1 *April*	GREENWOOD.
15 *dito*	KETELANUS.

Fig. 37. Schedule of meetings of the Sint Lukas Broederschap, Dordrecht, for the 1745 - 1746 season.

In 1736 it was necessary for Aart Schouman to blow new life into the brotherhood. The rules for that year [6] stipulated that:
(a) there should be only twelve members;
(b) meetings by rotation at members' homes during November - April, twice monthly on a Friday from 17.00 - 20.30 hrs (Figs. 36, 37);
(c) friends could be introduced to attend a meeting @ 6 stuyvers;
(d) the conversation should concern the art of painting, printmaking and drawing;

(e) 3 stuyvers fine for leaving before 20.00 or after 20.30 hrs;
(f) 6 stuyvers fine for absence by being out of town;
(g) one guilder and 4 stuyvers fine for absence while in town;
(h) the host must have some works of art for auction on penalty of 12 stuyvers;
(i) when nothing was sold the penalty to be 6 stuyvers; a commission @ 5% payable to the society by buyer and seller;
(j) the only food on offer to be bread and cheese, otherwise the penalty would be 30 stuyvers;
(k) the honorary printer of the society to be Joannes van Braam and the honorary copperplate engraver Arnold [recte: Aart] Schouman (see Fig. 35) - both to have free admission to the meetings on the understanding that they give their services free of charge [38].

Most of the members belonged to the category of town governors of Dordrecht, e.g., Mr Johan Hallincq, a sheriff during 1718-1720, 1724-1726, Mr Johan Diederik Pompe van Meerdervoort, sheriff 1739-1741, Mr Paulus Gevaerts, sheriff 1742-1744, C. B. Doll van Ouryck, alderman, M. van der Dussen, alderman [122].

In 1741, member Frans Greenwood wrote a eulogy which he dedicated to the Art Society on the occasion of the centenary of the original one; at the same time this was the silver jubilee of the new brotherhood. The poet complained about the decline in prosperity in Holland and the resulting unfavourable impact this had on Maecenati on whose patronage Art had always been dependent.

When the professional artist Aart Schouman, an associate of Sint Lukas and a great friend of Greenwood, left for 's-Gravenhage in 1748, the St Luke Art Brotherhood finally broke up. Eventually a new society of graphic artists, "Pictura", was founded in 1774 and this is still flourishing.

In Rotterdam a painters' guild was founded in the early 17th century and was known as the "Gilde van Sint Lucas" or "Broederschap van Sint Lukas". Prior to 1719 Greenwood mourned, in two poems, a dissent that had occurred in that society.

In 's-Gravenhage a "Pictura" brotherhood dated from around the middle of the 17th century. Aart Schouman was elected a Regent of that Pictura in 1748 (the year he settled in that town), followed by his nomination as Head in 1752 and finally as that of Dean of the brotherhood in 1762.

At the time there were quite a number of lovers and collectors of works of art in Dordrecht who supported local artists, e.g., C. Vriesendorp [127] and P. Repelaer van Spijkenisse. It is not surprising, therefore, that certain glasses engraved by Greenwood were or remained for a long time in possession of such families.

*   *   *

Frans Greenwood not only engraved glasses - a pastime which he took up when he was about 40 years old - but he also showed an interest (too keen, maybe) in collecting them as highlighted by the following extraordinary event [A275]. - On 16 December, 1724, eight men (Gijsbert de Lange, Cornelis van Brakel, Gerardus Vogel, Cornelis Blieck, Jacob van Koperen, Jan van den Anker, Jacob van Biesenbroeck en Michiel Baelde) declared before Notary Public Willem Boon, Rotterdam, that they were co-owners of ten glasses which used to be housed in the premises of Hermannus Croes, an innkeeper and wine-merchant on the Vissersdijk, Rotterdam, but which had been removed from there by Frans Greenwood of Rotterdam without permission from either the owners or Croes.

The eight men demanded that Greenwood should return the glasses to Croes and they requested the Notary to go to the house of Greenwood and hand him a copy of the notarial act describing his misdemeanour.

The following ten glasses were said to have been taken by Greenwood:

(1) An old-fashioned goblet.

(2) Goblet, wheel-engraved, inscribed "Het welvaren van de negotie" [The prosperity of commerce].

(3) Goblet, wheel-engraved, inscribed "'t Welvaren (or Welwezen) van 't Collegie" [The prosperity of the College (perhaps of The Noble College of Admiralty on the River Maas)].

(4) Goblet, inscribed "Vigilate Deo Confidentes" [Be vigilant while trusting in God]. - This was the motto of the Province of Holland during the time of the Dutch Republic.

(5) Goblet, wheel-engraved, inscribed "Oostbos" [East Wood]. - Oostbos, or Oostbosch, was the name of an estate and of a polder near Leidschendam, just east of 's-Gravenhage.

(6) Goblet, wheel-engraved, showing the "Brielse Hooft" [a headland at Brielle, island of Voorne, west of Rotterdam] and a sloop on the river [Maas].

(7) Goblet, wheel-engraved, inscribed "De wijn vendengie" [The wine vintage].

(8) Goblet, wheel-engraved, inscribed "Aurea Libertas" [Golden Freedom].

(9) Goblet, wheel-engraved, inscribed "Libertas Vita carior" [Freedom is life's greatest treasure]. - Note: "A wine-glass with straight-sided bowl of large size, engraved with an open bird cage and a bird above, inscribed within a label "Libertas vita carior", on a star-studded Silesian stem and folded foot" was in an auction at Sotheby's, London, 7.V.1937, lot 249.

(10) Goblet, wheel-engraved, inscribed "De groote visserij" [The herring fishery] with a scene of herring-fishing. - It is possible that this glass, like No. 6, has a Brielle connection because that town together with Delft, Rotterdam, Schiedam and Enkhuizen constituted the 'College van de Groote Visscherij'.

When Notary Public Willem Boon visited Greenwood on 28 December, 1724, he read him the contents of the notarial act and handed him a copy thereof. Frans Greenwood admitted that indeed he had those glasses except for numbers 2 and 7, and added - this almost sounds like a joke - that he also had a wine-glass inscribed "De absente Vrinden" [The absent friends] (various goblets with this inscription - usually commemorating the dead - are known). Subsequently Greenwood showed the glasses to Mr Boon.

No further documents about this incident were found.

Was this episode one of the reasons why Frans Greenwood left Rotterdam a year later ?

*   *   *

FRANS GREENWOOD AND POETRY

Writing poetry was much in vogue among Dutch burghers in the seventeenth and eighteenth centuries. It may be assumed that the children of Francis Greenewood all received a good education in Rotterdam. Frans happened to be born with an artistic bent which he developed to capacity. Like his friend Cornelis Boon, he was attracted to poetry but especially during the first half of his life.

A good many 18th-century poets, Greenwood among them, seem to have modelled their style of writing on that of Jan Antonisz van der Goes (1647-1684; he called himself Joannes Antonides) who in turn was a great admirer and friend of the famous old Joost van den Vondel. Greenwood befriended many of the leading poets of his day and when he went to live in Dordrecht, in 1726, he joined an informal circle of poets of good standing. In 1728 the poet Sybrand Feitama [33a] bemoaned in a sonnet the departure of poets from the "dejected river Maas", i.e., Rotterdam. - Ten Brinck [26] counted Greenwood among the best of the multitudinous 18th-century poets - few of whom were really outstanding.

Frans Greenwood did not date many of his poems. Among his earliest issued pen-fruits is the one in which he remembers the victory over French troops at Hochstet (near Blenheim) by allied forces under John Churchill, Duke of Marlborough, on 13 August, 1704. The following year he wrote a poem of welcome for that Duke on the occasion of his visit to Holland where he was hailed as a great victor.

Several of Greenwood's poems were at first printed privately so that they could be presented without delay to his poetic and other friends such as dedicatees; e.g., Hochstet in 1704 [41], Wilthof in 1714 [42], Geluk op reis [Successful journey] in 1715 [43] and at least two post-1719 poems: Aan een ongodist [To an atheist] [45, 72] and Avont-Zang [Evening song] [46]. His elegy on the death of his mother, together with one by Zeeus, was also published separately [52], and so was Greenwood's mournful poem on the death of his son [49].

Frans Greenwood's first collected poems appeared in 1719 (Fig. 38) [44]. In the introduction he justified the publication as follows: "Whatever one may say about me publishing a small and very modest book, I decided to do this not without reasons - the main one being that some of my friends at some occasion or other having seen a poem of mine that had not been printed, often implored me to write them a copy; sometimes, for the sake of courtesy, I could not refuse such a request. To obviate such copying, I considered having the poems published. And as I am intending to say farewell to the Parnassus [the field of poetry], if not entirely then certainly for some time, and I would not like to see - as is often the case nowadays - that my insignificant poems were to be copied by a second or third hand, I accepted the views and wishes of many of my good friends, especially my printer Arnold Willis, who suggested that my poems, of so little value, may find purchasers. The poem-loving reader should not think that I believe that my little book will please everyone. On the contrary, I know the world of poets too well to realise how very sensitive they are about things of this kind. But I find comfort in poets who have been praised very highly but could not escape the teeth of wrathful jealousy and of hair-splitting know-alls. I would like to add that this book could have been more voluminous if I had published everything that ever flowed from my pen. But I gathered that much of it would not have stood the test of time and it would have been too much trouble to make improvements. So I merely separated the goats from the sheep, exposing only the latter to the light. With this I present my piece of work and wish it well."

GEDICHTEN

VAN

FRANS GREENWOOD.

TE ROTTERDAM,

Gedrukt by ARNOLD WILLIS, Boekverkooper over den Rystuin. 1719.

Fig. 38. Title-page of Greenwood's first book of collected poems, published in 1719.

Greenwood dedicated this first book of poems to his friend the poet Jakob Zeeus, six years his junior, who died at the age of 32 on 27 November, 1718. Frans included a poem on a portrait of Zeeus without any indication of him having died (an elegy on the death of Zeeus [140] can be found in Greenwood's second anthology of 1760 [50]). The manuscript for the book must therefore have been ready for the printer at some time in 1718, before November. Zeeus, a bachelor living mainly at Zevenbergen (south of Rotterdam), began to ail in the spring of 1718 but he still managed to compose a poem - when he was "half alive, half dead" - for the birthday, in April, of Frans, ending it with "live long in happiness; remember me" [139]. Moreover, Zeeus gathered strength

TE ROTTERDAM,
Gedrukt by ARNOLD WILLIS, Boekverkooper.

Fig. 39. Title-plate by B. Picart, dated 1718, for Greenwood's anthology of 1719.

to write a eulogy - included in the 1719 book - on Greenwood and his poems [139] which contains the lines "Lately I lost courage but now, for medicine, I was poured a lavish measure of the effervescing nectar of your poetry . . . "

The 1719 book was quite well produced by Arnold Willis who was active as bookdealer and publisher in Rotterdam between 1711 and 1734. Although he became known as an archtypical unscrupulous publisher, by dabbling himself in poetry he counted Greenwood, Boon van Engelant, Zeeus, van Koeverden and other men of letters among his good friends. The book has an excellent etching of arcadian scenery as title-plate (Fig. 39) made in 1718 by the well-known French refugee engraver Bernard Picart (born in Paris in 1672 [73]) who lived in Holland from 1710 (after a short spell in 's-Gravenhage he moved to Amsterdam in 1711) until his death in 1733. Picart dealt in books and prints and made no fewer than 1,300 etchings and engravings; he illustrated also other books published by Willis so it seems that the latter, rather than Greenwood himself, commissioned him to etch the frontispiece. - Greenwood's first anthology contains 8 pastoral poems, 9 poems for weddings or wedding anniversaries, 9 for birthdays, 7 relating to deceased persons and 48 miscellaneous poems.

In 1722 Pieter Kraay presented the Millers' Guild of Rotterdam with an inverted silver cup surmounted by a windmill, made in 1721 by the renowned gold- and silversmith Hendrick van Beest (1680-1772) of Rotterdam [36, 81a, 113]. Such mill cups were made in Holland from the 16th century onwards. Whereas the mill is always constructed of metal, usually silver, the bowl was not infrequently a glass one. Mill cups belong to the category of drinking vessels designed to amuse onlookers: after having blown down a fixed metal tube to set the vanes in motion, one had to quaff the contents of the bowl before the sails ceased turning, lest . . . On this particular cup - which has an overall height of 254 mm - the engraved coat of arms of Pieter Kraay is flanked by a poem of Frans Greenwood which refers to the craft of the miller and to success in life; there is also the following dedication: "Gift / Van den Heere / Pieter Kraay / Aan het Rotterdamsche / Molenaarsgilden // Als Hooft Luyden / waaren / Jan van der Werf / Cornelus de Goeyer en / Lodewijk de Vos / 1722". Greenwood published the poem in 1760 in his second bundle [50], entitled 'On a silver mill, presented by Mr Pieter Kraai to the Millers' Guild of Rotterdam, cut thus: &c.' This could be interpreted that either Greenwood engraved the lettering ['having cut'] or that it should read 'being cut with'. There is no evidence that Frans Greenwood ever engraved silver; the letters, as well as the coat of arms, are very well executed and point to the work of a professional, presumably van Beest himself (who was indeed an expert engraver). Both dedication and verse are engraved by the same hand. The cup now belongs to the Rijksmuseum, Amsterdam (but is on extended loan to the Historisch Museum, Rotterdam) [36, 81a, 113].

*   *   *

Some Dutch townsfolk in search of arcadian amusement used to spend Whitsun in the country where one could witness or participate in "Pinkstervreugd" [Whitsun revelry] celebrations by villagers - even though it must have been known that as a rule drunken brawls ensued. Presumably in the early 1730s, Frans went to stay at a village inn of undisclosed location during Whitsuntide. The events he witnessed amused him so much that he recounted them in a long poem which he had published by Arnold Willis, Rotterdam, in 1733 [47] (Fig. 40). A second edition was issued by J. van Braam, Dordrecht, in 1760 [50], a third by J. C. van Kesteren, Amsterdam, in 1823 [100]. Apparently this 'Boere-Pinxtervreugt' was also published by G. Tielenburg, Amsterdam, @ 8 stuyvers [4], but no copy could be traced. A facsimile of 1733 was issued by Inmerc, Wormerveer, in 1975 [48].

F. GREENWOODS

B O E R E-

PINXTERVREUGT.

T E   R O T T E R D A M,

By **ARNOLD WILLIS**, Boekverkooper over
den Rystuin. **1733.**

Fig. 40. Title-page of Greenwood's Boere-Pinxtervreugt, 1733.

This satyre - modelled on Lucas Rotgans' "De Boerekermis" [Peasants' Fun Fair] of 1708 - on the manners and customs of rustics has been called an important socio-psychological essay [94].

Boere-Pinxtervreugt is illustrated with four unsigned etchings depicting some of the happenings described. One would surmise that at least sketches for the plates were made by Greenwood himself but it is far from certain whether he also made the etchings - which are of no outstanding quality. It is possible that either Kornelis Greenwood or Aart Schouman made the etchings; without any good reason De la Fontaine Verwey [34] opined that they were probably the work of Frans Greenwood. Three of the etchings in the Kramm auction of 1855 were attributed to Frans Greenwood. These statements, being mere guesswork, are far from conclusive. Comparison of the etchings with Schouman's 1736 etching of the Sint Lukas Broederschap (Fig. 35) reveals a similarity in execution; perhaps it may be suggested that the four etchings were made by young Aart Schouman.

Fig. 41. The four etchings (each measuring ca 11 x 16 cm) illustrating
Greenwood's Boere-Pinxtervreugt of 1733.

VERVOLG

VAN

F: GREENWOODS

GEDICHTEN,

EN

BOERE-

PINXTERVREUGT.

TE DORDRECHT,

By d'ERVE J: van BRAAM, 1760.

Fig. 42. Title-page of Greenwood's second anthology, published in 1760.

Plate 1 (Fig. 41) shows a drummer traversing a village to gather youngsters. To the left a country inn with Greenwood popping his head out of an upstairs window. Plate 2 depicts goose-shooting and in plate 3 the winner of that contest is addressing bystanders - he is standing on a barrel outside an inn with an owl as sign. Plate 4 shows a vicious scuffle, knives drawn and all, in the tap room of the inn at the end of the day [98].

*   *   *

The 1733 poem is dedicated to Willem Snellen (born 6.VIII.1683, a son of Jan Snellen, Rear-Admiral in the service of the Noble College of Admiralty on the Maas), who was married to Margaretha van 't Wedde. Their son Jan's second marriage resulted in a daughter Margaretha Cornelia who married François van Vollenhoven on 28 April, 1782. In 1877 their grandson Mr Samuel Constant Snellen van Vollenhoven (Rotterdam 1816 - 's-Gravenhage 1880) presented a fine leatherbound gold-embossed large (234 x 185 mm) copy of the first edition of Boere-Pinxtervreugt - being the author's presentation copy to Willem Snellen - to the Maatschappij van Nederlandsche Letterkunde in Leiden which later on donated it to the Library of the Rijks Universiteit, Leiden (inv. 1105 B 2). - S. C. Snellen van Vollenhoven was a wealthy non-practising jurist who devoted his life to entomology and the study of applied art; a highly skilled pictorial artist, he was chairman of the academy of art "Ars aemula naturae" during his residence in Leiden. He owned a goblet stipple-engraved by Greenwood (24.1) which, in 1876, he sold to the Nederlandsch Museum voor Geschiedenis en Kunst [now Rijksmuseum], Amsterdam.

* * *

In 1760, when he was 80 years old, Frans Greenwood published a "Vervolg der Gedichten" [A Continuation of Poems] together with the second edition of the popular Boere-Pinxtervreugt of 1733 [50]. Publisher this time was his friend Joannes van Braam in Dordrecht who utilised the same Picart 1718 title-plate. The short introduction - To the Reader - states that "The reason which compels me now to bring to light a further instalment of my poems are the same as those of 1719 and which can be found at the beginning of that volume (printed by Arnold Willis in Rotterdam), so in order to avoid a wearisome repeat I direct the curious reader to it. Furthermore, believing this will suffice as introduction, I wish him prosperity." - Following the introduction are three laudatory poems on the new bundle by his friends H. F. Ketelanus, Frans de Haes [54] and Niko-laes Versteeg. The 1760 book contains 56 mixed poems, 7 poems on portraits, 7 on birthdays, 10 on weddings or wedding anniversaries and 9 relating to deceased persons. Four of them, on pp. 24-26, 96, 181-186 and 190-192 had already been published by friends, namely by van Gool [40: pp. 341-343], van Gool [39: pp. xi-xii], Zeeus [140: pp. xvii-xxii] and Poot [91: pp. 197-200] respectively. A selection, without annotations or comments, of 14 poems from the 1719 bundle and 15 from the 1760 book was published in 1827 [51].

* * *

Having acquired the sword which was believed to have beheaded the great Dutch statesman Johan van Oldenbarnevelt in 1619, Greenwood wrote a poem on that evil sword in 1743; this is not included in his book of 1760. Subsequently Frans invited a number of his contemporaries to write a poem on the sword (to follow his introductory verse) in a special album [7] which was passed on from poet to poet, starting in Dordrecht in 1743 and returning there in March, 1745. A total of 47 poets obliged and their sequence in the album is:

D o r d r e c h t, 1743: F. Greenwood, H. F. Ketelanus, J. W. van Steenbergen, P. C. van Steenbergen nu de Court, Henr. van Bracht, Joannes van Braam. H e e n v l i e t: Kornelis Boon van Engelant. V l a a r d i n g e n : J. Badon, Klara Ghyben-Badon, Willem van der Linden, Jakob Brouwer, F. Froet, Katharina Froet, Jan Blijenburg, Arnold Hoogvliet. R o t t e r d a m : Frans de Haes, Dirk Smits (who dated his poem: 1743 - most of the subsequent authors also added a date), Willem van der Pot (4.I.1744), K. Westerbaen (27.I.1744), Nikolaes Versteeg (9.II.1744), Wouter de Kemp (9.III.44).

A m s t e r d a m : J. Elias Michielsz (30.IV.1744), B. Huydecoper, R. Blok (9.V.1744), B. de Bosch (14.V.1744), Dirk Willink (15.V.1744), Antoni Hartsen (20.V. 1744), Anna van Oostrum (23.V.1744), Philip Zweerts (1744), J. V. Stamhorst (30.V. 1744), A. Hobrink (6.VI.1744), Lucas Pater (15.VI.1744), Adriaan van Ommering Jacobsz. (19.VI.1744), H. van Elvervelt (6.VIII.1744), Joannes van der Heijde (7.VIII. 1744), Js. de Later (11.VIII.1744), Magdalena de Neve nu de Later (12.VIII.1744), Jacobus van der Streng (16.VIII.1744), Abraham de Haen de Jonge (19.VIII.1744), J. Haverkamp (13.IX.1744), Lambert van den Broek (25.IX.1744), Mattheus van den Broek (25.IX.1744), J. R. van Hoolwerff (4.X.1744), P. H. Bakker (31.I.1745), G. Klinkhamer (15.II.1745).
' s - G r a v e n h a g e : Mattheus de Ruusscher, J. V. Hoven (28.IX.1744 - this poem must have been written on a separate sheet as the album was in Amsterdam at the time), Aarn. Heckenhoek.

All contributors - except perhaps for two - deplored in their verses the lethal role the sword had played in the hands of evil men. Following Greenwood's poem, on the next page, is written in the same hand as that of the list of poets in front of the album: "Mr Herman Franciscus Ketelanus and Dr Jan Willem van Steenbergen each has clandestinely torn out his own verse." Then follows a poem by P. C. van Steenbergen née de Court [perhaps the wife of J. W. van Steenbergen] entitled "In reply to the verse of Mr H. F. Ketelanus on preceding p. 2" which alludes to opposite political views.

After its round-trip of nearly two years this fine collection of autographic poems by many leading and lesser poets of the day reached Dordrecht again. It was returned from Vlaardingen by Arnold Hoogvliet with the following covering letter (which gives us Greenwood's address in Dordrecht in that year):

Mr Frans Greenwood
in the Schryversstraat
*   in*
Dordrecht.   With a book

Mr F. Greenwood

Dear Sir and Friend,

*   This accompanies your album homeward, enriched with a good number of inscriptions, although to my surprise there are not among them any by my friends Messrs [Sijbrand] Feitama and [Jan] de Marre; although over two months ago I read at the Y [i.e., Amsterdam] poems on the same subject from their own hands, and I suspect there is no other reason than that one had discovered that all poems had in the meantime been copied by one of the contributors. At the right moment I shall try to obtain these verses separately so that I can send those to you - I saw that you had some others separately to be added as well to the album. I promise that the ones in your hands will be safe from mean theft.*
*   I do not think that I can do anything else in order to comply with my promise and remain with cordial greeting to Mr van Braam*
                              Dear Sir and Friend
                           Yours obedient servant
Vlaerdingen   *and friend*
17 March 1745   *Arnold Hoogvliet*

The special mention of Joannes van Braam, the publisher who in 1760 issued Greenwood's second anthology, could mean that Greenwood may have had plans to have all sword poems published by van Braam but that he refrained from doing so after learning that a number of the verses had already been copied without permission. Indeed, there is an old cahier in the Koninklijke Bibliotheek, 's-Gravenhage (Handschriften 135 D 2 - purchased from bookdealers M. Nijhoff in 1962) with eleven verses, namely those of Hoogvliet, de Haes, Smits, van der Pot, Huydecoper, de Bosch, Willink, Hartsen, Stamhorst, Pater and de Haen de Jonge - all written by the same hand, which is not one of the 47 original contributors.

The following two poems - "Dedication to The Netherlands" and "On the sword that clove the neck of Johan van Oldenbarnevelt" - are the introductory verses by Frans Greenwood:

T o e w y i n g
a a n
N e d e r l a n t .

Wie anders wyde ik zangen
dan u, o Nederlant ? geheng
Dat ik ze u onder d'oogen breng,
En laat ze het geluk erlangen
Bestraalt te worden met uw gunst,
Dewyl ze alleen aan u behooren
Van Dichters in uw' kreits gebooren,
En echte zoonen van de Kunst.
De stoffe moet u niet mishagen,
Het voorwerp hunner poëzy,
Ze zingen onbeschroomt en vry
Hoe elk uw vryheit kwam belagen
Toen fier Gewelt nam d'overhant,
En d'allerwenschelykste Vader
Des Vaderlants als een verrader
Uit bittren wrok geraakte aan kant.
Gy zaagt, o Neerlant, voor uwe oogen
Dat wrede en droevig schouspel aan,
De zon der vryheit onder gaan
En met een' dikken mist omtogen,
Het moortschavot tentoongestelt,
De onnozelheit by 't hooft gegrepen,
Het Heilloos zwaart op 't scherpst geslepen
Voor eedlen Oldenbarnevelt,
En zyn' gryze en zilvre hairen
Bepurpert met onschuldig bloet.
Wat kan de strydt wanneer ze woedt;
Zoo-rein-zoo-zuiver-van-gemoet
Rampzaligheên-en
Wat-kan-de-Nydt-al-onwil-baren-!
Een Ilias van rampen baren.
Men zegt dat op dien droeven dag,
Toen ge op 't schavot hem zaagt gedragen,
De zon haar' loop scheen te vertragen
En deinsde op 't nadren van den slag
Die 't waerig hooft van 't lichaam scheide.

Het hooft, dat knaging en verdriet
In zyne Rechters overliet
Toen elk zyn' val te laat beschreide.
't Ontzaglyk doch onschuldig staal,
In myn bewaring opgesloten,
Waar 't dierbaar bloet door is vergooten,
Noch diergelyk, moet andermaal
Geen staatsman door 't Gewelt doen sneven.
Bescherm dat onwaerdeerbaar pant,
Uw Vryheit, roemryk Nederlant,
Op dat ze ons nimmer mag begeven.

Frans Greenwood.

*　　*　　*

O p   h e t
Z w a a r t
d a t
J o h a n   v a n   O l d e n b a r n e v e l t
d e n   h a l s   d o o r k e r v d e .

Stokoude Staatsman, vrome Heldt,
Onschuldige Oldenbarnevelt,
Dit zwaart sloeg door uw' hals den Staat
Een diepe wonde in zynen Raadt,
Toen op het haagse moortschavot
Den boom uw's levens wierd geknot.

Frans Greenwood.

Fig. 43. Heading, in Frans Greenwood's handwriting, of above poem.

*　　*　　*

LIST OF DATED POEMS

A = Greenwood 1719 Gedichten
B = Greenwood 1733 Boere-Pinxtervreugt
C = Greenwood 1760 Vervolg der Gedichten
The figure following a bold capital letter is the page reference.

13.VIII.1704 - Victory at Hochstet **A**: 19
1705 - Marlborough in Holland **A**: 23
1713 - London Peace [of Utrecht] Medal **A**: 47
12.II.1714 - Death of Mrs van Ravestein **A**: 125 [= 115]
1714 - Whaling **A**: 57
1715 - Greenland whaling fleet **A**: 58
24.IX.1716 - Death of Ysbrant van der Elst **A**: 113
27.XI.1718 - Death of Jakob Zeeus **C**: 181
7.VI.1720 - Wedding of Adriaan Prins & Elizabeth Schepers **C**: 133
15.VII.1721 - Wedding of Frans Velters & Maria Thysen **C**: 138
5.X.1721 - Birthday of Maria Zydervelt **C**: 113
3.X.1722 - Birthday of Jan Theodoor, Baron van Freisheim **C**: 117
29.IX.1724 - Death of Kornelis van Arkel **C**: 187
4.X.1729 - Wedding of Arnold Willis & Alida Gramingh **C**: 146
31.XII.1733 - Death of Huibert Korneliszoon Poot **C**: 190
1733 - Boere-Pinxtervreugt **B**: 39 pp.
3.IV.1736 [actually later] - Death of Kornelis Greenwood **C**: 193
29.X.1737 - Death of Johan van den Broucke **C**: 196
9.I.1739 - Birthday of Adriaan Hallincq **C**: 125
21.XI.1739 - Birthday of Willem Beyen **C**: 128
4.VIII.1740 - Silver wedding anniversary of Huibert van Wetten & Adriana van Kampen **C**: 153
31.VIII.1740 - Death of Kornelis Terwe **C**: 203
7.I.1741 - Centenary of St Lukas Brotherhood Dordrecht **C**: 64
23.V.1741 - Death of Suzanna Catharina Albinus **C**: 204
17.IV.1743 - Birthday of Frans Greenwood **C**: 129
17.XII.1746 - Birthday of Mr N. N. (Jaap, chairman of the Wine Merchants' Guild) **C**: 121
7.III.1747 - Death of Elizabeth Maria de Bruin **C**: 207
28.V.1749 - Silver wedding anniversary of Caspar Balthazar Doll van Ouryk & Anthonia van Wezel **C**: 154
VII.1749 - Wedding of Jakob van der Heim & Maria Gevaerts **C**: 161
24.VII.1750 - Birthday of Adriana Anna Maria Greenwood **C**: 132
21.VIII.1750 - Golden wedding anniversary of Joannes van Braam & Maria Verhoef **C**: 160
23.II.1751 - Death of Joannes van Braam **C**: 208
3.X.1751 - Wedding of Paulus Gevaerts & Suzanna Adriana Beelaerts **C**: 169
2.IV.1754 - Wedding of Carel Bosschaert & Cornelia Apolonia Bosschaert **C**: 170

* * *

P E R S O N S   N A M E D   I N
G R E E N W O O D ' S   P O E M S

A = Greenwood 1719 Gedichten
B = Greenwood 1733 Boere-Pinxtervreugt
C = Greenwood 1760 Vervolg der Gedichten
The figure following a bold capital letter is the page reference.
b. = born
d. = died
m. = married

AGNOLO **C** 24, 25 - [Michelangelo ?]; painter

Johanna VAN AKEN **A** 60 - m. Mr Pieter de Bye VII.1714

ALBAAN **C** 65 - Francesco Albani, b. Bologna 1578, d. Bologna 1660; painter

Suzanna Catharina ALBINUS **C** 204, 205 - b. Leiden 1703, d. Dordrecht 1741,
    m. (1) Leonardus Hoeufft 1729, (2) Paulus Gevaerts XII.1739

duc d'ALVA **B** 15 - Fernando Alvarez de Toledo, Duke of Alva, 1507-1582;
    a barbaric and tyrannic Spanish general in the service of Philips II (still
    despised in The Netherlands)

ANGELO **C** 65 - presumably Michelangelo [Michelagniolo di Lodovico Buonarroti,
    1475-1564]; sculptor, painter, poet

ANTONIDES **C** 36 - Joannes Antonides van der Goes, b. Goes 1647, d. Rotterdam
    1684; poet

APEL **C** 24 - Apelles, legendary painter of ancient Greece, court painter to
    Alexander the Great

Kornelis VAN ARCKEL [van Arkel] **A** 96, **C** 187 - b. Amsterdam 1670, d. Rotter-
    dam 1724, m. Katharina Scheltinga VII.1717; Remonstrant teacher, poet

ARMIJN **C** 106 - Jacobus Arminius, b. Oudewater 1560, d. Leiden 1609;
    Remonstrant theologian

Heer A. B. **C** 93 - member of an art society in Dordrecht

K. V. B. **C** 34 - K. van Beer, b. Zoetermeer; maker of shoes and paltry rhymes

BEEFTINGH **C** 78 - Hendrik van Beeftingh, b. Rotterdam 1711, d. Rotterdam
    1797, m. Adriana Martina Brouwer VI.1740; high-ranking official in local govern-
    ment of Rotterdam

J. BEEKMAN **A** 87 - poet

Suzanna Adriana BEELAERTS **C** 169 - m. Paulus Gevaerts in Dordrecht 3.X.1751

BEKKER **A** 122 - Balthasar Bekker, b. Metslawier 1634, d. Amsterdam 1698;
    theologian

Mr M:V:B **C** 82 - "neef Max", cousin Maximiliaan van Berchem (see p. 63)

BERGHEM **C** 67 - Nicolaes Pietersz. Berchem, b. Haarlem 1620, d. Amsterdam
    1683; painter

Mr Engelbert VAN BERKEL **A** 82 - m. Theodora Petronella van Hogendorp;
    councillor & city-father of Rotterdam, governor of the Dutch East India Co.

Willem BEYEN **C** 128 - captain of the Noble College of Admiralty on the
    River Maas

Mr Kornelis BOON VAN ENGELANT **A** 118 - b. Rotterdam 1680, d. after 1746, son of Hugo Boon and Johanna van Heel; bailiff of Heenvliet, vassal of Voorne, poet

Kornelia BOS **A** 89 - m. Gysbert Peimans

Kornelis VAN DEN BOSCH **C** 35 - Leidschendam; poet

Mr Carel BOSSCHAERT **C** 170 - b. Rotterdam 1721, d. Dordrecht 1779, m. Cornelia Apolonia Bosschaert at Schiedam 2.IV.1754; jurist, pensionary of Schiedam and (since 1751) of Dordrecht

Cornelia Apolonia BOSSCHAERT **C** 170 - see above

Jakobus BOUTKAN **A** 59, 60 - m. Hester van der Kindert 14.VII.1712

Joannes VAN BRAAM **C** 62, 160, 208 - b. Dordrecht 1677, d. Dordrecht 1751, m. Maria Verhoef in Dordrecht 21.VIII.1700; bookdealer, publisher, poet

Gerard BRAKEL **C** 72 - owner of yacht 'Den Arion'

Kornelia BRAKEL **A** 67 - m. Joan[nes] van der Wallen

Johanna Katharina VAN BRAKEL **A** 125 [= 123] - wife of Jakob van Koperen

BREIDEL **A** 122 - poet

Mr Henrik BRENKMAN **A** 126 [= 116] - b. Rotterdam 1680, d. Rotterdam 1736; jurist, author

Mr Johan VAN DEN BROUCKE **C** 196 - b. Dordrecht 1693, d. Dordrecht 1737; official in local government of Dordrecht, writer of Latin poetry

BROUWER **C** 78 - Adriana Martina Brouwer, b. Rotterdam 1721, d. Rotterdam 1763, m. Hendrik van Beeftingh VI.1740

Elizabeth Maria DE BRUIN **C** 207 - b. Dordrecht 1747, m. Mr Hermanus Franciscus Ketelanus

Mr Johan VAN DER BURCH **C** 201 - b. Dordrecht 1660, d. Dordrecht 1732, m. Charlotte Elisabeth van Blyenburch; town official

VAN DER BURG **C** 101 [= 110] - Adriaen van der Burg, b. Dordrecht 1693, d. Dordrecht 1733; painter

Mr Pieter DE BYE **A** 60 - b. 's-Gravenhage 1687, d. 's-Gravenhage 1749, m. Joanna van Aken VII.1714; jurist, poet

DANTE **C** 184 - Dante Alighieri, b. Firenze 1265, d. Ravenna 1321; poet

DEZIDEER **C** 47 - Desiderius Erasmus, b. Rotterdam 1469, d. Basel 1536; humanist

Abraham DIERS DE RAS **A** 77 - father of Paul Diers de Ras

Paul DIERS DE RAS **A** 77 - second husband of Anna Greenwood (see p. 52)

Mr Caspar Balthazar DOLL VAN OURY[C]K **C** 154, 155 - b. 's-Gravenhage 1697, d. Dordrecht 1777, m. Anthonia van Wezel 28.V.1724; jurist, burgomaster of Dordrecht

Johan DOLL VAN OURYK **C** 158 - son of Caspar and Anthonia (above)

Kaspar DOLL VAN OURYK **C** 159 - ibidem

Marye DOLL VAN OURYK **C** 159 - daughter of Caspar and Anthonia

DOU **C** 67 - Gerard Dou, b. Leiden 1613, d. Leiden 1675; painter

Elizabeth Kristina VAN DER DUSSEN A 106 - m. Willem Schepers

VAN DYK C 25, 66 - Anthony van Dyck, b. Antwerpen 1599, d. London 1641; painter

Amaranta VAN DER ELST A 80 - m. Jakob Kristiaan Pielat

Willem VAN DER ELST A 113 - son of Ysbrant van der Elst

Ysbrant VAN DER ELST A 113 - d. Delft 24.IX.1716

Govert FLINK C 66 - Govert Flinck, b. Kleve 1615, d. Amsterdam 1660; painter

Johan Theodoor Baron VAN FREISHEIM C 117, 118, 120 - Jan Theodoor Baron van Friesheim, b. 1642, d. 's-Hertogenbosch 1733; military general-major, governor of Heusden

Joan[nes] Arnold GALLAS A 94 - m. Louiza Jozina Kools

Mr Johan GEVAERTS C 165 - town official & burgomaster of Dordrecht, official of the Noble College of Admiralty on the River Maas

Maria GEVAERTS C 161, 164 - Maria Arnoudina Gevaerts, daughter of Paulus Gevaerts, m. Mr Jakob van der Heim, a burgomaster of Rotterdam, VII.1749

Mr Paulus GEVAERTS C 169, 204 - b. 1697, d. 1770, m. (1) Suzanna Catharina Albinus (1703-1741) XII.1739, (2) Suzanna Adriana Beelaerts, Dordrecht, 3.X. 1751; Baron van Gansooyen, bailiff of Beyerlanden, town official & burgomaster of Dordrecht

Anna GLOVER A 74 - mother of Frans Greenwood (see p. 10)

Joannes Antonides VAN DER GOES A 118 - b. Goes 1647, d. Rotterdam 1684; poet

Johan VAN GOOL C 96 - b. 's-Gravenhage 1685, d. 's-Gravenhage 1763; painter

Alida GRAMINGH C 146 - a wealthy widow from Amsterdam, m. Arnold Willis 4.X.1729 [second wife]

Adriana Anna Maria GREENWOOD C 132 - cousin once removed of Frans Greenwood, b. 24.VII.1735 (see p. 62)

Anna GREENWOOD C 84 - daughter of Frans Greenwood (see p. 32)

Francis GREENWOOD A 75 - Francis Greenewood, father of Frans Greenwood (see p. 11)

Kornelis GREENWOOD C 193 - son of Frans Greenwood (see p. 34)

Mr Dirk GROENHOUT A 83, 84 - b. Rotterdam 1680, d. Rotterdam 1720, m. (1) Elisabeth Maria Roosmale 1709, (2) Bartha Maria Schepers; governor of Kapelle op den Yssel [Cappelle-op-den-IJssel, now Capelle aan den IJssel], burgomaster of Rotterdam, governor of the Dutch East India Company and of the Noble College of Admiralty on the River Maas

Huig DE GROOT C 46 - Hugo de Groot [Grotius], b. Delft 1583, d. Rostock 1645; savant, jurist, publicist, statesman

Jan DE GROOT C 46 - "a clever young man"

Pieter VAN HAGEN C 111 - Petrus Albertus van Hagen, lutenist, violinist; in 1731 Frans de Haes also poetically praised his playing

Arnold VAN HALEN C 44 - b. Amsterdam 1673, d. Amsterdam 1732; amateur painter and poet (see p. 37)

Adriaan HALLINCQ   C 125-127 - b. Dordrecht 1681, d. Dordrecht 1741, bachelor; jurist, alderman & burgomaster of Dordrecht, governor of the Noble College of Admiralty on the River Maas

DE HEEM   C 61 - either Cornelis de Heem, b. Leiden 1631, d. Antwerpen 1695, or Jan Davidsz. de Heem, b. Utrecht 1606, d. Antwerpen 1684; painters

Mr Jakob VAN DER HEIM   C 161, 164 - b. 's-Gravenhage 1727, d. Rotterdam 1799, m. Maria Arnoudina Gevaerts VII.1749; secretary of the Noble College of Admiralty on the River Maas

HELVETIUS   A 122 - Johan Frederik Helvetius, b. Köthen 1629, d. 's-Gravenhage 1709; writer, poet

Theodora Petronella VAN HOGENDORP   A 82 - m. Engelbert van Berkel

Marie / Mary VAN DEN HOLAART   A 74, 75, 113 - wife of Frans Greenwood (see p. 22)

Quirine VAN DEN HOLAART   A 81 - mother-in-law of Frans Greenwood (see p. 30)

HOOFT   C 36 - Pieter Cornelisz. Hooft, b. Amsterdam 1581, d. 's-Gravenhage 1647; man of letters, historian

Arnold HOOGVLIET   C 62, 108 - b. Vlaardingen 1687, d. Vlaardingen 1763, m. Ida van der Ruyt 30.XI.1735; clerk, bookkeeper, poet

HOUBRAKE   C 96 - Arnold Houbraken, b. Dordrecht 1660, d. Amsterdam 1719; painter, engraver, poet

H. VAN DER HULST   C 30 - Henrik van Hulst, b. Delft 1685, d. Paris 1754; painter, vulgar poet (honoured [?] Greenwood with a poem which has not been traced)

Geerlof DE JAGER   A 79, 79*, 80 - Maastricht; theologian

JORDAANS   C 66 - Jacob Jordaens, b. Antwerpen 1593, d. Antwerpen 1678; painter

Heer A. DE K.   A 122 - probably Adriaen de Kramer, a poetically-minded blacksmith

Heer H. K.   A 27

KALVYN   C 106 - Jean Chauvin or Calvin(ius), b. Noyon 1509, d. Genève 1564; Protestant reformer and theologian

Adriana VAN KAMPEN   C 153 - m. Huibert van Wetten in Dordrecht 4.VIII.1715

KARATS   C 65 - perhaps Agostino Caracci 1558-1602, Annibale Carracci 1560-1609 or Lodovico Carracci 1555-1618; painters

Mr Hermanus Franciscus KETELANUS   C 207 - b. Amsterdam 1712, d. Dordrecht 1761, m. (1) Elisabeth Maria de Bruyn Johansdr (d. 1747) 30.VIII.1735, (2) Geertruid Elisabeth Munninkhoven (from Wezel) widow of Jacob van de Wall 10.IX.1756; jurist, town official of Dordrecht, writer of Latin poetry

Klaas VAN KIETEN de Sparwouwer Reus   B 21 - Klaas van Kijten, the giant of Spaarnwoude

Hester VAN DER KINDERT   A 59, 60 - m. Jakobus Boutkan

Louiza Jozina KOOLS   A 94 - m. Joan[nes] Arnold Gallas

Jakob VAN KOPEREN A 125 [= 123] - m. Johanna Katharina van Brakel; Rear-Admiral of the Noble College of Admiralty on the River Maas

Pieter KRAAI C 20 - (see p. 75)

Broederen KRABETTEN C 74 - Dirk Pieters Crabeth, b. Gouda 1574 and his brother Wouter Pieters Crabeth, b. Gouda 1589; makers of stained-glass windows (Gouda)

Maria Justina KRAEY A 64 - m. Mr Samuel van der Lanen

LAIRES C 66 - Gerard de Lairesse, b. Liège 1641, d. Amsterdam 1711; painter

Mr Samuel VAN DER LANEN A 64 - m. Maria Justina Kraey; private secretary of the town of Haarlem

LEEUWENHOEK C 112 - Antoni van Leeuwenhoek, b. Delft 1632, d. Delft 1723; cloth merchant, famous naturalist

Joan[nes] LIEFTINK A 28 - captain of the Noble College of Admiralty on the River Maas

Louis / Luidewijk A 19, 22, 47, 120 - Louis XIV, King of France, 1638-1715

LUTHER C 106 - Martin Luther, b. Eisleben 1483, d. Eisleben 1546; German Protestant reformer

Heer M. M. C 103 - owner of horse "Zwaantje"

Adriaan MAAS C 48 - m. Sara Maria Verhoeven; owner of country house 'Zeevliet' [probably near IJsselstein]

MANDER C 96 - Carel van Mander, b. Meulbeke 1548, d. Amsterdam 1606; painter

Arnold MARCEL C 112 - b. Dordrecht 1672, d. Dordrecht 1748; philosopher, scientist, grinder and polisher of lenses - Aart Schouman made a mezzotint portrait of him

Hendrik VAN DER MARK A 43 - poet

Johan hertog van MARLBOROUG A 21, 23, 26, 120 - John Churchill, First Duke of Marlborough, b. Musbury (Devon) 1650, d. Windsor 1722

Aarnout VAN DER MEER C 94

Johan Diederik POMPE VAN MEERDERVOORT C 68 - (see p. 68)

MIERIS C 67 - either Frans van Mieris I, b. Leiden 1635, d. Leiden 1681, Frans van Mieris II, b. Leiden 1689, d. Leiden 1763 or Willem van Mieris, b. Leiden 1662, d. Leiden 1747; painters [probably Greenwood's friend Frans II]

David VAN MOLLEM C 27 - b. Utrecht 1670, d. near Utrecht 1746, son of Jacob van Mollem and Maria Sijdervelt, m. Jacomina van Oosterwijk in Amsterdam 28.XII.1698; owner of a large silkmill just outside the Weerdpoort, Utrecht, and of a nearby beautiful country-house 'De Zijdebalen'

Jacoba VAN MOLLEM C 140 - b. Amsterdam 1699, d. Utrecht 1735, daughter of David van Mollem, m. Jakob Sijdervelt 7.XII.1723

MOONEN C 36 - Arnold Moonen, b. Zwolle 1644, d. Deventer 1711; preacher, poet

NETSCHER C 67 - probably Caspar Netscher, b. Heidelberg 1639, d. 's-Gravenhage 1684; painter

NEWTON   C 112 - Isaac Newton, b. Woolsthorpe 1642, d. Kensington [London] 1727; natural philosopher

Geertruid NOORTHEI   A 50 - b. Rotterdam 1670, d. Rotterdam 1721, eldest daughter of Mr Daniël Noortheij, councillor & burgomaster of Rotterdam, and Maria Jacoba Schepers

Gysbert PEIMANS   A 89 - m. Kornelia Bos

Jakob Kristiaan PIELAT   A 80 - b. 's-Gravenhage ±1742, d. Waalwijk 1789, m. Amaranta van der Elst; jurist

POLIDOOR   C 65 - Polidoro da Lanciano, b. Lanciano 1515, d. Venezia 1565; painter

Huibert Korneliszoon POOT   C 190 - b. Abtswoude 1689, d. Delft 1733; poet - Greenwood's 'In Memoriam' was first published in Poot's posthumous third volume of poems [91]

Willem VAN DER POT   C 109 - b. Rotterdam 1704, d. Rotterdam 1783, m. Sara Bosch 23.XI.1729; merchant, poet

POTTER   C 61 - either Paulus Potter, b. Enkhuizen 1625, d. Amsterdam 1654, or Pieter Symonsz Potter, b. Enkhuizen ±1600, d. Amsterdam 1652; painters

Mr Adriaan PRINS   C 133 - b. Delft 1692, d. Rotterdam 1780, son of Adriaen Prins (d. 1705) and Adriana Jacoba de Groot, m. Elisabeth Schepers, Rotterdam 7.XI.1720; town official & burgomaster of Rotterdam, governor of the Dutch East India Company (his mother was a granddaughter of the well-known Hugo de Groot [Grotius])

J. QUIKKLENBERG   C 3 - Johan Frederik van Quickelenberg, b. 's-Gravenhage 1686, d. after 1721 probably in England (resided in Rotterdam 1715 - 1721); violinist.   Poot [90], in a poem, also praised his playing.

RAFAEL / RAFEL   C 24, 25, 65, 66 - Santi Raphael or Rafaello, b. Urbino 1483, d. Roma 1520; painter

Maximiliaan DE RAVE   A 1, C 11 - owned country-house 'Wilthof' (near 's-Grave-zande ?)

Johan VAN RAVESTEIN   A 125 [= 115] - his mother d. Rotterdam 1714

RENI   C 65 - Guido Reni, b. Bologna 1575, d. Bologna 1642; painter

Wilhelmus DE RIBB   C 36 - lived at Zaltbommel

ROMYN   C 65 - Giulio Romano, b. Roma 1492, d. Mantua 1546; painter

Michiel DE ROODE   C 44 - b. Amsterdam 1685, d. Amsterdam 1771 (see p. 37)

ROTGANS   B 3 - Lucas Jacobsz Rotgans, b. Amsterdam 1654, d. Amsterdam 1710; poet

RUBBENS   C 25, 66 - Peter Paul Rubens, b. Siegen 1577, d. Antwerpen 1640; painter

RUITER   A 28 - Michiel Adriaansz de Ruyter, b. Vlissingen 1607, d. Siracusa [Sicily] 1676; admiral

VAN RYN   C 66 - Rembrandt Harmensz van Rijn, b. Leiden 1606, d. Amsterdam 1669; painter, etcher

Pr. SCHEFFENS   A 7, 11, 12 - Pieter Scheffens, owned country-house 'Jeruzalem' in Schieland, northeast of Rotterdam

Katharina SCHELTINGA   A 96 - m. Kornelis van Arckel VII.1717

Bartha Maria SCHEPERS   A 83, 84 - m. Dirk Groenhout

Elizabeth SCHEPERS   C 133 - b. Rotterdam 1701, d. Rotterdam 1756, daughter of Bastiaen Schepers and Geertruyt Timmers, m. Mr Adriaan Prins (1692-1780) 7.XI.1720

Geertruid SCHEPERS   A 32 - b. Rotterdam 1718, daughter of Willem Schepers and Elizabeth Christina van der Dussen, m. Mr Jakob Visch

Willem SCHEPERS   A 106 - b. Rotterdam 1684, d. Rotterdam 1750, m. Elizabeth Christina van der Dussen; councillor & burgomaster of Rotterdam, member of the Noble College of Admiralty on the River Maas, steward and secretary of the Schieland Water Board

Johan SCHERMERS   A 49

SCHOUMAN   C 109 - Aart Schouman, b. Dordrecht 1710, d. 's-Gravenhage 1792; painter, etcher, glass engraver

Mr Willem VAN SCHUILENBURG   C 165 - burgomaster of Delft

Dirk SEELEN   A 17 - d. 1722; merchant, town-councillor of Rotterdam (see p. 125)

SLINGELANT   C 67 - Pieter Cornelisz van Slingelandt, b. Leiden 1640, d. Leiden 1691; painter

Willem SNELLEN   B 3, 4, C 40, 43 - owned country-house 'Overmeer' [just south of Amsterdam ?] (see p. 79)

Joannes VAN SPAAN   C 102 - b. Rotterdam 1725, d. Amsterdam 1789; clergyman in Hensbroek, Aalsmeer, Rijswijk, Dordrecht, Leiden and 's-Gravenhage, amateur poet - his portrait was stipple-engraved on a wine-glass almost certainly by David Wolff in the 1780s

Albertus Jeremias STAAL   A 51

Johan STEENIS   A 72 - owned a country-house on the Maas at Delfshaven

Mr Nicolaas STOOP   C 165, 204 - burgomaster of Dordrecht

Kornelis TERWE   C 203 - Kornelis Terwen, d. 1740

Maria THYSEN   C 138 - Maria Thijssen (from Surinam) m. Frans Velters 15.VII. 1721

TINTORET   C 65 - Jacopo Tintoretto, b. Venezia 1518, d. Venezia 1594; painter

TITIAAN   C 65 - Tiziano Vecellio, b. Pieve do Cadore ±1480, d. Venezia 1576; painter

VAILLANT   C 67 - either Bernard Vaillant, b. Lille 1632, d. Leiden 1698, or Wallerand Vaillant, b. Lille 1623, d. Amsterdam 1677; painters, engravers

VAN DE VELDEN   C 61 - either Adriaen van de Velde, b. Amsterdam 1636, d. Amsterdam 1672; Esaias van de Velde, b. Amsterdam 1591, d. 's-Gravenhage 1630; Jan Jansz van de Velde, b. Haarlem 1620, d. Enkhuizen 1662; Willem van de Velde I, b. Leiden 1611, d. Greenwich 1693 or Willem van de Velde II, b. Leiden 1633, d. Greenwich 1707; painters

Frans VELTERS   C 138, 139 - d. Leiden 1726, m. Maria Thijssen (from Surinam) 15.VII.1721; court-recorder at 's-Hertogenrade, bought estate Huis Ter Wegen (north of Leiden) 4.VIII.1723

Maria VERHOEF   C 160 - m. Joannes van Braam 21.VIII.1700

Sara Maria VERHOEVEN   C 48 - m. Adriaan Maas

Jan VERMEULEN   C 109 - b. Dordrecht 1674, d. Breda ±1750; painter, poet

VERRONEZE   C 65 - Paolo Caliari Veronese, b. Verona 1528, d. Venezia 1588; painter

Mr Jakob VISCH   A 32 - m. Geertruid Schepers

VISVLIET   A 122 - Jacobus Visvliet; preacher who wrote nonsensical poems and lost his sanity in 1711 - after a spell in a lunatic asylum at Koudekerk he was sent to work on a plantation in Surinam

Joan[nes] Eusebius VOET   C 83 - b. Dordrecht 1706, d. Dordrecht 1778, son of Karel Borchart Voet, m. (1) Sara van Outshoorn (d. Dordrecht 1748) 5.VIII.1725, (2) Elisabeth Ghyben (d. 1778) 16.II.1749; medical doctor, poet

Karel Borchart VOET   C 101 [= 110] - b. Zwolle 1671, d. Dordrecht 1744/1745, m. Jacomina Berg at Heino 30.VIII.1696; tax-officer in Dordrecht, painter, published (1725) two first-class volumes on Dutch beetles

A. DE VOGEL   A 55, 56

Gerard VOGEL   A 39, 40 - owned yacht 'd'Adelaar'

VOLLENHOVEN   C 36 - Johannes Vollenhoven, b. Vollenhove 1631, d. 's-Gravenhage 1708; preacher, poet

VONDEL   A 43, 117, 119,   C 36, 74 - Joost van den Vondel, b. Köln 1587, d. Amsterdam 1679; poet

Heer VOORDAAGH   C 74

H. G. VRYHOFF   C 95 - Hubertus Gregorius van Vryhoff; jurist, poet

Anton VAN DER WALLEN   A 36, 53, 102

Jakoba VAN DER WALLEN   A 38, 39, 102 - b. Rotterdam 1695, d. Rotterdam 1757, m. Theodorus van der Hoeven 20.VIII.1719

Joan[nes] VAN DER WALLEN   A 67 - m. Kornelia Brakel

VAN DER WERF   C 67 - either Adriaen van der Werff, b. Kralinger Ambacht 1659, d. Rotterdam 1722, or Pieter van der Werff, b. Kralinger Ambacht 1665, d. Rotterdam 1722; painters

Huibert VAN WETTEN   C 153 - m. Adriana van Kampen 4.VIII.1715; notary public in Dordrecht

Anthonia VAN WEZEL   C 154, 155 - b. Dordrecht 1707, d. Dordrecht 1772, m. Mr Caspar Balthazar Doll van Ouryk 28.V.1724

Willem / Vorst Willem   A 119. C   101 [= 110] - Prince Willem III of Orange, King of England, b. 's-Gravenhage 1650, d. Hampton Court 1702

Arnold WILLIS   C 59, 63, 146 - m. (1) Eremina Luygers 8.VII.1710, (2) Alida Gramingh 4.X.1729; publisher (see p. 75)

Kornelis & Johan DE WIT   A 13 - Cornelis de Witt, b. Dordrecht 1623, d. 's-Gravenhage 1672; Johan de Witt, b. Dordrecht 1625, d. 's-Gravenhage 1672; statesmen

Katharina Johanna DE WITH   A 117 [= 125] - b. Utrecht 1726/1727; poetess

WOUWERMAN **C** 61, 67 - either Jan Pauwel Wouwerman, b. Haarlem 1629, d. Haarlem 1666; Philips Wouwerman, b. Haarlem 1619, d. Haarlem 1668 or Pieter Wouwerman, b. Haarlem 1623, d. Amsterdam 1682; painters

Jakob ZEEUS **A** 119, **C** 36, 107, 181, 186 - b. Zevenbergen 1686, d. Zevenbergen 1718; notary, surveyor, poet

Jacob ZYDERVELT **C** 140 - Jacob Sijdervelt b. 1696, d. 1750, m. (1) Jacoba van Mollem (1699-1735) 7.XII.1723, (2) Maria van Oosterwijk (1711-1750) 7.I. 1738

Maria ZYDERVELT **C** 113 - Maria Sijdervelt b. 5.X. ?

*   *   *

Note: the following categories of names occurring in Greenwood's poems have not been listed: classical (nearly 200), geographical (85), poetic and fictional (60), biblical (12), societies (11) and houses (6).

*   *   *

Doll van Oury[c]k
  Caspar Balthazar 70 83 85 91
  Johan 85
  Kaspar 85
  Marye 85
Dostelwijt, Thomas 10
Dou 85
Dussen, van der
  Elizabeth Kristina 86 90
  M. 70
  Pieter 60
Duyvendyck, Frans 8
Dy[c]k, van 66 86

Edwards, John 33
Eem, van der 52
Eenhoorn, van
  Lambert 16
  Wouter Jan 16
Elgersma, M. 66
Elias Michielsz., J. 80
Ellemeet, Cornelis van 13
Elst, van der
  Amaranta 86 89
  Willem 86
  Ysbrant 83 86
Elvervelt, H. van 80
Erckenraadt 33
Eyk, Michiel Joost van 18
Eysch, Margriet den 16

Fahrensbach, F. 62
Fannius
  Adriaen Jr 20 49
  Adriaen Sr 20 49
  Daniël 49
Feitama, Sijbrand 72 80
Ferrand
  Estienne 51
  Francina Lucretia 51
  Francina Lucretia (née Saffin) 51
  Maria Jacoba 51
Fijt, J. 65
Firth, John 17 18
Flink, Govert 86
Fockert, Anthony de 33
Fontaine Verwey, de la 76
Freisheim, Johan Theodoor 83 86
Froet
  F. 79
  Katharina 79

Gallas, Joan Arnold 86 87
Gelder, Johan van 29

Gesmel, Gerrit 16
Gesquier, Petrus 57
Gevaerts
  Johan 86
  Maria 83 86 87
  Paulus 33 70 83 84 86
Ghijben, Elisabeth 91
Ghijben-Badon, Klara 79
Ghijs
  Adriaen 60
  Jacoba Elisabet 62 63
  Nicolaes 60
Gilles, Sam 14
Gips, Sebilla 33
Girodet, Jacques 19
Glover
  Anna 9 10 12 18 20 32 49 54
    55 57 59 86
  Benjamin 10
  Bridget 9 10
  Caterijna 9 10
  Catharijna 10
  Dorote 10
  Johannis 9 10
  Johannus 10
  John (Johan) 8 9 10 12
  Maria 10
  Richard 9 10
Godevaart 22
Godfrey, William 17
Goes, Joannes Antonisz van der 72 86
Goeyer, Cornelis de 75
Gool, Johan van 79 86
Goverts 22
Goyer, Willem de 18 19
Graeff, Jan de 16
Gramingh, Alida 83 86 91
Graswinkel 55
Graven, Marya de 10
Greene, Samuel 12
Greenewood
  Charles 8 10 13 14
  Ffransis 4 7
  Francis 4 8 10 11 12 13 14 15 16
    17 18 19 20 28 29 32 49 50 51
    53 54 55 57 59 60 86
  Henry 8 10 13
  James Jr 8 10 13
  James Sr 7 10
  John 8 10
  Thomas 8
  William 8 10
Greenwood
  Adriana Anna Maria 62 63 83 86

*　*　*

LITERATURE REFERENCES
- parts I & II -

1 A., J. - 1893 - Greenwood. -- Nederl. Leeuw 11: 4

2 AA, A. J. VAN DER - 1839-1851 - Aardrijkskundig woordenboek der Nederlanden. -- Gorinchem (J. Noorduyn). II (1840): x+865 pp.; VIII (1846): 796 pp.

3 AA, A. J. VAN DER - 1852 - Biographisch woordenboek der Nederlanden, bevattende levensbeschrijvingen van zoodanige personen, die zich op eenigerlei wijze in ons vaderland hebben vermaard gemaakt. -- Haarlem (J. J. van Brederode). III: 190+480+10 pp.

4 ABKOUDE, J. VAN & ARRENBERG, R. - 1788 - Naamregister van de bekendste en meest in gebruik zynde Nederduitsche boeken, welke sedert het jaar 1600 tot het jaar 1761 zyn uitgekomen, &c. Nu overzien, verbeterd en tot het jaar 1787 vermeerderd. -- Rotterdam (Gerard Abraham Arrenberg). (Ed. 2) x+598 pp.

5 ANONYMOUS - 1729 - Beschryving der stadt Delft, etc. Alles 't zamengestelt . . . door verscheiden Liefhebbers en Kenners der Nederlandsche Oudheden. -- Delft (Reinier Boitet). [xviii+]804[+14 pp. index], 21 pls.

6 ANONYMOUS - 1736 - Sint Lukas Regel voor de Dortsche Broederschap. -- Dordrecht (J. van Braam). 1 p., 1 fig.

7 ANONYMOUS [various authors] - 1743-1745 - Album met gedichten op het zwaard waarmede Johan van Oldenbarneveld onthoofd is te 's-Gravenhage op 13 Mei 1619. -- MS 32 sheets [Rijksmuseum, Amsterdam]

8 ANONYMOUS [various authors] - 1744-1749 - Album amicorum Mr Jacob Elias Michielsz. -- MS 53 sheets [Bibliotheek Rijks-Universiteit, Leiden; ex libris R. M. Buschhammer] (Greenwood's homage to Arnold Hoogvliet, folio 13, is published in Greenwood 1760: 108)

9 ANONYMOUS - 1773 - Arnoud van Halen's Pan Poëticon Batavûm verheerlijkt door Lofdichten en Bijschriften; Grootendeels uit het Stamboek van Michiel de Roode; en nu eerst in 't licht gebragt door het Genootschap, onder de Spreuk: Kunst wordt door arbeid verkreegen. -- Leyden. xxxvi+240[+8] pp., frontispiece

10 ANONYMOUS - 1884 - De Rijkdom van 's Gravenhage in 1742. -- Algem. Nederl. Familieblad (82): 4-6

11 ANONYMOUS - 1890 - Registration of Papists' Estates. Quarter Sessions Records. North Riding Record Society. -- London (Woodfall & Kinder). 8: 76-77

12 ANONYMOUS - 1892 - Schas. -- Algem. Nederl. Familieblad 9: 252

13 AUCTION CATALOGUE BEIJERS - 1875 - Catalogue de la bibliothèque et de la collection artistique délaissée par M. C.-Kramm, 7-15.XII.1875. -- Utrecht (J. L. Beijers). viii+391 pp., frontispiece portrait

14 AUCTION CATALOGUE MULLER - 1874 - Collections artistiques formées par feu M. A. van der Willigen, oncle et neveu, à Harlem. Premier partie. 20-21.IV. 1874. -- Amsterdam (F. Muller). 47 pp.

14a AUCTION CATALOGUE MULLER - 1902 - [not seen]

15 AUCTION CATALOGUE ROOS, DE VRIES & BRONDGEEST - 1818 - Catalogus van . . . het alomberoemde Pan Poëticum Batavum, &c. 9.IV.1818 -- Amsterdam. ii+41 pp.

16 AUCTION CATALOGUE SCHEURLEER - 1792 - Catalogus eener fraaye verzameling van teekeningen en prenten, etc. nagelaaten door wijlen den Heere Aart Schouman. 10.XII.1792. -- 's Haage (B. Scheurleer). 88 pp.

17 AUCTION CATALOGUE DE VRIES - 1909 - Catalogue d'une précieuse collection de portraits gravés de Néerlandais et de personnes qui ont été en rapport avec les Pays-Bas. Collection A. J. Nijland à Utrecht. 23.II.1909. -- Amsterdam (R. W. P. de Vries), La Haye (M. Nijhoff). 233 pp.

18 AUCTION CATALOGUE DE VRIES, ROOS & BRONDGEEST - 1849 - Catalogus van . . . het Pan Poëticon Batavum &c. 16.X.1849. -- Amsterdam. viii+48 pp.

19 BACKER, J. A. - 1789 - De jonge reiziger door Nederland. -- Amsterdam (D. M. Langeveld). I: 422 pp., 1 pl.

20 BELONJE, J. - 1941 - Bijdorp te Voorschoten. -- Nederl. Leeuw 59(8): col. 351

21 BICKER CAARTEN, A. - 1946 - Molenleven in Rijnland. Bijdrage tot de kennis van het volksleven in de streek rondom Leiden. -- Leiden (A. W. Sijthoff). 155 pp., frontispiece, illus.

22 BIDLOO, L. - 1720 - Panpoëticon Batavûm, kabinet, Waar in de Afbeeldingen van Voornaame Nederlandsche Dichteren, Versameld, en Konstig Geschilderdt door Arnoud van Halen, En onder Uytbreyding, en Aanmerkingen, over de Hollandsche Rym-Konst, geopendt, door Lamb. Bidloo. -- Amsterdam (Andries van der Damme). [iv+]283[+8] pp.

23 BIJLEVELD, W. J. J. C. - 1921 - Uit de oude registers van Voorschoten. -- Nederl. Leeuw 39(10): cols 270-279

24 BOON VAN ENGELANT, C. - 1724 - Gedichten van Mr. Cornelis Boon van Engelant. -- Leyden (Gerard Potvliet). I: 12+328[+vii] pp. (Ed. 2: 1732)

25 BREMAN, P. & RIJKEN, J. - 1983 - Dichters in Dordt. -- Dordrecht (Gemeentelijke Archiefdienst & Openbare Bibliotheek). 50 pp., illus.

26 BRINCK, J. TEN - 1897 - Geschiedenis der Nederlandsche Letterkunde. -- Amsterdam (Elsevier). xii+698 pp., frontispiece, 297 text-figs., 108 pls.

27 BRUIJNING, C. F. A. & VOORHOEVE, J. - 1977 - Encyclopedie van Suriname. -- Amsterdam & Brussel (Elsevier). 716 pp., illus.

28 BURGH, W. F. VAN DER - 1947 - Een drinkgebruik in Hollandsch polderland in oude tijden. -- Leidsch Jb. 39: 115-126, 1 pl.

29 COOL, W. - 1914 - Bij de nieuwe Oostbrug. -- Rotterdamsch Jb. (2)2: 108-126

30 DALEN, J. L. VAN - 1927 - De Groote Kerk (Onze Lieve Vrouwenkerk) te Dordrecht. -- Dordrecht (Dordrechtsche Drukkerij en Uitgevers Mij.). xv+309 pp., frontispiece, 78 figs.

31 DALEN, J. L. VAN - 1931, 1933 - Geschiedenis van Dordrecht. -- Dordrecht (C. Morks Czn). I (1931): 1-528, figs. 1-94; II (1933): 529-1200, figs. 95-190

32 EEGHEN, P. VAN - 1958 - Geldgebrek en genealogie. -- Nederl. Leeuw 75(6): cols 295-307

33 EIJNDEN, R. VAN & WILLIGEN, A. VAN DER - 1817 - Geschiedenis der vaderlandsche schilderkunst, sedert de helft der XVIII eeuw. -- Haarlem (A. Loosjes, Pz). II: 514 pp., pls. A-D

33a FEITAMA, S. - 1764 - Nagelaten dichtwerken van S. F. onder de zinspreuk Studio Fovetur Ingenium. -- Amsteldam (Pieter Meyer). p. 293

34 FONTAINE VERWEY, E. DE LA - 1934 - De illustratie van letterkundige werken in de XVIIIe eeuw. Bijdrage tot de geschiedenis van het Nederlandsche boek. -- Amsterdam (H. J. Paris). 191 pp., pls. I-XVI

35 FREDERIKS, J. G. & BRANDEN, F. J. VAN DEN - 1892 - Biographisch woordenboek der Noord- en Zuidnederlandsche Letterkunde. -- Amsterdam (L. J. Veen). 918 pp.

36 FREDERIKS, J. W. - 1958 - Dutch silver. II. Wrought plate of North and South-Holland from the Renaissance until the end of the eighteenth century. -- The Hague (Martinus Nijhoff). xxxv+211 pp., 313 pls.

37 GEERARS, C. M. - 1954 - Hubert Korneliszoon Poot. Neerlandica Traiectina I. -- Assen (van Gorcum & Comp. N. V.). iv+527 pp., frontispiece

38 GIJN, S. VAN - 1908 - Dordracum illustratum. Verzameling van kaarten, teekeningen, prenten en portretten, betreffende de stad Dordrecht. -- Dordrecht (De Dordrechtsche Drukkerij- en Uitgeversmaatschappij). II: xiv+278+lviii pp., figs. 35-60

39 GOOL, J. VAN - 1750 - De nieuwe schouburg der Nederlantsche Kunstschilders en schilderessen: Waer in de Levens- en Kunstbedryven der tans levende en reets overleedene Schilders, die van Houbraken, noch eenig ander Schryver, zyn aengeteekend, verhaelt worden. -- 's Gravenhage (gedrukt voor den autheur). I: [xii+]480 pp., pls. A-G (Greenwood's sonnet-eulogium, pp. xi-xii, also published, with slight modifications, in Greenwood 1760: 96)

40 GOOL, J. VAN - 1751 - Ibidem. II: xii+576 pp., pls. A-O (Greenwood's poem, pp. 341-343, also published in Greenwood 1760: 24-26)

41 GREENWOOD, F. - [1704] - Ter Gedachtnisse van de Overwinninge, door de krygsmagten der bondtgenoten, verkregen by Hochstet den 13 van Oogstmaant 1704. -- [Privately published]. 4 pp. (also published in Greenwood 1719: 19-23)

42 GREENWOOD, F. - 1714 - Wilthof. Lustplaats van den Heere Maximiliaan de Rave. -- [Privately published]. 8 pp. (also published in Greenwood 1719: 1-3)

43 GREENWOOD, F. - 1715 - Geluk op reis, aan de uitgaande Groenlantsche vloot. -- [Privately published; Rotterdam, printed by Arnold Willis]. 1 p. (also published in Greenwood 1719: 58-59)

44 GREENWOOD, F. - 1719 - Gedichten van Frans Greenwood. -- Rotterdam (Arnold Willis). [xii+]126[+4] pp., title-pl. [by B. Picart, 1718]. - There is some faulty page numbering: extra pp. *79, 80, 81, 82 between 78 and 79 proper; p. 125 (following 114) to be 115; 126 (preceding 117) to be 116; 125 (following 122) to be 123; 117 (following 124) to be 125; 118 (following the latter page) to be 126

45 GREENWOOD, F. - post-1719 - Aan een ongodist. -- [Privately published]. 3 pp. (also published in Greenwood 1760: 49-51)

46 GREENWOOD, F. - post-1719 - Avont-zang. -- [Privately published]. 4 pp. (also published in Greenwood 1760: 97-101)

47 GREENWOOD, F. - 1733 - Boere-Pinxtervreugt. -- Rotterdam (Arnold Willis). 39 pp., 4 pls. (Ed. 2: 1760; Ed. 3: 1823 in L. Rotgans et al.)

48 GREENWOOD, F. - 1733 - Boere-Pinxtervreugt. -- Rotterdam (Arnold Willis). 39 pp., 4 col. pls. -- Wormerveer (reprinted by Inmerc B. V., 1975)

49 GREENWOOD, F. - 1736 - Lykklagt over myn zeer lieven zoon, Kornelis Greenwood, overleden in Suriname den IIIden April MDCCXXXVI in den ouderdom van XXVII. Jaren VII. Maanden en I. Dag. -- [Privately published]. 3 pp. (also published in Greenwood 1760: 193-195)

50 GREENWOOD, F. - 1760 - Vervolg van F: Greenwoods Gedichten, en Boere= Pinxtervreugt. -- Dordrecht (J: van Braam). [viii+]208[+4] pp., title-pl. [of Greenwood 1719] & Boere-Pinxtervreugt (Ed. 2) 39 pp., 4 pls.

51 GREENWOOD, F. - 1827 - In: Keur van Nederlandsche Letteren. -- Amsterdam (M. Westerman). I(7)40: 3-72

52 GREENWOOD, F. & ZEEUS, J. - [1712] - Lykgedichten op het afsterven van jufvrouwe Anna Glover, huisvrouwe van den Heere Francis Greenwood. -- [Privately published]. 6 pp. (Greenwood's poem also published in Greenwood 1719: 75-77)

53 GREENWOOD, I. J. - 1868 - Pedigree of Greenwood (North American branch). -- New York [Privately published]. 1 p.

54 HAES, F. DE - 1764 - De nagelaten gedichten, en Nederduitsche spraekkunst, van wylen den Heer Frans de Haes. -- Amsteldam (Pieter Meijer). [vi+]300[+vi] +17[+3] pp.

55 HALL, H. VAN - 1963 - Portretten van Nederlandse beeldende kunstenaars. -- Amsterdam (Swets en Zeitlinger). xii+419 pp.

56 HARTSINCK, J. J. - 1770 - Beschryving van Guiana, of de Wildekust, in Zuid-America. -- Amsterdam (Gerrit Tielenburg). II: 521-977, 6 pls.

57 HAZEWINKEL, H. C. - 1942 - Geschiedenis van Rotterdam. -- Amsterdam (N. V. Uitgevers Mij. "Joost van den Vondel"). III: 533 pp., illus.

58 HEEREN, J. J. M. - 1919 - Het "Panpoëticon Batavum". -- Oud-Holland 37: 230-240

59 HOET, G. - 1752 - Catalogus of naamlyst van schilderyen, met derzelver pryzen Zedert een langen reeks van Jaaren zoo in Holland als op andere Plaatzen in het openbaar verkogt. -- 's Gravenhage (P. G. van Baalen). I: xii+650 pp.; II: iv+562 pp.

60 HOOGEWERFF, G. J. - 1947 - De geschiedenis van de St. Lucasgilden in Nederland. -- Amsterdam (P. N. van Kampen & Zoon N. V.). 245 pp., 16 figs.

61 HOOGVLIET, A. - 1753 - Vervolg der mengeldichten van Arnold Hoogvliet. -- Rotterdam (Philippus & Jakobus Losel). [xxvi+]216 pp., 1 pl.

62 HORSMAN, P. J. - 1975 - Jacob Hoolaart (1713-1789). Oeuvre-catalogus. -- Dordrecht (Gemeentelijke Archiefdienst). 24 pp., 8 figs.

63 HUDIG, F. W. - 1929 - Delfter Fayence. Ein Handbuch für Sammler und Liebhaber. -- Berlin (Richard Carl Schmidt & Co.). 348 pp., 291 figs.

64 IMMERZEEL, J. - 1842 - De levens en werken der Hollandsche en Vlaamsche kunstschilders, beeldhouwers, graveurs en bouwmeesters, van het begin der vijftiende eeuw tot heden. -- Amsterdam (J. C. van Kesteren). I: xxxii+300 pp., frontispiece, illus.

65 JAGER, H. DE - 1879 - De Waalsche Gemeente te Brielle. - Navorscher 29 (N. S. 12): 57-64

66 JAGER, H. DE - 1891 - De Brielsche Vroedschap in de jaren 1608-1794. -- Algem. Nederl. Familieblad 8: 181-184

67 JAGER, H. DE - 1892 - De Brielsche Vroedschap in de jaren 1608-1794. -- Algem. Nederl. Familieblad 9: 173-176

68 JONGE, C. H. DE - 1947 - Oud-Nederlandsche majolica en Delftsch aardewerk. Een ontwikkelingsgeschiedenis van omstreeks 1550-1800. -- Amsterdam (Scheltema en Holkema). xii+445 pp., 8 col. pls, 302 figs.

69 K. - 1909 - Greenwood. -- Nederl. Leeuw 27: 60

70 KASTEELE, P. R. D. VAN DE - 1882 - Aperceaux, Greenwood. -- Navorscher 32 (N. S. 15): 138

71 KLOOSTER, L. J. VAN DER - 1965 - Het inrijhek van huize Bijdorp te Voorschoten. -- Leids Jb. 57: 158-160, fig. 45

72 KNUTTEL, W. P. C. - 1902 - Catalogus van de pamfletten-verzameling berustende in de Koninklijke Bibliotheek. -- 's Gravenhage (Algemeene Landsdrukkerij). IV (1714-1775): 414 pp.

73 KOENEN, H. J. - 1846 - Geschiedenis van de vestiging en den invloed der Fransche vluchtelingen in Nederland. -- Leiden (S. en J. Luchtmans). xviii+452 pp., frontispiece

74 KRAMM, C. - 1858, 1861 - De levens en werken der Hollandsche en Vlaamsche kunstschilders, beeldhouwers, graveurs en bouwmeesters, van den vroegsten tot op onzen tijd. (Strekkende tevens tot vervolg op het werk van J. Immerzeel, Jr). -- Amsterdam (Gebr. Diederichs). II (1858): 313-640; V (1861): 1281-1600

75 KUILE, E. H. TER - 1944 - De Nederlandsche monumenten van geschiedenis en kunst. VII. De provincie Zuidholland. Eerste stuk: Leiden en westelijk Rijnland. -- 's-Gravenhage (Algemeene Landsdrukkerij). xiv+260 pp., 41 figs., 186 pls.

76 KUNZ, G. G. - 1977 - Oude- en Nieuwe Gasthuis 1252-1977. -- Delft (Elmar B. V.). 80 pp., illus.

77 L. - 1909 - Greenwood. -- Nederl. Leeuw 27: 22, 121

78 LAVAUX, A. DE - 1737 - Generale Caart van de Provintie Suriname, Rivieren & Districten met alle d'ontdekkingen van Militaire Togten mitsgaders de groote der gemeetene Plantagien gecarteerd op de naauwkeurigste waarneemingen. [a large map printed on silk]

79 LAVAUX, A. DE & LETH, H. DE - ±1770 - Algemeene kaart van de Colonie of Provintie van Suriname, met de rivieren, districten, ontdekkingen, door militaire togten, en de grootte der gemeeten plantagien, etc. - Amsterdam (Petrus Schenk en Zoon)

80 LINDE, J. M. VAN DER - 1966 - Surinaamse suikerheren en hun kerk. -- Wageningen (H. Veenman en Zonen N. V.). 263 pp., 8 pls.

81 MAAS, J. VAN DE [J. L. van Dalen] - n. d. - Dordtsche Schetsen. CLXX. Aanteekeningen over Dordrecht in de 18e eeuw.

81a MEYERMAN, A. M. & SCHADEE, N. I. - 1986 - Kunst in een Historisch Museum. In: Een Paleis in Rotterdam. Historische verzamelingen in het Schielandshuis. -- Rotterdam (Stichting Vrienden van het Schielandshuis): 52-67, illus.

82 MOES, E. W. - 1897 - Iconographia Batava. Beredeneerde lijst van geschilderde en gebeeldhouwde portretten van Noord-Nederlanders in vorige eeuwen. -- Amsterdam (F. Muller & Co.). I: 530 pp.

83 MOLHUYSEN, P. C. & BLOK, P. J. - 1911-1937 - Nieuw Nederlandsch biographisch woordenboek. -- Leiden (A. W. Sijthoff's Uitgevers-Maatschappij N. V.). [10 vols] I (1911): ix+1600 cols; II (1912): ii+1600 cols; III (1914): iii+1600 cols

84 MOQUETTE, H. C. H. - 1917 - Catalogus van de portretverzameling.

Archief der Gemeente Rotterdam. -- Rotterdam (P. van Waesberge & Zoon).
vii+389 pp.

85 MOQUETTE, H. C. H. & DROOGENDIJK, J. M. - 1928 - Rotterdamsche
straatnamen geschiedkundig verklaard. -- Rotterdam (W. L. & J. Brusse's Uitgevers-
maatschappij). xxxvi+338 pp., 30 pls.

86 MULLER, F. - 1853 - Beschrijvende catalogus van 7000 portretten, van Nederlanders, en van buitenlanders, tot Nederland in betrekking staande, &c. --
Amsterdam (F. Muller). xl+408 pp.

87 NAGLER, G. K. - 1837 - Neues allgemeines Künstler-Lexicon. -- München
(E. A. Fleischmann). V: 574 pp.

88 OUDSCHANS DENTZ, F. - 1941 - Nederlandsche grafzerken in Suriname. --
Nederl. Leeuw 59(9): cols 382-386; 59(11): cols 443-448

89 OVERVOORDE, J. C. - 1899 - Catalogus van de prentverzameling der gemeente Dordrecht. -- Dordrecht (Morks & Geuze). 332 pp.

90 POOT, H. K. - 1722 - Gedichten van Hubert Korneliszoon Poot, met kunstige
printen versiert. -- Delf (Reinier Boitet). [xvi+]444[+4] pp., title-pl., illus.
(Ed. 2: 1726)

91 POOT, H. K. - 1747 - Vervolg, of derde en leste deel der gedichten van
Hubert Korneliszoon Poot. Hier is by gevoegt het leven des dichters. -- Delf
(Reinier Boitet). (Ed. 2). [x+]268 pp.

92 POSTMA, C. - 1948 - Copy poorterboek der stad Rotterdam 1699-1750 (vervolg). -- Gens nostra 3(6): 82-87

93 R. R. - 1877 - Geslacht Fannius. -- Navorscher 27 (N. S. 10): 430, 583

94 RAVESTEYN, W. VAN - 1946 - Iets over politieke poëzie in het begin der
achttiende eeuw. -- Rotterdams Jb. (5)4: 49-65

95 REANEY, P. H. - 1958 - A dictionary of British surnames. -- London
(Routledge and Kegan Paul). lix+366 pp.

96 REDMONDS, G. - 1973 - English surnames series. 1. Yorkshire, West Riding. --
London & Chichester (Phillimore & Co. Ltd). xiv+314 pp., 8 maps

97 RIEMSDIJK, B. W. F. VAN - 1903 - Catalogus der schilderijen, miniaturen,
pastels, omlijste teekeningen, enz. in het Rijks-Museum te Amsterdam. --
Amsterdam (Roeloffzen-Hübner en van Santen). xxviii+348 pp.

98 RIJN, G. VAN - 1901 - Atlas van Stolk. Katalogus der historie-, spot- en
zinneprenten betrekkelijk de geschiedenis van Nederland verzameld door A. van
Stolk Cz. -- Amsterdam (F. Muller & Co.). - V: 151 [No. 3925]

99 ROEVER, N. DE - 1888 - Aert Schouman volgens zijne aanteekenboekjes. --
Oud-Holland 6(3): 33-44

100 ROTGANS, L., BARTELINK, J., GREENWOOD, F. & HOVEN, J. VAN - 1823 -
De Oud-Hollandsche Kermisparnas, of de Kermisdichttafereelen van L. Rotgans,
J. Bartelink, F. Greenwood en J. van Hoven. Nieuwe druk. -- Amsterdam (J. C.
van Kesteren). 8+124 pp. (F. Greenwood's Boere-Pinxtervreugt [Ed. 3]: 73-97
[without plates])

101 SCHAS, L. D. J. - 1916 - 64 Kwartieren van Lodewijk Diederich Johan Schas,
Leonard Jacob Lodewijk Schas en Daniel Francis Marinus Schas. [a broadsheet,
privately published)

102 SCHAS, L. D. J. - 1921 - Saffin - Schas. -- Nederl. Leeuw 39(5-6): col 143

103 SCHAS, L. D. J. - 1929 - Het geslacht Schas. -- Den Haag [Privately published]. 33 pp.

104 SCHEEN, P. A. - 1946 - Honderd jaren Nederlandsche schilder- en teekenkunst. De romantiek met voor- en natijd (1750-1850). -- Den Haag (Uitgevers= bureau "Boek en Periodiek"). [iii+]381+xl pp., 417 figs.

105 SCHEEN, P. A. - 1969 - Lexicon Nederlandse beeldende kunstenaars 1750-1950. -- 's-Gravenhage (P. A. Scheen N. V.). I: viii+752 pp., 954 figs.

106 SCHEEN, P. A. - 1981 - Lexicon Nederlandse beeldende kunstenaars 1750-1880. -- 's-Gravenhage (P. A. Scheen B. V.). xiii+687 pp., 889 figs.

107 SCHILTKAMP, J. A. & SMIDT, J. TH. DE - 1973 - West Indisch Plakaatboek. Suriname (1667-1816). -- Amsterdam (S. Emmering). xxxv+1425 pp., 16 figs., 1 map

108 SCHOLTEN VAN ASCHAT, M. - 1912 - Fannius. -- Navorscher 61: 574-575

109 SCHOUMAN, A. - 1733-1738 - Memori Boek van mijn desiepelen die ik heb onderwesen. -- MS

110 SCHOUMAN, A. - 1748-1765 - Kladboek dienende tot het ander dat ik in s'Haage heb, van 't Jaar 1748. -- MS

111 SMITS, D. - 1753 - Nagelaten gedichten van Dirk Smits. -- Rotterdam (Jakob Burgvliet). I: [iv+]358[+vii] pp.

112 SMITS VAN NIEUWERKERK, J. A. - 1874 - De Dordrechtsche Schilderschool, bevattende Levensberichten der Hollandsche en Vlaamsche Kunstschilders, Beeldhouwers, Graveurs en Bouwmeesters, in Dordrecht geboren of gewoond hebbende van den vroegsten tijd tot op 1 October 1874. -- Dordrecht (H. R. van Elk). 68 pp.

113 SNOEP, D. P. & THIELS, C. - 1973 - Adriaen van der Werff. -- Rotterdam (Historisch Museum). 64 pp., 59 figs.

114 SOMEREN, J. F. VAN - 1890 - Beschrijvende catalogus van gegraveerde portretten van Nederlanders. -- Amsterdam (F. Muller). II: 416 pp.

115 SPAAN, G. VAN - 1738 - Beschryvinge der stad Rotterdam, en eenige omleggende dorpen, verdeeld in III. boeken. -- Rotterdam (Philippus Losel). (Ed. 3). [xx+]429 pp., frontispiece, 15 pls.

116 SPEX, J. - 1755 - Gedichten van Jakob Spex. -- 's Gravenhaege (Pieter Gerard van Balen). [x+]350[+12] pp., 2 pls.

117 STEDMAN, J. G. - 1796 - Narrative of a five years' expedition against the revolted negroes of Surinam, in Guiana, on the wild coast of South America; from the year 1772 to 1777; &c. -- London (J. Johnson). I: xix+414 pp., pls.

118 THIEL, P. J. J. VAN, BRUYN KOPS, C. J. DE, CLEVERINGA, J., KLOEK, W. & HEYN, A. V. - 1976 - Alle schilderijen van het Rijksmuseum te Amsterdam. Volledig geïllustreerde catalogus. -- Amsterdam (Rijksmuseum), Haarlem (de Haan). 911 pp., illus.

119 THIEME, U. & WILLIS, F. C. - 1921 - Allgemeines Lexikon der bildenden Künstler von der Antike bis zur Gegenwart. -- Leipzig (E. A. Seemann). 14: viii+600 pp.

120 UNGER, J. H. W. - 1892 - Bronnen voor de geschiedenis van Rotterdam. I. De Regeering van Rotterdam 1328-1892. -- Rotterdam (P. van Waesberge & Zoon). 600 pp., pls. I-XXIII

121 VERSTEEG, N. - 1764 - Het leven van Dirk Smits. In: Nagelaten gedichten van Dirk Smits. -- Rotterdam (Jakob Burgvliet). III: appendix pp. 3-40, 1 pl.

122 VETH, G. H. - 1890 - Iets over de confrerie van St. Lucas en de latere kunstgenootschappen te Dordrecht. -- Arch. Nederl. Kunstgeschiedenis 7: 81-110

123 VETH, G. H. - 1892 - Aanteekeningen omtrent eenige Dordrechtsche schilders. -- Oud-Holland 10: 1-16.

124 VOORT, J. P. VAN DE - 1974 - Nederlands kapitaal voor West-Indië in de 18de eeuw. -- Spiegel Historiael 9(2): 94-101, figs. 1-10

125 VOU, J. DE - 1694 - Rotterdam met al syn gebouwen net op maet geteekent en gesneden. [map]

126 VRIES, J. DE - 1808-1809 - Antwoord op de vraag: welke zijn de vorderingen, welke is de verachtering der Nederduitsche dichtkunde, gedurende de achttiende eeuw, in vergelijking van vroegere tijdperken ? -- Amsterdam (J. Allart). x+322+407 pp.

127 VRIESENDORP, J. - 1901 - Geslacht Vriesendorp. -- Navorscher 51: 547-552

128 WAGNER, J. D. - 1878 - Geslacht Fannius. -- Navorscher 28: 252-253

129 WALLER, F. G. - 1938 - Biographisch woordenboek van Noord Nederlandsche graveurs. Bewerkt door W. R. Juynboll. -- 's-Gravenhage (Martinus Nijhoff). xix+551 pp., pls. I-LX

130 WALSON, C. J. - 1967a - De straat waarin ik woon (42). -- Dordtenaar 11.III.1967

131 WALSON, C. J. - 1967b - De straat waarin ik woon (45). -- Dordtenaar 15.IV.1967

132 WEEL, E. VAN - 1944 - Aperceaux. -- Mededeelingen Nederl. Gen. Geslacht-en Wapenkunde (6): xxvii

133 WEIGEL, R. - 1856 - Rudolph Weigel's Kunstlager-Catalog. Abtheilung 27. -- Leipzig (R. Weigel). 376 pp.

134 WIERSUM, E. - 1907 - Het vermoeden van overleven. -- Navorscher 57(1): 33-40

135 WIERSUM, E. - 1910 - Jan Bisschop. -- Rotterdamsch Jb. 8: 50-74, 1 pl.

136 WITSEN GEYSBEEK, P. G. - 1822 - Biographisch, Anthologisch en Critisch Woordenboek der Nederduitsche Dichters. -- Amsterdam (C.L. Schleijer). II (Cab.-Gyz.): xxiv+456 pp.

137 WOLBERS, J. - 1861 - Geschiedenis van Suriname. -- Amsterdam (reprint 1970, S. Emmering). vi+849+viii pp., frontispiece

138 WURZBACH, A. VON - 1906 - Niederländisches Künstler-Lexikon. -- Wien & Leipzig (Halm & Goldmann). I: viii+iv+778 pp.

139 ZEEUS, J. - 1721 - Gedichten van Jakob Zeeus. Met veele kopere Kunstplaten versiert. -- Delf (Reinier Boitet). [xxxvi+]552[+viii] pp., illus.

140 ZEEUS, J. - 1726 - Overgeblevene gedichten van Jakob Zeeus. -- Rotterdam (Arnold Willis). xliii+[xxxviii+]288+liii pp.

*   *   *

ARCHIVAL REFERENCES

Amsterdam

Gemeentelijke Archiefdienst

N. A. (Notarieel Archief):

A1 = 5260: -	A4 = 7961:228	A7 = 8630:1196	A10 = 8763:78
A2 = 7624:455	A5 = 8039:171	A8 = 8630:1205	A11 = 8763:79
A3 = 7636:728	A6 = 8398:41	A9 = 8630:1235	A12 = 8763:81

Delft

Gemeentelijke Archiefdienst

A13 = Dopen Nieuwe Kerk
A14 = Dopen Oude Kerk
A15 = Ondertrouwboek Nieuwe Kerk
A16 = Ondertrouwboek Oude Kerk

A17 = Trouwboek Gerecht
A18 = Begraafboek Nieuwe Kerk
A19 = Huizenregister

Dordrecht

Gemeentelijke Archiefdienst

A20 = Gaardersarchief 39.3
A21 = Begrafenis Register Groote Kerk (1751-1771) DTB 11.52
A22 = Begrafenis Register Nieuwe Kerk (1794-1811) DTB 11.72
A23 = Weeskamer 38.63

O. R. A. (Oud Rechterlijk Archief):

A24 = 834:4	A25 = 841:23	A26 = 842:311

O. N. A. (Oud Notarieel Archief):

A27 = 765:215	A30 = 958:35	A33 = 1047:4	A36 = 1096:115
A28 = 770:246	A31 = 958:36	A34 = 1051:72	A37 = 1096:116
A29 = 853:27	A32 = 1046:49	A35 = 1096:104	A38 = 1237:163
			A39 = 1304:9

's-Gravenhage

Algemeen Rijksarchief

Rechterlijk Archief Voorschoten:

A40 = 16:22	A41 = 16:35v	A42 = 17:67	A43 = 18:130	A44 = 19:122

Rechterlijk Archief Wassenaar:

A45 = 20:208	A47 = 20:345	A49 = 21:93v	A51 = 23:38	A53 = 106:22
A46 = 20:209	A48 = 21:70	A50 = 22:102	A52 = 106:21	

Gaardersbescheiden Wassenaar:

A54 = 9:I:6	A55 = 9:II:88

Gemeentelijke Archiefdienst

A56 = DTB [Baptisms, Marriages, Funerals]

R. A. (Rechterlijk Archief):

A57 = 644

N. A. (Notarieel Archief):

A58 = 334:271	A61 = 921:851	A64 = 4012:199	A67 = 4426:746
A59 = 657:945	A62 = 1008:202	A65 = 4286:111	
A60 = 921:827	A63 = 1066:428	A66 = 4292:24	

L e i d e n

G e m e e n t e l ij k e   A r c h i e f d i e n s t

A68 = Attestatieboek F 1803   A71 = Huwelijken Waalse Kerk
A69 = Dopen Waalse Kerk   A72 = Weeskamer Archief 118-17C
A70 = Kerkelijk Ondertrouw Register

N. A. (Notarieel Archief):

A73 = 1345:111	A76 = 1533:72	A79 = 1824:22	A82 = 1828:146
A74 = 1345:131	A77 = 1726:79	A80 = 1824:23	A83 = 1829:120
A75 = 1533:8	A78 = 1727:79	A81 = 1827:145	A84 = 1831:11
			A85 = 1833:83

H o o g h e e m r a a d s c h a p   v a n   R ij n l a n d

A86 = Archief Driemanspolder 17

R o t t e r d a m

G e m e e n t e l ij k e   A r c h i e f d i e n s t

A87 = Doop Register Gereformeerde Gemeente
A88 = Trouwboek Gereformeerde Gemeente
A89 = Doden Register
A90 = Weeskamer 349, Seclusieboek
A91 = Weeskamer, Boedelregister (1700-1805) 491:500
A91a= Weeskamer, Register Voogdijen 557: 164, 198

Schepen Archief:

A92 = Besoigneboek 1710-1722	A95 = Giftenboek 53:532
A93 = Giftenboek 45:524	A96 = Giftenboek 60:539
A94 = Giftenboek 49:528	A97 = Giftenboek 63:542

Oud Stads Archief, Bestuur:

A98 = 445:348-349   A99 = 2046

O. N. A. (Oud Notarieel Archief):

A100 = 279:53	A113 = 441:52	A127 = 595:158	A141 = 935:1
A101 = 332:730	A114 = 444:100	A128 = 595:181	A142 = 935:921
A102 = 334:299	A115 = 475:182	A129 = 595:214	A143 = 964:495
A103 = 335:95	A116 = 480:105	A130 = 595:225	A144 = 964:1095
A104 = 436:136	A117 = 480:148	A131 = 595:275	A145 = 964:1339
A105 = 436:159	A118 = 484:73	A132 = 595:281	A146 = 964:1343
A106 = 436:162	A119 = 499:728	A133 = 595:345	A147 = 964:1407
A107 = 438:185	A120 = 499:732	A134 = 621:115	A148 = 967:117
A107a= 438:186	A121 = 499:985	A135 = 636:27	A149 = 969:245
A108 = 438:187	A122 = 502:398	A136 = 683:70	A150 = 969:381
A109 = 439:57	A123 = 595:55	A137 = 733:293	A151 = 1015:494
A110 = 439:58	A124 = 595:59	A138 = 733:315	A152 = 1224:103
A111 = 439:59	A125 = 595:60	A139 = 733:332	A153 = 1263:4
A112 = 439:97	A126 = 595:92	A140 = 856:5	A154 = 1263:25

A155 = 1263:43	A190 = 1487:165	A225 = 1647:13	A260 = 1978:8
A156 = 1263:261	A191 = 1487:194	A226 = 1648:19	A261 = 1979:122
A157 = 1271:70	A192 = 1489:22	A227 = 1648:306	A262 = 1980:52
A158 = 1271:149	A193 = 1489:146	A228 = 1650:149	A263 = 1986:7
A159 = 1271:150	A194 = 1489:193	A229 = 1653:139	A264 = 2021:94
A160 = 1271:155	A195 = 1489:196	A230 = 1653:219	A265 = 2065:279
A161 = 1271:260	A196 = 1489:219	A231 = 1661:381	A266 = 2065:292
A162 = 1273:103	A197 = 1490:184	A232 = 1684:162	A267 = 2087:16
A163 = 1273:108	A198 = 1490:271	A233 = 1685:93	A268 = 2089:133
A164 = 1273:109	A199 = 1492:133	A234 = 1734:145	A269 = 2097:441
A165 = 1273:211	A200 = 1492:248	A235 = 1791:73	A270 = 2100:209
A166 = 1273:232	A201 = 1493:212	A236 = 1791:74	A271 = 2100:235
A167 = 1274:11	A202 = 1494:114	A237 = 1791:76	A272 = 2124:158
A168 = 1274:203	A203 = 1495:7	A238 = 1794:33	A273 = 2213:69
A169 = 1275:45	A204 = 1496:261	A239 = 1794:212	A274 = 2218:140
A170 = 1275:104	A205 = 1497:39	A240 = 1814:21	A275 = 2222:258
A171 = 1275:155	A206 = 1497:57	A241 = 1814:98	A276 = 2231:74
A172 = 1275:226	A207 = 1539:47	A242 = 1814:102	A277 = 2253:91
A173 = 1275:263	A208 = 1539:130	A243 = 1814:110	A278 = 2262:22
A174 = 1275:264	A209 = 1539:185	A244 = 1814:175	A279 = 2278:11
A175 = 1275:274	A210 = 1553:1099	A245 = 1814:194	A280 = 2282:30
A176 = 1275:284	A211 = 1569:188	A246 = 1815:143	A281 = 2283:21
A177 = 1276:179	A212 = 1586:55	A247 = 1815:146	A282 = 2286:32
A178 = 1278:118	A213 = 1616:35	A248 = 1816:42	A283 = 2308:54
A179 = 1278:198	A214 = 1616:43	A249 = 1816:77	A284 = 2315:169
A180 = 1280:53	A215 = 1616:53	A250 = 1816:121	A285 = 2315:225
A181 = 1280:62	A216 = 1618:332	A251 = 1818:96	A286 = 2318:237
A182 = 1280:87	A217 = 1619:489	A252 = 1819:179	A287 = 2324:116
A183 = 1281:72	A218 = 1619:514	A253 = 1821:61	A288 = 2324:191
A184 = 1283:89	A219 = 1636:16	A254 = 1822:41	A289 = 2557:195
A185 = 1283:229	A220 = 1636:27	A255 = 1829:158	A290 = 2574:24
A186 = 1284:5	A221 = 1636:121	A256 = 1829:159	A291 = 2632:223
A187 = 1316:133	A222 = 1638:37	A257 = 1832:153	A292 = 2632:224
A188 = 1360:62	A223 = 1643:45	A258 = 1835:17	A293 = 3303:71
A189 = 1361:56	A224 = 1643:189	A259 = 1937:12	A294 = 3356:47

Schiedam

Gemeentearchief

A295 = Doopboek Nederlandsche Hervormde Kerk 10

Giftteboek:

A296 = 355:13   A297 = 355:135v   A298 = 356:57   A299 = 357:1v
A300 = 357:228

O. N. A. (Oud Notarieel Archief):

A301 = 831:31

*   *   *

III

G L A S S   E N G R A V I N G

*   *   *

F R A N S   G R E E N W O O D :   G L A S S   E N G R A V E R

It is not always easy to recollect the impetus which enkindled an interest in a certain subject. In the case of Frans Greenwood, the absence of any pertinent documentation combined with a considerable time-lag makes it quite impossible to determine the influence which sparked him off to indulge in glass engraving. - A guess or two may be ventured.

Among Greenwood's wide circle of friends and acquaintances was the prosperous van der Wallen family whose gifted daughter Jakoba (Rotterdam 1695-1757) so much impressed Frans with her drawing and singing that, prior to 1719, he praised these qualities in a poem each (1719: 38, 39); his friend Hubert Poot also wrote a eulogy on her singing [90]. Apart from painting, singing and playing the harpsichord, Jakoba was also said to have engraved glass (Schotel 1841: 118) although no identifiable engravings from her hand have been recorded. One may wonder whether it was Jakoba van der Wallen who induced widower Greenwood to take up diamond-point engraving.

A little more plausible, perhaps, could be the assumption that Frans was for some time acquainted with François Crama (1637-1718), a writing-master at the Latin School in Leiden and an expert calligrapher of glass [until recently his work on glass had erroneously been attributed to his daughter Elizabeth (1672-1721); see Auction Catalogue Christie, London, 19 June 1984: 54, sub lot 309]. Crama had certain ties with Abraham Apourceaux (e.g., the latter witnessing the baptism of Crama's daughter Marie in 1688) who happened to be (a) an uncle of Maria Hosteyn of Leiden who in 1708 married Charles, a brother of Frans Greenwood, and (b) the father of Joost Apourceaux who became associated with Sara Greenwood, a sister of Frans. There seems little doubt that Greenwood met Crama at least when attending the wedding of his brother Charles which took place in Leiden in the Walloon Church with which François Crama, being a catechist, was closely connected. Even though François Crama is known to have engraved glass mainly calligraphically, he may have taught Frans Greenwood the principles of diamond-point engraving; as a matter of fact, Greenwood did use some limited calligraphy in several of his engravings (Figs. **84, 86, 103, 118**).

It would be logical to assume that Greenwood at first applied the technique of line-engraving because at the time that was still the only diamond-point method in use. In fact: little in use - during the first two decades of the 18th century glass engraving in Holland had reached its nadir. Greenwood's earliest known engraving (1720) is indeed entirely composed of scratched lines, without a stipple; it is signed "frans Greenwood pinxit 19 Jan: 1720." It is worth noting that Frans never used 'pinxit' in connection with his stipple-engravings, only 'fecit' (often abbreviated). Some years earlier (1718 at the latest) Greenwood had presented a Brotherhood in Rotterdam with "the love of David and Jonathan depicted on a glass"; it cannot be ascertained whether or not he himself had engraved the glass. In the relevant poem (1719: 18) he referred to that engraving [of two boys] as resembling a drawing and it is fairly certain, therefore, that this particular goblet was line-engraved.

Johan van Gool ('s-Gravenhage 1685-1763), writing in the 1740s, was the first to publish (1751: 345-346) a short account of Greenwood's stipple-engraving: "He has invented an unusual method (as never seen before) of drawing upon wine= glasses with a diamond, not like the well-known wheel- or line-work which engraves the darker parts, leaving glass for the lightest areas blank, but just the opposite: his engraved parts are the lightest while blank glass represents the darker areas of a design. This creates the effect of drawing with white chalk upon dark brown paper. This method requires much time, patience and aptitude and therefore will not readily find followers except as a purely pleasurable pursuit; in order to make a profit from the craft one would have to charge high prices which is seldom done nowadays."

Regrettably, none of the diamond-point engravers ever recorded technical details of their craft, relatively simple though the method may be. It is certain that a natural diamond splinter was used (Fig. 57), set to the tip of a stylus. - Willem Jacobszoon van Heemskerk (1613-1692), the glass calligrapher, used to stuff a goblet with a skein of black wool during engraving in order to increase visibility of marks left by the diamond. Other engravers will also have worked against a dark background (nowadays usually matt-black cotton velvet). - Magnifying glasses will have been used when stippling fine details. Greenwood and Schouman were each acquainted with the scientist Arnold Marcel (Dordrecht 1672-1748), well known as a polisher of lenses. In a poem on a portrait of Marcel - possibly the mezzotint by Aart Schouman - Greenwood (1760: 112) referred to Marcel's accomplished polishing of magnifying glasses, one of which he was perhaps using himself.

The vessels which Greenwood first practised stippling on have not been preserved but his earliest dated (1722) stipple-engravings are already quite successful. In one of them, a horse (goblet 22.1), he still used line-work for mane and tail; in another (22.2) for plants and tendrils. Later on he applied scratches occasionally mainly to increase density or to attain full opacity, e.g., in hair of putti and in plants (38.1), plants and hooves (*41.2), leaf-nerves (*47.4, 47.5), in various objects (42.1, 48.1); single lines also serve as a frame (48.1).

In certain engravings by later stipplers the outlines of objects - starting points - are still more or less discernible. If Greenwood also first finely pricked in the outlines [very likely he did], he was most skilful in subsequently merging them with adjacent areas of stipples, thus virtually obliterating the contours (cf. goblet X.5).

In comparison with the work of stipple-engravers of the second half of the eighteenth century - the period of luxuriant blossoming of that technique - Greenwood's stipples are relatively rather coarse (indicative of a firm hand) although the stippling is mostly quite or very dense. Eventually he could at times produce a reasonably fine stipple (e.g., *44.1, 44.2) but he also executed offhand some simple designs in comparatively sparse stippling or with lettering lacking great precision (46.1, 47.3). Facial features - only two of Greenwood's human effigies are in full profile, which is not too difficult - did not always come off well, while fingers sometimes tend to resemble carrots. Characteristically, a hand is not infrequently at a marked angle with the lower arm.

In his early engravings (20.1, 22.1, 22.2, 22.3, 22.4, 22.5) Greenwood left the background blank; some 25 years later he did the same with his simple single motif designs of rose (46.2, 46.3, 46.4, 47.2, 49.1, *49.2), orange (*47.4, 47.5), lyre (46.1) and palette (47.3). These engravings are not contained within a frame. In all other engravings the background is most laboriously stippled in. If he chose to frame an engraving, Greenwood used either a single line or a straight band - nothing elaborate. Of his stippled-background engravings two-thirds are frameless, the remainder are within simple lines or bands.

According to van Gool (l. c.), Greenwood also used to paint miniatures but examples thereof have not come to light. In a way that craft is comparable with his glass engravings, many of which are pictorial, often actually miniatures of prints made of paintings popular at the time.

Greenwood favoured the portrayal of human subjects: of the 56 engravings catalogued, 41 belong to that category while 8 have a botanical theme, 5 a zoological one and 2 are of inanimate objects. Until the mid-1740s, wine drinkers - including Bacchus (30.1, *46.6) the most appropriate subject to be engraved on the bowl of a wine-glass - were his favourite subjects (24.1, 28.1, *28.2, 38.1, *38.2, 38.3, 42.1, 42.2, 43.3, 43.4, 45.1). Then, during 1746 and 1747, Greenwood engraved a number of relatively simple designs of flowers (46.2, 46.3, 46.4, 47.2), fruit (*47.4, 47.5), lyre (46.1) and palette (47.3). Finally, 1747 saw the first of several scenes expressing human relationships (*47.6, 47.7, *47.8, 48.1, *48.2, 55.1). Frans was in his late sixties when he applied his diamond to depict representations of the phenomenon of innate magnetism between man and woman.

Noteworthy is the long period 1731 - 1737 from which no glasses genuinely engraved by Frans Greenwood are known.

No fewer than some fifteen of the designs exist in duplicate albeit usually with some variation: 24.1 - 38.3 / 28.1 - *28.2 / 38.1 - *38.2 / 39.1 - 40.1 / 41.1 - *41.2 / 42.2 - 45.1 / 43.1 - *43.2 / *44.1 - 44.2 / 46.3 - 46.4 / 46.8 - 47.1 / *47.4 - 47.5 / 47.7 - *47.8 / 48.1 - *48.2 / 49.1 - *49.2 and possibly 43.5 - 46.7. It appears that either these engravings gave Greenwood much satisfaction or that he was not quite content with the first version he had stippled. Perhaps an admirer of his art asked Frans for the favour of a copy -- after all, Greenwood's stippling is quite masterly !

* * *

A certain Jac. A. (1893) quoted a newspaper article of 21.IV.1892 in which the question was asked: "Is it true that a cheerful Frans, named Greenwood, living in Dordrecht in the 18th century, etched glasses in taverns for want of money ?"

Answer: extremely unlikely !

* * *

Fig. 44. Frans Greenwood's last complete stipple-engraving, dated 1755 (when he was 75 years old), which is still wholly characteristic of his craftsmanship. Note: utilisation of entire height of bowl; dense stippling with full tonal range; stippled background with silhouetted trees; absence of noticeable outlines; absence of frame; hand at marked angle with lower arm; carrot-like fingers; the off the shoulder [? night]dress which the seductively voluptuous woman is wearing is partially in folds and quite leaves her bosom bare.

GREENWOOD'S SIGNATURES ON GLASS

Nearly all Greenwood engravings are fortunately signed and most of them are dated as well. With one exception (goblet A), the authenticity of those signatures appears to be beyond any suspicion [it would not be too difficult to fake one]. Two unsigned engravings (*41.2, *49.2) are attributed to Frans Greenwood with a fair degree of certainty; each is on a goblet with a replacement foot. A third unsigned and undated engraving (*48.2) could not be traced. Of the seven signed but undated engravings four have a damaged or missing stem and/or foot. These goblets perhaps met with an unfortunate accident during engraving, Greenwood subsequently having had no wish to sign or date the imperfect media. The six signed and dated damaged glasses - breakage or chipping here pertaining to stem and/or foot, not to the bowl - were probably maltreated after they had left the hands of the engraver.

Almost two-thirds of the signatures are in script, the remainder [starting in 1741] in Roman letters. Early engravings are signed either on a stem knop (22.4, 22.5, 38.1 [date only]) or below the design (20.1, 22.1, 22.2, 28.1, 38.1). Most later work is signed opposite the design. Greenwood did not sign his name on the foot of a goblet. The full Christian name (Frans) is used on only seven goblets, namely during 1720 - 1722 and 1742 - 1744.

As far as has been possible to check (exceptions being goblets 22.3, 38.3, 43.5), the following variations in signature and 'fecit' occur (a = on stem knop; b = below design; c = obliquely below design; d = opposite design) [numbers are those of goblets enumerated in the catalogue]:

in script

Mostly in single line letters (down strokes often scratched), used during the first twenty years (Figs. 45 - 47). Such letters tended to spall badly, causing them to resemble multiple-scratch letters which Greenwood used during 1744 - 1755 (Figs. 48 - 50). One signature (*47.8) is in stippled letters.

frans Greenwood pinxit 20.1 b

Frans Greenwood f. 22.5 a

frans Greenwood fec.^{t} 22.1 b

Frans Greenwood fec^t 22.4 a

Frans Greenwood fecit. *44.1 d

F: Greenw.^{d} 24.1 d

F. Greenwood. 39.1 d

f: Greenwood. f. 22.2 b

F. Greenwood f 38.1 b

F: Greenwood f: 30.1 d

F: Greenwood f:^{t} *46.6 d

F G fec^t *28.4 d

F. Greenwood fec.^{t} *28.2 d, 43.1 b, *47.4 d, *47.8 d, 49.1 d

F: Greenwood fec.^{t} 28.1 b

F. Greenwood fec.^{t} Dord.^{t} 48.3 d

F. Greenwood fecit 46.5 d, 47.1 d, 47.5 d, 47.6 d, 47.7 d, 48.1 d, 55.1 d

in roman

Except for one name in open letters within a stippled area (28.3), one in stipple (42.1) and 'fecit' (usually in single line script), Roman letters are all in multiple scratches and were used by Greenwood during 1741 - 1747 (Figs. 51, 52).

Frans Greenwood 42.2 c

Frans Greenwood fecit 44.2 d

F. Greenw^d 28.3 b

F. Greenwood 42.1

F. Greenwood fec.^{t} 43.3 d, 43.6 b, 46.1 d, 46.2 d, 47.2 d, 47.3 b

F. Greenwood fecit 41.1 d, 43.4 d, 45.1 d, 46.3 d, 46.4 b, 46.7 d, 46.8 d

Fig. 45.   Goblet 22.1

Fig. 46.   Goblet 24.1

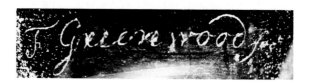

Fig. 47.   Goblet *28.2

Fig. 48.   Goblet 46.5

Fig. 49.   Goblet 49.1

Fig. 50.   Goblet 55.1

Fig. 51.   Goblet 44.2

Fig. 52.   Goblet 45.1

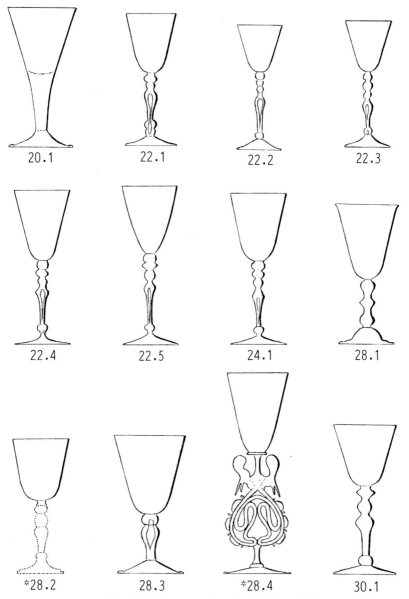

Fig. 53. Contours of goblets 20.1 - 30.1

Fig. 54. Contours of goblets 38.1 - *44.1

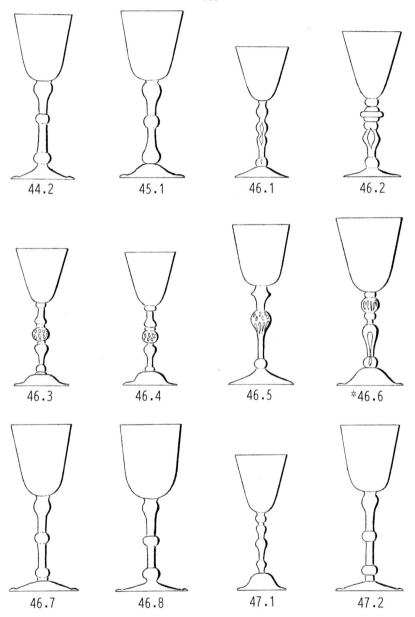

Fig. 55. Contours of goblets 44.2 - 47.2

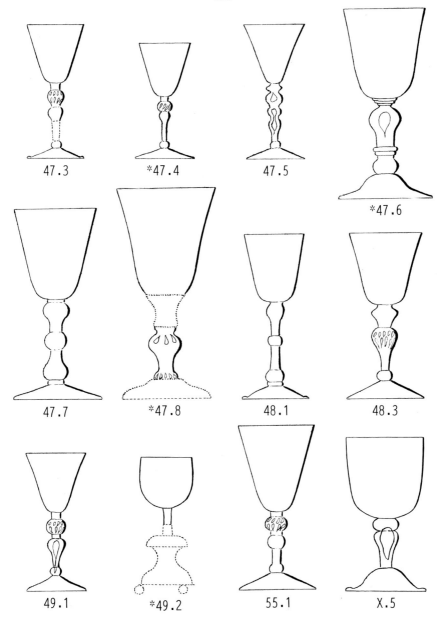

Fig. 56. Contours of goblets 47.3 - X.5

TYPES OF GOBLETS ENGRAVED

As far as is known, Greenwood used only wine-glasses for his engravings. He favoured sturdy lead-crystal goblets, varying in height from 173 to 317 mm (an average height of 225 mm); this sensible preference will be one of the reasons why a fair number of them are extant. Except for one façon-de-Venise goblet (of soda glass [*28.4]), all glasses used for his stipple-engravings have knopped stems, some with air beads or tears but none with a twist stem. - The vexing question of the provenance of these glasses can still not be answered satisfactorily. Many of them may well be of Netherlandish manufacture; the bowl : stem ratio is often ideal - certainly from an engraver's point of view - which on the whole is not a characteristic of glasses produced in England at the time. Apart from other localities in Holland, there were various glasshouses in Dordrecht during the eighteenth century.

For easy comparison the outlines - drawn to the same scale - of all known Greenwood goblets are shown in order of date of engraving (figs. 53 - 56 on pp. 118 - 121) [the first two ciphers of the goblet number denote the year of the 18th century]; repaired or replaced parts of goblets are shown in broken lines.

Apart from eight singular goblets (20.1, 28.1, 28.3, *28.4, 46.2, *47.6, *49.2, X.5), Frans Greenwood used four main types for his engravings:

(a) Slender teared-knopped stems, foot not folded; used early on from 1722 - 1724 (22.1, 22.2, 22.3, 22.4, 22.5, 24.1) and once again in 1739 (39.1).

(b) Multiknopped stems without tears or with only a single tear in a knop; foot not folded, rarely domed; engraved from 1728 till 1747 (*28.2, 30.1, 42.2, 43.1, 43.3, 43.4, 43.6, *44.1, 46.1, 47.1, 47.5).

(c) Stem composed of a central knop between a baluster below and an inverted baluster above, foot usually folded; this sturdy type of goblet was a favourite of the engraver from 1738 - 1748 (38.1, 38.3, 41.1, *41.2, 42.1, 44.2, 45.1, 46.7, 46.8, 47.2, 47.7, 48.1).

(d) Multiknopped stems with multiple tears in one of the knops, foot usually not folded but may be domed; Greenwood used these from 1746 - 1755 (46.3, 46.4, 46.5, *46.6, 47.3, *47.4, *47.8, 48.3, 49.1, 55.1).

*   *   *

VERBEELDINGEN
EN
BYSCHRIFTEN,
DOOR MY OP WYNKELKEN MET EEN DIAMANT
GETEKENT EN BESCHREVEN.

Fig. 57. "Designs and inscriptions drawn and inscribed by me with a diamond on wine-goblets." - This heading for a group of eight poems (Greenwood 1760: 76) proves that Greenwood used a diamond to engrave glass. References to that usage also occur in poems by his friends (pp. 38, 40, 42, 44).

KEY   FOR   THE   IDENTIFICATION   OF
GLASS-ENGRAVINGS   BY   F.   GREENWOOD

How   to   use   the   key:

- if diagnosis agrees with engraving: (a) code-number of goblet follows or
                                                    (b) if it does not, proceed to next diagnosis
- if diagnosis does not agree with engraving: proceed to diagnosis with number
  indicated in brackets

* undated, year of engraving estimated
X undatable
[ ] only known from literary or archival sources
+ goblet damaged (usually only slightly)
- not in W. Buckley 1930, 1931, 1935

 1 (2) line-scratch engraving -- **20.1**
 2 (1) stipple engraving
 3 (6) inanimate objects
 4 (5) lyre, inscribed "Poësis" -- **46.1**
 5 (4) palette, inscribed "Pictura" -- **47.3+**
 6 (3) objects from the living world
 7 (75) human beings included
 8 (13) youngsters only
 9 (12) putti
10 (11) three putti, without inscription -- **38.1**
11 (10) three putti, inscribed "Krakeelt &c." -- [***38.2**-]
12 (9) two children -- [**X.3**-]
13 (8) adult(s)
14 (60) one adult
15 (43) man
16 (40) without other company
17 (18) portrait of J. van den Vondel -- [**X.1**-]
18 (19) sailor, inscribed "'t Is een ontuchtig &c." -- [**X.2**-]
19 (20) bareheaded, holding a berkemeier -- **43.3**
20 (17) not bareheaded
21 (22) wearing a crown of vine leaves (Bacchus) -- **30.1**
22 (21) wearing a cap or hat
23 (35) wearing a cap
24 (29) holding a drinking-glass
25 (26) a berkemeier -- **28.1**
26 (25) a roemer
27 (28) dated 1742 -- **42.2+**
28 (27) dated 1745 -- **45.1-**
29 (24) not with a drinking-glass
30 (31) holding a bottle -- ***28.2+**
31 (32) holding a dagger or sword -- **46.7-** ?[**43.5**-]
32 (30) holding a tobacco pipe
33 (34) without inscription -- **46.8**
34 (33) inscribed "Gelyk de rook &c." -- **47.1**
35 (23) wearing a hat
36 (37) holding a Passglas -- **43.4**
37 (36) holding a berkemeier
38 (39) without inscription -- **38.3+**
39 (38) inscribed "Aanzien &c." -- **24.1**
40 (16) one man with youngsters or animals

41 (42) with two cherubs -- **22.5**
42 (41) with two donkeys -- ***28.4**
43 (15) woman
44 (45) empty-handed, unfinished engraving -- **X.5**
45 (46) holding a cornucopia, inscribed "Vrientschap" -- **22.2**+-
46 (47) playing a lute -- **22.3**
47 (48) painting, holding a palette -- **22.4**+
48 (49) holding a flower, inscribed "Verwekte 't schoon &c." -- **28.3**
49 (50) hooded woman seated at a table, inkstand -- **43.6**
50 (55) holding a fish
51 (52) a roemer in other hand -- **42.1**+-
52 (51) a platter in other hand
53 (54) plain background -- ***44.1**+-
54 (53) wall, urn, tree in background -- **44.2**-
55 (44) shepherdess, holding rose and crook -- **48.3**
56 (57) woman as Venus with satyr(s) -- [**X.4**-]
57 (56) woman holding three babies
58 (59) inscribed "O Gevaerts &c." -- **39.1**
59 (58) inscribed "O Beeftingh &c." -- [**40.1**-]
60 (14) two adults
61 (66) men
62 (65) playing trick-track
63 (64) without inscription -- **43.1**
64 (63) inscribed "'t Verkeeren &c." -- [***43.2**-]
65 (62) Bacchus, Silenus, &c., inscribed "Het druivenbloet &c." -- ***46.6**
66 (61) man and woman
67 (68) seated, with dog and cat -- ***47.6**+
68 (71) half-length nudes, in a park
69 (70) dated 1747 -- **47.7**
70 (69) undated -- ***47.8**+
71 (74) full-length nude shepherd and shepherdess
72 (73) dated 1748 -- **48.1**
73 (72) undated -- [***48.2**-]
74 (67) old man ogling younger woman -- **55.1**
75 (7) without human beings
76 (83) with animal(s)
77 (78) various birds -- **46.5**-
78 (77) one horse
79 (80) background blank -- **22.1**-
80 (79) background hilly
81 (82) inscribed "Vryheit" -- **41.1**+-
82 (81) without inscription -- ***41.2**+-
83 (76) botanical objects
84 (94) rose
85 (88) without insects, inscribed "Nulle Roze &c."
86 (87) inscription below rose, signature opposite -- **46.3**-
87 (86) inscription opposite rose, signature below -- **46.4**
88 (89) with one butterfly, inscribed "Geen Rozen &c." -- **46.2**
89 (85) with butterfly and damselfly
90 (91) with chrysanthemum and tulip -- **47.2**-
91 (90) without other flowers
92 (93) dated 1749 -- **49.1**
93 (92) undated -- ***49.2**+-
94 (84) oranges
95 (96) dated 1747 -- **47.5**
96 (95) undated -- ***47.4**-

CATALOGUE OF GOBLETS
ENGRAVED BY FRANS GREENWOOD

The numbering of the chronologically arranged goblets is based on the year of engraving: the numeral before the full stop is that of the year (in the eighteenth century), the cipher following the full stop is the number for the individual glass engraved in that year. For an undated engraving the presumed year is preceded by an asterisk. The five engravings which could not be dated are listed last and coded with an X number.

Measurements are in millimeters; calculated measurements [which require checking] are in brackets. H = height of goblet; the diameter of a bowl is the outer one. - The description of a knopped stem follows a downward direction. - Left (sinister) and right (dexter) as seen from the viewpoint of the spectator (but, e.g., a "right hand" is of course a person's right hand).

About two-thirds of the goblets catalogued have been examined; descriptions of the other glasses are based on [published] photographs (which cannot always show an engraving satisfactorily or in its entirety).

The outlines of the goblets are shown in Figs. 53 - 56 on pp. 118 - 121; no separate reference is made to these in the descriptions.

Illustrations of the engravings are provided mainly to aid identification; some of them are of an unsatisfactory standard (better ones not having been obtainable). Extremely useful and pleasing as they may be, relatively few photographs of engravings do fully justice to Frans Greenwood -- there simply is no substitute for an actual engraved goblet.

It is deplorable that glasses engraved by Greenwood - and indeed by other stipple-engravers as well - which are housed in public collections are frequently far from ideally exhibited (poor lighting, a pale background or placing at the back of a deep cabinet).

*   *   *

(pre-1719 - a dubious attribution)
"De liefde van David en Jonathan op een glas afgebeelt, door my aan de Broederschap gegeven." (The love [friendship] of David and Jonathan depicted on a glass, presented by me [Frans Greenwood] to the Brotherhood.) In the relevant poem, on a birthday of Dirk Seelen, Greenwood referred to this engraving as being exe - cuted in the manner of a drawing; this would seem to allude to a diamond-point line-engraving. Although it is by no means certain that Greenwood had engraved the goblet himself, he may well have done so.

OWNERSHIP At the latest in 1718 Frans Greenwood presented this wine-glass either to a Brotherhood (St Lucas ?) in Rotterdam or perhaps more specifically to Dirk Seelen, a prominent member of that fraternity. Various 18th-century glasses engraved with representations of the friendship between David and Jonathan [often two boys shown to be shaking hands] have survived but it may not be possible to ascertain whether one of them is this particular goblet.

REMARK Dirk Seelen Sr, a merchant and town-councillor, was a man of means; in 1694, for instance, he advanced money for the building of a sugar refinery in Rotterdam. After the death of his first wife he married Susanne van de Velde (widow of Adriaen Boon) in 1698. Seelen died in his house at Wijnhaven, Rotterdam, on 20 May, 1722.

LITERATURE Greenwood 1719: 18, footnote.

Fig. 58. Bowl of goblet 20.1   Fig. 59. Bowl of goblet 20.1

20.1 (Figs. 58, 59)

Four grotesque men, copied from Jacques Callot's *Balli di Sfessania*, encircling the bowl. They are (a) Scapino with (b) Capitan Zerbino playing the game of mora (or morra - one player guessing the number of fingers held up simultaneously by another player) in which a bottle of wine, seen standing on the ground between them, seems to be at stake, (c) Smaraolo cornuto or the horned Smaraolo [his companion Ratsa di Boio is omitted] and (d) Maramao.

Engraving entirely in scratched lines, quite dense; spalling along many lines.

SIGNED (in single-line letters, hardly spalled, just below the figure of Maramao): frans Greenwood pinxit / 19 Jan: 1720.

GOBLET H 210. **Bowl** drawn funnel, ⌀ 108. **Stem** plain. **Foot** conical, folded, pontil mark fairly smooth, ⌀ 104.

A heavy glass, apparently the only plain-stemmed goblet ever used for engraving by Greenwood.

OWNERSHIP W. Buckley, Basingstoke / Victoria and Albert Museum, London (C.434-1936 - presented by Mrs B. T. Buckley in 1936)

REMARKS During some 200 years, from about 1550-1750, troupes of the then famous Italian Comedy, or Commedia dell'Arte, travelled and performed all over Europe. Although the plot for the plays they enacted was usually written out, it was common practice for the actors to improvise the dialogue. Certain characters recur almost invariably in these plays and among them are the prototypes of the Punch and Judy show. The influence of the Commedia dell'Arte can be traced throughout European art and literature. The various characters, or masks, performing in these theatrical variety acts inspired artists to copy them. Murano glassmakers fashioned Commedia figures and such characters were also painted in enamel on beakers. Several porcelain manufacturers also made copies of players. Among the graphic representations of Commedia players the best known are those by the great French engraver Jacques Callot of Nancy (1592-1635) who spent some time in Italy. During a stay in Firenze [Florence] he sketched a number of masks and on his return to Nancy, in 1621, Callot made etchings of 24 scenes depicting the *Balli di Sfessania* (Dances of Sfessania).

Greenwood gave Maramao one forward-pointing feather on his cap instead of two backward-pointing ones and he changed the long squirt which, in the original print, Maramao is holding into a long staff with a double hook at the end which, so it seems, Maramao stealthily employs to hook the bottle - around the neck of which a large ring - standing between Scapino and Zerbino. This perhaps symbolises the old adage "When two dogs fight for a bone, a third will run away with it" (cf. 38.1, *38.2). In all other respects the four engraved figures are quite exact copies of Callot's etchings but in mirror image; however, Greenwood left out Callot's backgrounds. The four engraved figures all being somewhat smaller (at various reductions) than the print ones, Greenwood did not straight-forwardly trace the latter.

Could there have been a connection between this glass and the St Lucas Guild of Rotterdam which was originally founded in 1609 ? Apart from painters, sculptors and printers, all kinds of glassworkers were admitted as members. This diversity led to much dissension as is clear from two poems by Greenwood written some time during the first two decades of the 18th century. Eventually, on 26 January, 1720, St Lucas issued an entirely new set of rules for membership. It is noteworthy that exactly a week previously Greenwood finished - in any case dated - this particular engraving. Was the goblet meant to be a present for the newly re-established guild or was it a masterpiece to be submitted for election as member and consequently inscribed by the engraver as "pinxit" perhaps to gratify painter-electors ?

LITERATURE Hudig 1926: xxvii. Buckley 1926: 74 (No. 67), pl. 67. Anonymous 1929a: fig. 156; 1929b: fig. 155. Hudig 1929: fig. 7. Buckley 1929: 308 (No. W); 1930a: 290 (No. W); 1930b, c: 12 (No. 1), pl. 5, 5A; 1939: 72, 270 (No. 380), pl. 134. Charleston 1957: 240, fig. 11. Elville 1961: fig. 105. Savage 1965a, b, ? 1968, 1969: fig. 77; 1972: fig. 80. van Hall 1976: 309, fig. 1. Fleming & Honour 1977: fig. p. 351. Matcham & Dreiser 1982, 1983: upper fig. p. 119.

*   *   *

22.1 (Fig. 60)
A horse galloping in a direction obliquely towards the left. A few small plants to the right, background otherwise blank.
In stipple but mane and tail in lines.

SIGNED (in single-line small script, below design):

frans Greenwood fec.ᵗ 1722.

GOBLET **H** 197. **Bowl** pointed round funnel, ⌀ 81. **Stem** knop / knop / single-teared inverted baluster / double base knop. **Foot** conical, ⌀ 80.

OWNERSHIP R. Kneppelhout van Sterkenburg, 's-Gravenhage / Rijksmuseum, Amsterdam (R. B. K. 16529 - purchased from the former owner in 1951)

REMARKS A galloping or springing horse is usually a symbol of Freedom. Its portrayal in the eighteenth century does not, as is often assumed, always relate to the so-called White Horse of Hannover. A rearing or charging horse is in fact in a very conventional pose in numerous prints of the 17th and 18th centuries. - Two decades later Greenwood engraved two other prancing horses (41.1, *41.2). The Dutch Republic enjoyed an unaccustomed blessing of peace during the thirty years following the Treaty of Utrecht in 1713. Neither in 1722 nor in 1741 did national events call for a very special celebration of liberty.

LITERATURE Anonymous 1952: 15, fig. Schrijver 1961: 118, pl. 14b. Anonymous 1962a: 58 (sub No. 304). Braat 1962: 16. Schrijver 1963: 131, pl. 14b; 1969: 143, pl. 15b. Newman 1977: lower fig. p. 299. Ritsema van Eck 1980: left-hand fig. p. 288.

Fig. 60. Bowl of goblet 22.1   Fig. 61. Bowl of goblet 22.2

22.2 (Fig. 61)

A standing woman, face in profile to sinister, emblematic of Copia or Abundance. Wearing a floral crown and flowing robes which leave the bosom bare, she is holding with the right arm an adorned cornucopia overflowing with vine-leaves, tendrils, grapes and several apples or pomegranates. With her left hand she raises a metal tazza burdened with grapes, vine-leaves and tendrils. At her feet, to the left, a bound sheaf of corn, to the right a plant. Background blank. - Some line-work, mainly in plants.

INSCRIBED (in scratched unlinked Italic capital letters, opposite design low down on bowl):
V R I E N T S C H A P

SIGNED (in single-line script with scratches along downstrokes, below design): f: Greenwood. f. 1722.

GOBLET **H** 187. **Bowl** pointed round funnel, ∅ 70. **Stem** three knops / slender single-teared inverted baluster / base knop. **Foot** conical, pontil mark smooth, ∅ 70 [a small chip on edge].

OWNERSHIP An old Dordrecht family (since about 1830) / F. Laméris, Amsterdam / private collection, The Netherlands

EXHIBITED 39e Oude Kunst- en Antiekbeurs, Stedelijk Museum Het Prinsenhof, Delft, 15-29.X.1987.

REMARKS This is the earliest of the Greenwood goblets known to bear an inscription. The Italic lettering is similar to that used by the engraver also in later years, for instance for manuscript headings of poems (Figs. 82, 83).
    Frans Greenwood, a widower since 1711, used to have a wide circle of friends and acquaintances in Rotterdam and elsewhere and it cannot now be established with any certainty whose friendship in particular was symbolically enshrined in this goblet. Could it have been his good friend Arnold Willis, the publisher of Greenwood's first book of collected poems (1719) ? Or perhaps Maria Sijdervelt, a maiden whose desirable qualities had been extolled by Frans in a poem for her birthday in 'wine month' [October], 1721 ? (cf. Remarks sub 28.3)

Fig. 62. Bowl of goblet 22.3   Fig. 63. Bowl of goblet 22.4

Some drinking-glasses dedicated to friendship were already engraved in Holland in the 1680s but not until the second half of the eighteenth century did engraved 'Vriendschap' wine-glasses become really popular there.

LITERATURE Anonymous 1987a: 49, figs. pp. 51, 58; 1987b: fig. p. 191; 1987c: fig. p. 38; 1987d: fig. p. 41; 1987e: 32-33, 3 figs.; 1987f: pl. p. [30]. Smit 1987: 4 pp., 6 figs.

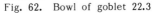

*   *   *

22.3 (Fig. 62)
A knee-length portrait of a seated woman, face ¾ to sinister with head slightly tilted. She is dressed in a loose-fitting garb leaving right breast bare and is playing a 20-stringed lute. A number of tall cypresses in the background and, to the right, a large sculptured lidded garden urn. Background otherwise blank.

SIGNED (below design ? [no information could be obtained]):
F. Greenwood 1722

GOBLET **H** 190. **Bowl** pointed round funnel, ϕ (72). **Stem** three knops / slender single-teared inverted baluster / teared base knop. **Foot** conical, ϕ (71).

OWNERSHIP Hessisches Landesmuseum, Kassel

REMARKS This could be either a representation of Hearing as one of the Five Senses, of Music personified as one of the Seven Liberal Arts or of the Muse Polyhymnia. It is extremely unusual to reverse the functions of the hands for the playing of a stringed instrument; this engraving is therefore very likely the mirror-image of a print. The strings of this lute are divided into six pairs of unisons and eight single strings for basses.

LITERATURE Schmidt 1914: 14. Hudig 1926: xxvii. Buckley 1930b: 11 (No. 2), pl. 6; 1930c: 12 (No. 2), pl. 6.

*   *   *

22.4 (Fig. 63)
A standing barebosomed woman wearing flowing drapes; on each side of the head a small Mercurial wing. She is looking downwards to sinister while holding an almost circular palette with her left hand and pointing with her right index-finger

Fig. 64. Bowl of goblet 22.5   Fig. 65. Bowl of goblet 24.1

to a painting of a colonnade with two pedestalled garden urns which is standing on an easel before her. Behind the easel the pedestal of a statue hidden from sight by the painting. To the right a round pedestal behind which, on another but rectangular pedestal, an armless bust of a Satyr. On the ground two masks beneath the easel and, to the right, a seated monkey holding a paint brush in a rectangular paintbox to the left of which a large shell. Background blank.

SIGNED (in single-line script, on upper knop of stem):
Frans Greenwood / fect 1722

GOBLET **H** (230). **Bowl** pointed round funnel, ⌀ (86). **Stem** knop / angular knop / swelling knop / elongate single-teared inverted baluster / base knop. **Foot** conical, ⌀ (85) [quite a large piece missing].

OWNERSHIP Jhr Dr J. P. Six / Mrs Six van Hillegom / Jhr J. Six van Hillegom, Amsterdam

REMARK As symbolised by the monkey, the design is presumably emblematic of the art of painting and sculpture.

LITERATURE de Castro 1883: 281. Gerspach 1885: 292. Schmidt 1914: 14. Hudig 1926: xxvii. Buckley 1930b: 11 (No. 4), pl. 8; 1930c: 12 (No. 4), pl. 8. Haynes 1944: pl. IV. Charleston 1957: 240, fig. 12.

* * *

22.5 (Fig. 64)

A nude male figure representing Apollo, face in near-profile to sinister, wearing a laurel crown. He is seated, with left leg crossing the right one, on drapery spread over clouds and is playing with his right hand a six-stringed lyre. While held with his left hand, the instrument is resting on cloth draped over Apollo's lap. The left arm of the lyre is surmounted with a griffin's head. Below Apollo to the right a cherub [Cupid], seen from behind with a quiver of arrows on its back and with a bow and arrow at the ready, apparently aiming at Apollo's bottom. Another cherub, full-face, to the left of the god's right foot, holding up a laurel crown with its left hand and clasping another in its right hand. Background blank.

Fig. 66. Bowl of goblet 24.1   Fig. 67. Bowl of goblet 24.1

SIGNED (in single-line script, on upper knop of stem):
Frans Greenwood f. 1722.

GOBLET H 238. **Bowl** funnel, ∅ 90. **Stem** three knops / slender single-teared inverted baluster / base knop. **Foot** conical, pontil mark fairly smooth, ∅ 87.

OWNERSHIP Freiherr Alexander von Minutoli, Liegnitz, Silesia [now: Lignica, Poland] / Brandenburgisch-Preussische Kunstkammer, Berlin (M 631 - purchased from von Minutoli in 1869 for RM 90) / Kunstgewerbemuseum, West Berlin (since 1876).

REMARKS Apollo, also called Phoebus, was a son of Zeus and Leto who became well-known as one of the twelve gods of the Olympus. He was the god of music, poetry and the fine arts as well as leader of the nine Muses. The lyre was his attribute as patron of poetry, Mount Parnassus his favourite residence. When, according to Ovidius, Cupid struck Apollo with a golden arrow to prove its power, he fell in love with nymph Daphne, a daughter of a river god. Daphne escaped the suitor by being changed into a laurel bush.
    Laurel crowns were awarded for achievements in the arts.
    According to Schmidt (1914) the design was copied from an etching by Samuel Bottschild (1641-1706) published in 1693. Indeed, Greenwood's engraving is quite an accurate copy of the print [254 x 183 mm] which bears the legend "Dum mihi torpenti virtutes premia Sordent / Heu ! miser im belli victus ab hoste cado." - Could the sentiment expressed in etching and text reflect an amorous event in the life of the poet-engraver ?

LITERATURE Pazaurek 1902: 26, footnote. Anonymous 1907: 148. von Falke 1910: 126; n.d.: 69. Schmidt 1911: fig. 10; 1912: fig. 212; 1914: 14; 1922: fig. 227. Hudig 1926: xxvii. Buckley 1930b: 11 (No. 3), pl. 7; 1930c: 12 (No. 3), pl. 7. Haynes 1944: fig. III. Dreier 1981: 39, fig. 17.

*   *   *

24.1 (Figs. 46, 65-67)
A half-length portrait of a man, face ¾ to dexter, wearing a hat with upturned brim and raising a prunted berkemeier with his left hand. Drapery in the stippled background as well as a pillar to the right; part of a monumental garden scene to the left.

INSCRIBED (in Roman capitals, low down on pedestal of right pillar):
Aanzien / doet / Gedenkēn [Out of sight, out of mind]
The final letter of 'Gedenken' is within the densely stippled side of the pedestal and therefore hardly visible; Greenwood consequently placed a dash over the
penultimate letter to turn that 'e' into 'en', as was commonly done in old script.

SIGNED (in single-line script with scratches along downstrokes, opposite design
at bottom of bowl):

F: Greenw.^{d} / 1724

GOBLET H 225. **Bowl** pointed round funnel, ϕ 86. **Stem** three knops / elongate
single-teared inverted baluster / base knop. **Foot** conical, ϕ 85.

OWNERSHIP S. C. Snellen van Vollenhoven, Leiden / Rijksmuseum, Amsterdam
(NM 2925 - purchased from the previous owner in 1876)

EXHIBITED Tentoonstelling Breekbaar Licht, Stedelijk Museum Het Prinsenhof,
Delft, 26.X - 10.XII.1957

REMARKS The engraving occupies about three-quarters the circumference of the
bowl. - Schmidt (1914) noticed that the design was copied from a print [253 x
175 mm] by Abraham Blooteling (1640-1690) after a painting by Jan van Mieris
(1660-1690). Blooteling's print (Wessely 1867: 82 [No. 116]; Buckley 1930b, c:
pl. 9A) shows a somewhat happier looking man than Greenwood managed to engrave. Greenwood made another copy in 1738, this time quite successful but
with a different background and without an inscription (38.3).
The toper's garment is characterised by longitudinal slashes, fashionable in
the middle of the seventeenth century; similar jackets can be seen on 28.1, *28.2,
38.3, 42.2 and 45.1.
The inscription - an old Dutch adage recorded as early as 1550 - literally
means 'In sight, in mind'. In 1676 Willem Jacobszoon van Heemskerk calligraphically adorned a bulbous bluish-green bottle with the same saying.

LITERATURE de Castro 1883: 281. Gerspach 1885: 292. Schmidt 1914: 14.
Hudig 1926: xxvii. Buckley 1930b: 11 (No. 5), pl. 9; 1930c: 12 (No. 5), pl. 9.
Haynes 1944: fig. V. van Gelder 1955: pl. XXX(1). Bolten 1957: (No. 97).
Braat 1962: 16, fig. 9. van Gelder & Jansen 1969: 76, fig. 211. Schack 1976:
fig. 64.

*   *   *

28.1 (Fig. 68)
A half-length portrait in left-side view of a man, wearing an unadorned cap
askant, his head turned towards spectator and holding in his left hand a prunted
berkemeier to which he is pointing with his right hand. Background stippled with
the bough and foliated branch of a tree, a conifer-tree left and right and to the
right the left half of a large garden urn. The design framed to the right by a
vertical stippled band 3 mm wide, increasing to 4 mm lower down; left side not
framed.

SIGNED (in single-line script lightly written with little spalling, below design):

F: Greenwood fec^t 1728

GOBLET H 210. **Bowl** pointed round funnel, a little flared, ϕ 95 [a horizontal
50 mm long scratch ±25 mm below rim]. **Stem** inverted baluster / central knop /
baluster. **Foot** domed, folded, pontil mark fairly rough, ϕ 87 [a few scratches on
the foot below design].

Fig. 68. Bowl of goblet 28.1   Fig. 69. Bowl of goblet *28.2

OWNERSHIP   W. Buckley, Basingstoke (WB 381) / Victoria and Albert Museum, London (C.435-1936 - presented by Mrs B. T. Buckley in 1936)

REMARKS   The design is somewhat reminiscent of "The jolly drinker" by Judith Leyster (1609-1660) [Rijksmuseum, Amsterdam, inv. A 1685].
   The garment worn resembles that on 24.1, *28.2, 38.3, 42.2 and 45.1.
   The toper's left hand and the berkemeier are very similar to those on 24.1 and 38.3.
   The sitter is obviously the same man as the one depicted on *28.2 which engraving, however, shows a more successful execution of facial features.

LITERATURE   Hudig 1926: xxvii.   Buckley 1926: 75 (No. 68), pl. 68.   Schmidt 1927: 37 (No. 68), pl. 68.   Thorpe 1927: fig. [6] p. 78.   Anonymous 1929a: fig. 157;   1929b: fig. 156.   Buckley 1929: 306 (No. R);   1930a: 289, pl. CXX (No. R); 1930b: 12 (No. 6), pl. 10;   1930c: 13 (No. 6), pl. 10;   1939: 270, pl. 135.   Honey 1946: 134, pl. 59A.   Stone & Stone 1953: fig. p. 19.   Robertson 1954: pl. 45.   Charleston 1957: 240, fig. 13.   Hayward 1960: fig. 3.   Savage 1965a, b: fig. 78.   Davis, F. 1966: fig. 107.   Savage 1968: fig. 78.   Wilkinson 1968: fig. 69.   Robertson 1969: pl. 50.   Savage 1972: fig. 81.   Vose 1975: 181, fig.

*   *   *

*28.2   (Figs. 47, 69)
A half-length portrait of a smiling man with head turned towards spectator, wearing a plumed cap askant and holding in his left hand a bulbous wine-bottle encased in wicker-work to which he is pointing with his right hand.   Some trees silhouetted in stippled background; the bough of a tree to the right, far left the end of a crumbling garden wall.

SIGNED   (in single-line script with much spalling, opposite design):

F. Greenwood fec^t.

GOBLET   H 202.   **Bowl** round funnel, ϕ 88.   **Stem** a four-knopped metal replacement.   **Foot** a silver replacement, terraced near edge, ϕ 70.

OWNERSHIP   Private museum of Repelaer van Spijkenisse, Haarlem / H. P. van de Wall Repelaer van Puttershoek, Dubbeldam / H. P. van de Wall Repelaer, Dubbeldam / auction Christie, Amsterdam, 24.IX.1985 (unsold) / private collection, The Netherlands

Fig. 70. Bowl of goblet 28.3   Fig. 71. Bowl of goblet 28.3

EXHIBITED Herdenkingstentoonstelling Aart Schouman, Dordrecht's Museum, Dordrecht, 27.VIII - 2.X.1960 / Tentoonstelling Diep in het Glas kijken, Museum Mr Simon van Gijn, Dordrecht, 17.XII.1987 - 27.III.1988

REMARK The subject is very similar to that on 28.1 which, however, did not come off quite as well as the present engraving.

LITERATURE Buckley 1930b: 14 (No. 26), pl. 30; 1930c: 15 (No. 26), pl. 30. Bol 1960: 94 (No. 185). Auction Catalogue Christie 1985b: 31 (lot 70), pl. p. 30. Liefkes 1987: 58 (No. 68), 3 figs.

*   *   *

28.3 (Figs. 70, 71)
A half-length figure, with bared left breast, of a goddess of river Maas [Meuse] portrayed as Flora with garlanded hair and holding up in her right hand a large flower at which she is gazing. To the right and behind her a wall and flower vase. On opposite side a view of a park with a fountain, steps with urns, and groups of trees. The design occupies the entire circumference of the bowl.

INSCRIBED (on the foot of the goblet):
Verwekte 't schoon der Bloemgodin / Oit aan den Tyber grooter min, /
Dan nu 't op 't glas door Greenwoods hant / De Maasstroomgodin zet in Brant ? /
Maar, Schoonheit, wat is toch uw roem ? / De teerheit van een glas, of bloem ?/
K. Boon van Engel[ant]
[Did the beauty of the Flower Goddess / on the Tiber ever exite greater love / Than now ignited in the Goddess of River Maas / By Greenwood's hand on this glass ? / But, Beauty, what really is your fame ? / The fragility of a glass or the delicacy of a flower ? / K. Boon van Engel(ant)]

SIGNED (in open letters within a stippled area below park scenery):
F. Greenw^{d} / 1728

GOBLET H 208. **Bowl** round funnel, ϕ 114. **Stem** knop / inverted baluster containing a large tear. **Foot** conical, folded, ϕ (113).

OWNERSHIP H. A. Steengracht van Duivenvoorde, 's-Gravenhage / auction Muller, Amsterdam, 8.V.1913 (Hfl. 1,175) / H. Stibbe, Berlin / J. Mühsam, Berlin

(1913 - 1927) / The Metropolitan Museum of Art, New York (27.185.207 - Munsey bequest of 1931)

EXHIBITED   Sammlung Jacques Mühsam, Königliches Kunstgewerbemuseum, Berlin, 1914

REMARKS   In Roman mythology Flora is a goddess of flowers and spring-time; she had an old temple on the Collis Quirinalis in Rome. Her festival, Floralia, was held annually on April 28th (the foundation date of her temple) and lasted for six days till May 3rd. The festivities included theatrical performances and circus games and were characterised by excessive merriment and licentiousness.
The identity of the "goddess of [or: living along] river Maas" remains a real mystery. The engraving and inscribed hexastich perhaps allude to Maria Zydervelt (or Sijdervelt), a maiden whose desirable qualities were poetically extolled in print by both Boon van Engelant and his good friend Frans Greenwood in the early 1720s. In a poem on a birthday of hers in "wijnmaand" [wine month = October], Boon van Engelant (1732: 126-128) praised Maria's beauty and other attributes which, he said, challenge the rose in Flora's Court. Greenwood (1760: 113-117) versified in similar vein, likewise for a birthday (specifically that of 5 October, 1721); his poem was probably first published separately for the occasion. Both poets end their homages by wishing, possibly wishfully, that Maria would come across a suitable husband before long. [This particular Maria is not included in the Sijdervelt genealogy (1978, Jb. Centr. Bur. Geneal. 32: 121-146)].
Boon van Engelant's hexastich is not included in his published works.
The portrayed woman is rather reminiscent of one of the Magdalens painted by Gerard Dou [W. Martin, 1902, *Gerard Dou*].

LITERATURE   Auction Catalogue Muller 1913a: 65 (lot 871), pl. [17]. Anonymous 1914: 59. Schmidt 1914: 14, 19 (No. 27), pl. 2 No. 27. Comstock 1926: figs. 9, 10. Hudig 1926: xxvii. Anonymous 1928: 1 fig. Avery 1928: 14, fig. 12. Buckley 1930b: 12 (No. 7), pl. 11;   1930c: 13 (No. 7), pl. 11. Thorpe 1930: 325, 2 figs. Avery 1936: 30, fig. 27. Honey 1946: 134. Vávra 1953: pl. 86 figs. 226, 227; 1954a, b: pl. 90 figs. 217, 218. McNab Dennis 1972: 437, fig. 14.

*   *   *

*28.4   (Figs. 72, 73)
A landscape with, to the right, a large old pollarded willow split wide open behind which, to the right, part of a fence of three horizontal planks in front of a tree with a foliate branch extending over design to the left. There are various other trees and plants as well as the back view of two donkeys one of which burdened with packs, the other supporting a hatted rider. Background all in stipple; large plants in foreground. Design occupying nearly two-thirds the circumference of the bowl and framed between two scratched vertical lines widening to 2 mm at top of bowl.
Some line-scratching in saddles.

SIGNED   (with obvious difficulty in single-line script, badly spalled, opposite design at bottom of bowl about 10 mm above merese):

F G fec[t]

GOBLET   **H** 302. **Bowl** pointed round funnel resting on a merese at top of stem, ⌀ 91. **Stem** composed of a strand of twisted opaque white and (especially on one side, the right when looking at design) clear bluish-green threads in clear glass, with impressed projections of clear glass at the edges. **Foot** conical, narrowly folded, pontil mark rough, ⌀ 103.

Fig. 72. Bowl of goblet *28.4   Fig. 73. Bowl of goblet *28.4

REMARKS   This is a light-weight [soda glass] Netherlandish façon-de-Venise
wine-glass (Flügelglas), probably of the second half of the 17th century. The bowl
is very seedy, containing numerous small vertical-oval air bubbles.

Not surprisingly, this is the only known stipple-engraved Flügelglas; such a
cumbersome goblet with a hard and rather thin bowl is an extremely awkward
object to engrave. It is amazing that Greenwood managed to complete this
veritable tour de force without accidents. He did not write his signature in full
because it was clearly difficult enough to scratch in just the initials.

Could this be the "old-fashioned goblet" removed by Greenwood from the
premises of Herman Croes, Rotterdam, in 1724 (cf. p. 71) ?

OWNERSHIP   W. Buckley, Basingstoke (WB 379) / Victoria and Albert Museum,
London (C.433-1936 - presented by Mrs B. T. Buckley in 1936)

LITERATURE   Buckley 1930c: 15 (No. 27), pls 31, 32; 1939: 270, pl. 133.
Haynes 1944: pl. VIII. Honey 1946: 134. van Hall 1976: fig. 2.

                            *   *   *
30.1 (Fig. 74)
A seated nude Bacchus, face $\frac{3}{4}$ to dexter, wearing a crown of vine-leaves and
holding up with his left hand a ribbed stemmed metal tazza burdened with grapes
and with his right hand a bunch of grapes. To the left a garden urn on a pedestal behind which a large silhouetted tree trunk; background entirely in stipple.
Design not framed.

Stippling quite coarse.

SIGNED (in single-line script, opposite design at bottom of bowl):
F: Greenwood f: 1730.

GOBLET H 228. **Bowl** pointed round funnel, ⌀ 97. **Stem** angular knop / knop /
inverted baluster / base knop. **Foot** rather flat, pontil mark fairly rough, ⌀ 97.

OWNERSHIP   A. van Hoboken van Cortgene, Rotterdam / Museum Boymans -
van Beuningen, Rotterdam (140 - presented by A. van Hoboken van Cortgene 1922)

REMARK   For another Bacchus [God of Wine] by Greenwood see *46.6.

LITERATURE   Hudig 1926: xxvii. Buckley 1930b: 12 (No. 8), pl. 12; 1930c:
13 (No. 8), pl. 12. Isings 1966a, b: fig. 108.

Fig. 74. Bowl of goblet 30.1   Fig. 75. Bowl of goblet 38.1

38.1 (Fig. 75)
Three naked putti, the left one of whom, face in profile to dexter, is standing
and drinking from a bulbous bottle the handle of which is tied to a stick held in
the left hand by the middle putto with face ¾ to dexter, who has fallen to the
ground and is looking up at the third putto who is standing and is shown obliquely
from behind. Stippled background with trees and hills; to the left some rocks
and vegetation.
    The hair of the putti is in stipple and lines; there are also some short lines
in, e.g., the plants.

SIGNED (in single-line script, within stippled foreground):
F. Greenwood f
(in single-line on central knop of stem, straight below signature):
1738

GOBLET H 249. **Bowl** round funnel, ⌀ 92. **Stem** inverted baluster enclosing
a large tear / single-teared central ball knop / baluster [forming a base knop].
Foot conical, folded, pontil mark fairly smooth, ⌀ 97.

OWNERSHIP Felix Slade, London / British Museum, London (69.6-24.89 -
F. Slade bequest of 1869)

REMARK The sentiment expressed in this and the following engraving (*38.2)
is that of the 16th-century adage "Two dogs fight for a bone, and a third runs
away with it."

LITERATURE Bate 1905, 1913: 87, pl. L fig. 193. Hudig 1926: xxvii. Buckley
1930b: 13 (No. 23), pl. 27; 1930c: 15 (No. 23), pl. 27.

                    *   *   *

*38.2 (Fig. 76)
According to Greenwood himself (1760), he decorated a goblet with "Twee
kindertjes worstelende om een wynkruik, terwyl 'er een derde mee heen loopt."
[Two children fighting for a pitcher of wine while a third runs away with it.]
This engraving may therefore be assumed to be similar to that of the previous
glass (38.1).

INSCRIBED (see Fig. 76)

TWEE KINDERTJES WORSTELENDE OM EEN WYNKRUIK, TERWYL'ER EEN DERDE MEE HEEN LOOPT.

Krakeelt om weinig noch om veel,
Maar neemt genoegen met uw deel;
Want twist ge uit hebtzucht onder een,
Een derde loopt'er licht meê heen.

Fig. 76. Inscription on goblet *38.2 (Greenwood 1760: 77). [Quarrel about neither much nor little, / But be satisfied with your share; / For a third will quietly make off with it / If greed causes you to quarrel with someone.]

OWNERSHIP This glass has not been recorded since 1760 and, if still extant, its depository is unknown.

LITERATURE Greenwood 1760: 77.

* * *

38.3 (Fig. 77)
A half-length portrait of a man, face ¾ to dexter, wearing a hat with upturned brim and raising a prunted berkemeier with his left hand. Background stippled with trees.

SIGNED F. Greenwood 1738

GOBLET H 250. **Bowl** round funnel, ∅ (87). **Stem** inverted baluster / central knop / base knop [stem broken below central knop but repaired with a metal collar]. **Foot** conical, folded, ∅ (91).

Fig. 77. Bowl of goblet 38.3

OWNERSHIP Private collection, The Netherlands (±1929] / H. Schieffer, Amsterdam (1930) / ?

EXHIBITED Tentoonstelling van Oude Kunst, Rijksmuseum, Amsterdam, 1929

REMARK See notes sub 24.1 which carries exactly the same subject (but with an inscription and a different background). This later engraving is more successful, especially as regards the facial expression.

LITERATURE Hudig 1926: xxvii. Anonymous 1929c: 138 (No. 730a). Buckley 1930b: 12 (No. 9), pl. 13; 1930c: 13 (No. 9), pl. 13.

* * *

Fig. 78. Bowl of goblet 39.1   Fig. 79. Bowl of goblet 39.1

39.1 (Figs. 78, 79)
A frontal view of a standing woman with flowers in her hair, wearing flowing
robes which leave the left breast bare. She is holding three very tiny babies
on her right arm while her left hand is stretched out over a garlanded flaming
brazier standing to her left. Her bare right foot is treading on a serpent.
Two billing doves in front of the brazier. Background architectural and with
drapery above which forms a large knot to top left. Design not framed.

INSCRIBED (in single-line script but downstrokes scratched, opposite design):
ô Gevaerts en Albyn, / Uw' Echt moet dúúrzaam zyn; / Gezegent úit den hoogen/
Met welvaart en vermogen, / En onder úw gezin / Zy eendragt, vrede en min.
[Oh, Gevaerts and Albinus, / Your marriage should be lasting; / Blessed heavenly
from above / With prosperity and fortune, / And in your family / Be harmony,
peace and love.]

SIGNED (in single-line script but 'G' scratched, opposite design below
inscription):
F. Greenwood.

GOBLET H 205. **Bowl** pointed round funnel, ∅ 80. **Stem** two knops / slender
baluster with an elongate tear / two teared base knops. **Foot** conical, pontil
mark rather rough, ∅ 82.

OWNERSHIP Deutz van Lennep, Meerenberg estate, south of Heemstede /
A. Vecht, Amsterdam / auction Sotheby, London, 10.XI.1938 (unsold) / Vecht
collection, Amsterdam

EXHIBITED Tentoonstelling van Oude Kunst, Rijksmuseum, Amsterdam,
VII - IX.1936

REMARKS The design is presumably meant to be an allegory of unfailing Love
and Charity. Billing doves are symbolic of lovers' embraces. The brazier is an
attribute of Constancy and alludes to the constancy of the Roman hero Mucius
Scaevola who once thrust his right hand into the flames of an altar fire.
Treading on a snake signifies the vanquishing of evil.
    Exactly the same design was engraved on goblet 40.1.
    The inscribed poem has not been published by Greenwood.

Paulus Gevaerts (1697-1770), once a burgomaster of Dordrecht, married widow Suzanna Catharina Albinus (1703-1741) in December, 1739. She was a daughter of Bernardus Albinus, a medical professor in Leiden, and Suzanna Catharina Ring; her eldest brother Bernhard Siegfried Albinus (1697-1770) was a famous physician and anatomist. When living at Huys-Te-Paauw, south of Wassenaar [later on the residence of Prince Willem Frederik Karel of Orange-Nassau (1797-1881)], she married Leonardus Hoeufft, Seignior of Buttinge and Santvoort [province of Zeeland], in 1729; the husband died after some years. Her second marriage, to Paulus Gevaerts (already widowed twice), did not comply with Greenwood's wish for long duration: Suzanna died on 23 May, 1741, which moved Greenwood to write a poem on her death (1760: 204). - Ten years later, in Dordrecht on 3.X. 1751, Paulus Gevaerts married a fourth wife, Suzanna Adriana Beelaerts.

LITERATURE Buckley 1931: 49 (No. 32), pl. 30. Anonymous 1936a: 155 (No. 768); 1936b: 156 (No. 768). Auction Catalogue Sotheby 1938: 49 (lot 138), fig. 138. Haynes 1944: fig. VI.

* * *

40.1 (Figs. 80 - 83)
Although the goblet itself is not known to be extant, this is the only glass for which the original unpublished design has been found, namely a pen-and-wash drawing in Indian ink, probably by Aart Schouman, with an inscription by Frans Greenwood (Figs. 81 - 83). The design "Een zinnebeelt des huwelyks" [An allegory of marriage] (Greenwood 1760: 78) is similar to that executed on goblet 39.1, q.v. Schouman's original sketch will very likely have been used for both glasses.

EEN ZINNEBEELT DES HUWELYKS.

ô **B**EEFTINGH, ramp noch druk

Stoore ooit uw trougeluk,

Maar heil moet het beftralen

En op u nederdalen.

Smaakt dan in overvloet,

Met fchoone B R O U W E R 't zoet

Der zuivre liefdevlammen,

Tot aanwas uwer ftammen.

Fig. 80. Inscription of goblet 40.1 (Greenwood 1760: 78). [Oh, Beeftingh, may disaster or stress / Never disturb your married bliss, / But Fortune should shine upon it / and descend upon you. / Then, with beautiful Brouwer, / Taste liberally the sweetness / Of the pure flames of love, / Thus proliferating your kin.]

Fig. 81.   Original sketch, probably by Aart Schouman (cf. Fig. 21 on p. 41), for the design on goblet 40.1 [and 39.1].   The engraving on 39.1 is a mirror-image; a smaller (and more detailed) copy will have been made of the design which was then either copperplate-etched or by some means directly transferred on to the bowl of the goblet.

ô BEEFTINGH, ramp noch druk

Stoore ooit uw Troügelük;

Maar heil moet het bestralen

En op U Nederdaalen.

in den Echt vereenigt
den 22: in Junij
1740.

Fig. 82. MS inscription [part] for goblet 40.1 (cf. Fig. 80). - Greenwood added "in den Echt verEenigt / den 22e in Junij / 1740." [joined in marriage / 22nd June / 1740].

REMARKS   Hendrik van Beeftingh (Rotterdam 18.IV.1711 - 10.IX.1797) occupied a variety of official posts, including that of Burgomaster, in the municipality of Rotterdam.   He owned a collection of paintings and drawings and was an amateur draughtsman himself.   On Wednesday 22 June, 1740, he married Adriana Martina Brouwer (Rotterdam 14.V.1721 - 23.IV.1763), a granddaughter of the famous painter Adriaen van der Werff (1659-1722).   Among their children was Elizabeth Catharina (Rotterdam 19.VII.1751 - 18.V.1835) who married, in Rotterdam on 13.VIII.1775, Pieter van IJzendoorn (Rotterdam 11.IV.1749 - 's-Gravenhage 17.XII. 1818, buried in Rotterdam 22.XII.1818); there were seven children.

The original design (Figs. 81 - 83) was discovered by Mr Ch. Thiels, conservator at the Historisch Museum, Rotterdam, among documents relating to the IJzendoorn family.

It may be noted that in 1728 IJzendoorn became affiliated with Sijdervelt through marriage at Simonshaven.   Sijdervelt and Simonshaven are subjects of several poems by Greenwood.

There are numerous interconnections the knowledge of which may be useful when trying to discover for whom or for which occasion a certain glass was engraved.

LITERATURE   Greenwood 1760: 78.

*   *   *

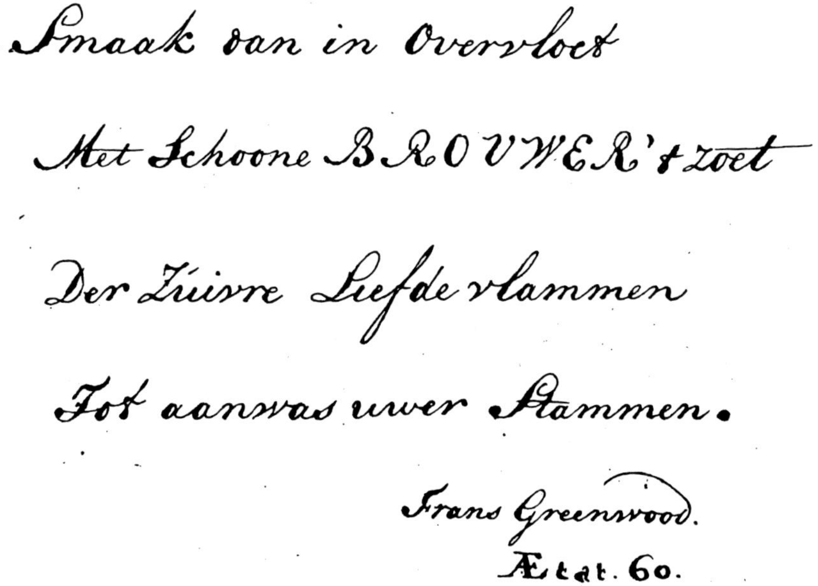

Smaak dan in Overvloed

Met Schoone BROUWER'tzoet

Der Zuivre Liefde vlammen

Tot aanwas uwer Stammen.

Frans Greenwood.

Ætat. 60.

Fig. 83. MS inscription [part] for goblet 40.1 (cf. Fig. 80). - Greenwood added "AEtat. 60.", thereby confirming 1680 as year of birth.

41.1 (Figs. 84 - 86)
A prancing horse in side-view to sinister. Below the body of the horse a hilly landscape in the distance. Trees to the right in the cloudy background which is entirely stippled. The engraving, contained by a thin vertical line to the right, occupies nearly half the circumference but almost the entire height of the bowl.

Fig. 84. A copy of the inscription on goblet 41.1.

Fig. 85. Bowl of goblet 41.1   Fig. 86. Bowl of goblet 41.1

INSCRIBED (in stippled calligraphic capital script with much scrollwork, opposite design - Figs. 84, 85):
V R Y H E I T

SIGNED (in scratched Roman letters but "fecit" in single-line script, below inscription):
1741. F. Greenwood fecit

GOBLET H 212. **Bowl** pointed round funnel, ⌀ 95. **Stem** inverted baluster / central knop / baluster [stem broken below central knop (in the 1940s); repaired with a metal collar]. **Foot** domed, pontil mark fairly rough, ⌀ 91.

OWNERSHIP A. Vecht, Amsterdam / private collection, The Netherlands

REMARK The design is said to be based upon a print by Antonio Tempesta (1555-1630). - For a similar goblet with exactly the same horse and a similar background but without signature, date and inscription, see *41.2. See also 22.1.

LITERATURE van Gelder 1959: fig. 64. Anonymous 1962a: 58 (sub No. 304). Braat 1962: 24, fig. 21.

*   *   *

*41.2 (Figs. 87, 88)
A prancing horse in side-view to sinister. Below the body of the horse a hilly landscape in the distance. Trees to the right in the cloudy background which is entirely stippled. Fruiting orange branches to the left, right and below the design which to the left and right is furthermore flanked by giant grass blades. The design occupies about ¾th the circumference and almost the entire height of the bowl.
    There are engraved lines in the dense parts of plants and of hooves but not in the horse's mane or tail.

SIGNED Neither signed, nor dated.

GOBLET H 251. **Bowl** round funnel, ⌀ 96. **Stem** inverted baluster / central knop / baluster. **Foot** conical, [a 19th-century glass replacement], ⌀ 90.

Fig. 87. Bowl of goblet *41.2

OWNERSHIP   auction Sotheby, London,
30.VII.1957 (£50   - together with a tazza)
/ H. Phillips, London / W. A. Evill /
Fitzwilliam Museum, Cambridge (C.8-1963
- W. A. Evill bequest of 1963)

REMARKS   Cf. 22.1 and 41.1.
Greenwood (1760: 78) referred to a goblet
engraved with "De vryheit verbeelt door
een ongetoomt paert." [Freedom represented by an unbridled horse] with a poem
of six lines which may have been inscribed on the original foot of this glass
(Fig. 88).

LITERATURE   Greenwood 1760: 78.
Auction Catalogue Sotheby 1957: 4 (lot 4).
Anonymous 1962a: 58 (No. 304). Schnitzer
1978: 114 (No. 295), fig. 295.

DE VRYHEIT VERBEELT DOOR EEN ONGE-
TOOMT PAERT.

ô Nederlant , alom vermaert,

Dit vrye en ongetoomde paert

Is 't zinnebeelt van uwe vryheit.

Geen fcheuring breekt den eendragtsbant

Die zulk een heillot houdt in ftant:

Zoo bloei den Staat in vrede en blyheit.

Fig. 88.   Inscription which was perhaps engraved on the foot, now lost, of
goblet *41.2 (Greenwood 1760: 78). [Oh, Netherlands, universally renowned, /
This free and unbridled horse / Is the symbol of your freedom. / No discord
breaks the bond of unity / Which maintains its prosperity: / Thus flourishes
the State in peace and joy.]

*   *   *

EEN HARINGVERKOOPSTER.

ô Zegenryke Visfchery,

Wat fchaft ge ons jaarlyks lekkerny!

Uw' haring , die geliefde visch,

Wekt eet en drinklust aan den disch,

Fig. 89. Inscription which perhaps was engraved on the foot, now lost, of goblet 42.1 (Greenwood 1760: 76). [Oh, greatly blessed fishery, / What delicacies you provide each year ! / Your herring, that beloved fish, / Whets one's appetite for food and drink.]

42.1 (Figs. 89, 90)
A half-length portrait of a woman, face ¾ to sinister, wearing a bonnet, earrings and a peasant dress, holding up in her left hand a half full roemer and with her right hand a herring by its tail. She is shown in an arched window frame with fruiting vines flanking the sides; drapery in the background to the right and a table-cover draped over the sill.
Hair partly in line-work; lines also in foot of roemer, in table-cover, in fringe of right sleeve, in tendrils of vine and, rather indistinctly, in the dense part of the frame on the right. There are two inadvertent scratches over the frame to the right of the roemer.

SIGNED (in stippled letters, opposite design low down on bowl):
F. Greenwood / (in scratched script, between small scrolls) fecit 1742

GOBLET H 287. **Bowl** round funnel, ø 99. **Stem** inverted baluster / central knop / baluster [the knops and most of the remaining part of the stem enveloped in 19th-century parcel-gilt silver mounts, embossed and chased and with a Dutch control mark]. **Foot** a metal replacement [similar to the stem mounts], ø 101.

OWNERSHIP auction Sotheby, London, 3.VI.1974 (£4,200) / A. C. R. Dreesmann

REMARKS The subject is reminiscent of a fish-seller painted by Gerard Dou (1613-1675) (cf. W. Martin, 1902, *Gerard Dou*: No. 41 [= No. 257 in the Dutch edition]).
Greenwood (1760: 76) referred to a goblet which he had engraved with "Een haringverkoopster" [A herring saleswoman] with a poem (Fig. 89) which was perhaps engraved by Greenwood on the now missing foot of the glass. There are two other goblets with a herring seller (*44.1, 44.2) but those do not include a roemer of wine to which the poem alludes ("food and drink").
This goblet, or *44.1, may be the "haringwijfje" [herring wife] owned in the middle of the 18th century by bachelor Pauls Schepers (one of the Directors of the United Dutch East India Company), Rotterdam, who bequeathed it (together with two other Greenwood glasses: 46.8 or 47.1, 48.3) in his testaments of 27.II.1755, 31.VII.1755 and 7.III.1757 (Gemeentelijke Archiefdienst, Rotterdam:

Fig. 90. Bowl of goblet 42.1   Fig. 91. Bowl of goblet 42.2

O.N.A. 2282:30, 2283:21, 2286:32) to his second cousin Gerard Schepers (Rotterdam 1720-1757; married Jacoba Prins 1746) who, however, died on 23.III.1757, shortly before the death of Pauls Schepers on 13.IV.1757.

LITERATURE Greenwood 1760: 76. Auction Catalogue Sotheby 1974: 24 (lot 115), frontispiece. Davis, F. 1974: 142, fig. 1. Edelstein 1974: 439, pl. [part]. Wellensiek & Keyszelitz 1974: 264.

*   *   *

42.2 (Fig. 91)
A half-length portrait of a smiling man, face $\frac{3}{4}$ to dexter, wearing a slashed cap decorated with two ostrich feathers; his jacket is also slashed [see Remarks sub 24.1]. He is holding a half full roemer in his left hand. Background entirely stippled with a bough of a tree to the left and silhouetted trees in the distance. To the right the design is contained by a vertical stippled thin frame line.
Lines in feathers; hair stippled over fine lines.

SIGNED (in scratched Roman letters, in right-hand lower corner of design): Frans / Greenwood. / 1742.

GOBLET H 216. **Bowl** round funnel / bucket, $\emptyset$ 95. **Stem** knop / angular knop / knop / inverted baluster / double base knop. **Foot** rather flat, pontil mark fairly smooth, $\emptyset$ 97 [a piece missing].

OWNERSHIP E. van Rijckevorsel, Rotterdam / Museum Boymans - van Beuningen, Rotterdam (141 - presented by E. van Rijckevorsel in 1928)

REMARK Buckley (1930) considered the engraving to be "distinctly below the standard of the work on any of the other [Greenwood] glasses, for which reason I do not feel assured that it was executed by Greenwood." It is difficult to understand and to justify Buckley's opinion. Greenwood engraved the same design three years later (45.1 - not known to Buckley) but somewhat less successfully.

LITERATURE Zwartendijk 1919: 56. Hudig 1926: xxvii. Buckley 1930b: 12 (No. 10), pl. 14; 1930c: 13 (No. 10), pl. 14. Braat 1962: 48.

*   *   *

Fig. 92. Bowl of goblet 43.1   Fig. 93. Bowl of goblet 43.3

43.1 (Fig. 92)

Two rather angry-looking men, each wearing a cap, in a room bending over a games board on a small low trestle-table, playing 'verkeeren' or trick-track. The player standing behind the table is about to move a piece with his left hand, the other man is seated and holding dice in his right fist. A third man, wearing a beret, seen in the stippled background between the two players, is leaving the room through a door. A shadow falls partly on to the board, to the right of which a tobacco pipe. On the background wall, to the left, a picture below which in small open lettering "Droevig / verlies" ("es" botched) [a sad loss] below which a placard in three columns starting with a large initial A. To the right a slate. Design not framed.

Lines in caps and in some other objects.

SIGNED (in single-line script, below design):

F. Greenwood / fec.^{t} 1743.

GOBLET **H 216**. **Bowl** bucket-shaped round funnel, ϕ 94. **Stem** annular knop / angular knop / knop / inverted baluster / base knop. **Foot** conical, pontil mark smooth, ϕ 96.

OWNERSHIP Deutz van Lennep, Meerenberg estate, south of Heemstede / A. Vecht, Amsterdam / auction Sotheby, London, 10.XI.1938 (unsold) / Vecht collection, Amsterdam

EXHIBITED Tentoonstelling van Oude Kunst, Rijksmuseum, Amsterdam, VII - IX. 1936 / Fourth international Exhibition C.I.N.O.A. "Art dealer and collector", Historisch Museum, Amsterdam, 27.III - 31.V.1970

REMARK Trick-track is a form of backgammon in which both pegs and pieces are used.

LITERATURE Buckley 1931: 49 (No. 28), pl. 26. Anonymous 1936a: 155 (No. 767); 1936b: 156 (No. 767). Auction Catalogue Sotheby 1938: 49 (lot 139), fig. 139. Glerum 1970: 67 (No. 195), fig. on p. 266.

*   *   *

TWEE AAN 'T VERKEERBORT.

't Verkeeren neemt altoos een' keer,
Dan geeft het en dan neemt het weêr.
't Gaat even zoo met 's waerelts goet:
Een onophoudlyke ebbe en vloedt.

Fig. 94. Inscription on goblet *43.2 (Greenwood 1760: 77). [When playing trick-track one's luck fluctuates, / Now one wins, then one loses. / The same applies to wordly possessions: / A constant ebbing and flowing.]

*43.2 (Fig. 94)
According to Greenwood himself (1760: 77), he engraved a goblet with "Twee aan 't verkeerbort" [Two playing trick-track]. The design may be assumed to be similar to that of the previous goblet (43.1) but now supposedly with the poem published by Greenwood.

INSCRIBED (see Fig. 94)

OWNERSHIP This glass has not been recorded since 1760 and, if still extant, its depository is unknown.

REMARK The verse recalls the calligraphic inscription diamond-point engraved by François Crama on a bulbous blue bottle in 1687: "Het werelds goet is eb en vloed" [The world's fortunes ebb and flow].

LITERATURE Greenwood 1760: 77.

*   *   *

43.3 (Fig. 93)
A half-length portrait of a bareheaded jolly man, face $\frac{3}{4}$ to dexter, with tousled hair, dressed in 17th-century attire with open neck; he is holding a berkemeier in his left hand. Silhouetted trees in stippled background.
    Stippling rather coarse.

SIGNED (in scratched Roman letters ('fect' in single-line script), opposite design):
F. Greenwood fec.[t] / 1743.

GOBLET H 207. **Bowl** pointed round funnel, ϕ 91. **Stem** six-knopped, the upper three forming a bobbin. **Foot** rather high conical, ϕ 92.

OWNERSHIP D. H. de Castro, Amsterdam / Koninklijk Oudheidkundig Genootschap, Amsterdam (KOG 1552 - D. H. de Castro Dz. legacy of 1890) / Rijksmuseum, Amsterdam (KOG loan since 1896)

REMARK The sitter is evidently the same as the one on goblet 43.4 and the engraving may therefore be assumed to be based on a painting by Arie de Vois.

LITERATURE de Castro 1883: 280. Anonymous 1891: 11. Pareau 1896: 23-24 (No. 2). Pazaurek 1902: 26, footnote. Schmidt 1914: 14. Hudig 1926: xxvii. Buckley 1930b: 13 (No. 13), pl. 17; 1930c: 14 (No. 13), pl. 17. Hudig, C. J. 1955: fig. 87. Braat 1962: 16.

Fig. 95. Bowl of goblet 43.4   Fig. 96. Bowl of goblet 43.6

43.4 (Fig. 95)
A half-length portrait of a hatted man, face ¾ to dexter, dressed in 17th-century attire, holding a Passglas in his right hand. A bough of a tree to the left and other trees silhouetted in the stippled background.

SIGNED (in finely scratched Roman letters, 'fecit' in single-line script, opposite design):
F. Greenwood / fecit 1743

GOBLET H 204. **Bowl** pointed round funnel, ⌀ 94. **Stem** a bobbin of three ball knops / annular knop / base knop. **Foot** high conical, ⌀ 84.

OWNERSHIP Private museum of Repelaer van Spijkenisse, Haarlem /
H. P. van de Wall Repelaer, Dubbeldam / H. van de Wall Repelaer, Dubbeldam /
private collection, The Netherlands

EXHIBITED Tentoonstelling Het Hollandsche interieur in de XVIIIe eeuw, Rijksmuseum, Amsterdam, 14.III - 3.V.1931 / Herdenkingstentoonstelling Aart Schouman, Dordrecht's Museum, Dordrecht, 27.VIII - 2.X.1960

REMARK A painting by Arie de Vois (1632-1680) in the Rijksmuseum, Amsterdam [inv. A457] shows a merry musician with a violin under his left arm and quite a large roemer in his right hand. If that picture was the original for the engraving, then the design was modified substantially. Arie de Vois painted the same man also in the guise of "The smoker" (Rijksmuseum, Amsterdam, inv. C260). Cf. remark sub 43.3.

LITERATURE Buckley 1930b: 12 (No. 12), pl. 16; 1930c: 13 (No. 12), pl. 16.
Anonymous 1931: 18 (No. 49). Bol 1960: 94 (No. 183).

*   *   *

43.5
A warrior wearing a cuirass.

SIGNED F. Greenwood fec. 1743

OWNERSHIP van Hoëvell Sr (? Jacob Diederik Baron van Hoëvell [28.VIII.1814-11.XII.1885], rector of the Latin School in Dordrecht) / van Hoëvel Jr [in 1907]

Fig. 97. Bowl of goblet *44.1   Fig. 98. Bowl of goblet 44.2

REMARK   This engraving, only known from a short published note, could be very similar to the one on goblet 46.7 which shows a fearsome-looking man wearing a breastplate.

LITERATURE   van Hoëvell 1907: 114.

*   *   *

43.6 (Fig. 96)
A half-length portrait of a hooded woman, almost full-face slightly to sinister, seated on a chair at a table and holding a small glass in her left hand while apparently stirring in it with an object held in her right hand.   Below the hands the wide dress-sleeves [not a bag].   On the table a lighted candle, a sheet of paper and a rectangular inkstand with a quill in the inkpot.   Background stippled with some drapery to top left.   The design framed by an ovoid thin stippled line.

SIGNED   (in scratched Roman letters, "fect" in single-line script, below design):
F. Greenwood fec.^{t} / 1743.

GOBLET   **H** 230. **Bowl** pointed round funnel, ϕ 97. **Stem** three knops the middle of which teared and annular / teared inverted baluster / teared base knop.
Foot conical, ϕ 99.

OWNERSHIP   Graaf A. van Rechteren Limpurg / A. Vecht, Amsterdam / auction Sotheby, London, 10.XI.1938 (unsold) / Vecht collection, Amsterdam

EXHIBITED   Tentoonstelling Oude Kunst, Rijksmuseum, Amsterdam, VII - IX.1936

REMARKS   Pelliot (1936) noted that this engraving is a mirror-image of a work by Caspar Netscher (1639-1684) [which in the catalogue raisonné of Netscher's paintings by Hofstede de Groot (1913) is probably No. 413g (p. 275): Portrait of a lady seated at a table.] - Cornelis Ploos van Amstel (1726-1798) made an undated [after 1756] mezzotint which he presumably based on a print similar to the one copied by Greenwood (Laurentius et al. 1980: 280, No. 57, fig.).

LITERATURE   Buckley 1930b: 12 (No. 11), pl. 15; 1930c: 13 (No. 11), pl. 15. Anonymous 1936a: 155 (No. 769); 1936b: 156 (No. 769). Pelliot 1936: 88. Auction Catalogue Sotheby 1938: 48 (lot 137), fig. 137. Anonymous 1954: 81, fig. Berryer 1954: 38.

Fig. 99. Bowl of goblet *44.1   Fig. 100. Bowl of goblet 44.2

*44.1 (Figs. 97, 99)
A half-length figure of a fisherwoman looking ¾ to sinister with a downward gaze, wearing a wide-brimmed hat and a low-cut bodice exposing cleavage. She is holding with her right hand an oval metal platter with zigzag border decoration, on which a herring; with her left hand she is holding a pendent herring by its tail. To the left of the woman on a table a spray of two flowering lilies and one in bud in a jug standing behind a pail of herrings. Background entirely in stipple, plain.

SIGNED (in script, scratched lines with small flourishes from F, G, d and f, opposite design low down on bowl):
Frans Greenwood fecit.

GOBLET **H** 243. **Bowl** round funnel, ∅ 89. **Stem** weak knop / angular knop / knop / inverted baluster / base knop [the knops and the remaining parts of the stem were at some time encased with 19th-century parcel-gilt mounts, embossed and chased and with a Dutch control mark (these mounts were removed in 1974)]. **Foot** a metal ornamental replacement, similar to the now discarded stem mounts. The metal mounts slightly less elaborate than those on glass 42.1.

OWNERSHIP auction Sotheby, London, 3.VI.1974 (£2,500) / Viscount Newport, Earl of Bradford, Weston Park, Shifnal / auction Christie, London, 4.VI.1985 (£32,400) / H. Hübner, Würzburg / ?

EXHIBITED Weston Park, Shifnal, 1983 / Christie's, Amsterdam, 23-29.IV.1985 / Haus der Kunst (31. Deutsche Kunst- und Antiquitäten-Messe), München, 24.X - 2.XI.1986

REMARK See notes sub 42.1 and 44.2 (the latter very similar).

LITERATURE Auction Catalogue Sotheby 1974: 26 (lot 116), fig. 116. Riley 1975: fig. 5. Auction Catalogue Christie 1985a: 62-63 (lot 30), 2 figs. Davis, F. 1985: 215, fig. 1. Watts 1986: 2 figs. on p. 87.

*   *   *

44.2 (Figs. 51, 98, 100)
A half-length figure of a fisherwoman looking ¾ to sinister with a downward gaze, wearing a wide-brimmed hat and a low-cut bodice exposing cleavage. She is holding with her right hand an oval metal platter on which a herring while her left hand is holding a pendent herring by its tail. Background entirely in stipple: a wall with lower part of a window and to the right a garden urn in which some plants, as well as two tree trunks and other vegetation. The design, which is not framed, occupies a little over half the circumference of the bowl.
Stippling quite fine; here and there some short lines.

SIGNED (in Roman letters of short scratches, "fecit" in single-line script, opposite design):
Frans Greenwood fecit / 1744

GOBLET H 247. **Bowl** round funnel, ∅ 92. **Stem** inverted baluster / central knop / baluster / base knop. **Foot** fairly high conical, folded, pontil mark rather rough, ∅ 98.

OWNERSHIP Members of the Vriesendorp family - who originally came to Dordrecht from Westphalia. Already in 1690 mention was made of a sugar refinery of Vriesendorp & Co. which was in operation until 1732, with Hendrik Vriesendorp as director from 1701 until his death in 1728. Shortly after his death his widow, Aletta Vriesendorp née Melanen, bought a house in Steegoversloot, the street in which Frans Greenwood (who was the same age as Aletta) eventually came to live. It may be assumed that they knew each other well. In 1733, Greenwood's friend Aart Schouman painted portraits of Aletta, aged 53, and of her son Hendrik, aged 18. Aletta, who died in 1760, probably became the first owner of this Greenwood goblet [one of his best engravings] which, remarkably, remained in the Vriesendorp family until 1985 / Museum Mr Simon van Gijn, Dordrecht (16485 - purchased in 1985)

EXHIBITED Tentoonstelling Flonkering van de wijn [Sparkling of wine], Museum Mr Simon van Gijn, Dordrecht, 28.X.1967 - 8.I.1968 / Tentoonstelling Diep in het Glas kijken, Museum Mr Simon van Gijn, Dordrecht, 17.XII.1987 - 27.III.1988

REMARKS Interestingly, the present location of the goblet in a way perpetuates the Vriesendorp connection as the late Simon van Gijn's wife was Cornelia Agatha Vriesendorp whom he had married in 1864.
    Fishwives of Scheveningen, nr 's-Gravenhage (and presumably elsewhere) used to wear wide-brimmed hats such as the one depicted on this and the previous glass. On the flattened top they carried wide flat fish-baskets; the wide brim, effectively an umbrella, protecting the wearer against drips from the basket. As early as 1654 the Dutch poet Jacob Cats (1577-1660) published a poem "On a woman from Scheveningen carrying a basket of fish on her head".
    The three Greenwood fishwives (42.1, *44.1, 44.2) have in common that each is holding a herring by its tail. In Dutch painting such a display has been interpreted as having licentious implications but Greenwood may not have had such symbolism in mind. His poem, quoted sub 42.1 (Fig. 89), only sings praise of purely epicurean delights. It is interesting, though, that on the previous glass (*44.1) Greenwood added lilies, a symbol of purity. [A painting of a woman selling fish, by Adriaen van der Werff, likewise includes a spray of lilies.]
    The herring industry or the 'Groote Visscherij' [Great Fishery] has played a very important role in the Dutch economy especially since the 17th century.

LITERATURE Ruempol 1967: 16 (No. 54), 1 pl. van Roosendaal 1967: 219, fig. 1. Smit 1982a, b: fig. 1. Anonymous 1985a: 1. Domela Nieuwenhuis 1986: 30, pl. p. 31. Liefkes 1987: 57 (No. 67), 2 figs.

Fig. 101. Bowl of goblet 45.1

Fig. 102. Bowl of goblet 46.1

45.1 (Figs. 52, 101)
A half-length portrait of a smiling man, face ¾ to dexter, wearing a slashed cap adorned with two ostrich feathers, and a jacket which is likewise slashed. He is holding a half full roemer in his left hand. Background entirely in stipple with a bough of a tree to the left and silhouetted trees in the distance.

SIGNED (in Roman letters of scratched stipples, 'Fecit' in script, opposite design):
F. Greenwood Fecit / 1745

GOBLET H 250. **Bowl** round funnel, ⌀ 94. **Stem** inverted baluster / central knop / baluster. **Foot** fairly high conical, folded, pontil mark fairly rough, ⌀ 98.

OWNERSHIP auction Sotheby Mak van Waay, Amsterdam, 1.X.1984 (Hfl. 129,920)/ J. A. Limburg, Brouwershaven / auction Sotheby, London, 13.VII.1987 (£35,200) / Private collection, England

REMARK This is the same subject as that on goblet 42.2 but executed somewhat less successfully, notably as regards the eyes.

LITERATURE Auction Catalogue Sotheby Mak van Waay 1984: 20 (lot 95), pl. p. 21. Anonymous 1985b: 100, fig. Auction Catalogue Sotheby 1987: 40-41, (lot 202), col. pl. p. 41. Fogg 1987: 293, col. fig.

*   *   *

46.1 (Figs. 102, 103)
A lyre between two laurel branches against a blank background.
    The engraving is rather coarse and not of fine quality; the lyre is comparatively sparsely stippled and the lettering lacks precision. The scratched lines representing the strings of the lyre are spalled a good deal. The work was perhaps carried out hurriedly which could explain the rather unfinished appearance of the engraving.

INSCRIBED (in scratched script, opposite design, with large flourishes flowing from the first letter and trailing from the last):
Poësis.

SIGNED (in Roman letters, 'fect' in script, within lower scroll of inscription):
F. Greenwood / fec^t 1746

Fig. 103. Bowl of goblet 46.1   Fig. 104. Bowl of goblet 46.2

GOBLET H 196. Bowl round funnel, ∅ 82. **Stem** knop / knop / inverted baluster/ ball base knop (a single elongate tear connecting second knop with baluster knop). **Foot** conical, ∅ (82).

OWNERSHIP Gemeentemuseum, Arnhem (2310)

REMARK The lyre, a stringed instrument of ancient Greece, is the attribute of Apollo and therefore also of Poetry personified, as well as of Erato, the Muse of lyric poetry. Engraved in homage to Poetry, this glass was perhaps presented by Greenwood to a fellow-poet or to a literary society.

LITERATURE Hudig 1926: xxvii. Buckley 1930b: 13 (No. 17), pl. 21; 1930c: 14 (No. 17), pl. 21. Braat 1962: 26.

*   *   *

46.2 (Fig. 104)
A semi-pendent full-blown rose with some leaves and to the left a small Lepido-pterous insect [a non-existent species]. Background blank.

INSCRIBED (in scratched script, opposite design):
Geen Rozen / zonder doornen [No roses without thorns]

SIGNED (in scratched Roman letters, "fect" in single-line script, below the inscription):
F. Greenwood / fec^t 1746

OWNERSHIP Bayerische Landesgewerbeanstalt, Nürnberg (G 3006 - obtained before 1884)

REMARK The adage on this goblet - meaning: no pleasures without displeasures (or perhaps implying that even the most perfect woman is not without imperfect-ions) - is an old one and known in various languages. - It looks as if Green-wood gave vent to feelings by engraving a rose on no fewer than five glasses, two of them with the French version Nulle Roze sans épine (46.3, 46.4) while on the other two (49.1, *49.2) an inscription was apparently superfluous.

LITERATURE Friedrich 1884: 227-228. Garnier 1886: 299. Pazaurek 1902: 26. Schmidt 1914: 14. Hudig 1926: xxvii. Buckley 1930b: 12 (No. 15), pl. 19; 1930c: 14 (No. 15), pl. 19. Berryer 1954: 40.

Fig. 105. Bowl of goblet 46.3   Fig. 106. Bowl of goblet 46.4

46.3 (Fig. 105)
A pendent full-blown rose with stalk and some leaves to the right. Background blank.

INSCRIBED (in scratched script, below design):
Nulle Roze sans épine [No rose without a thorn]

SIGNED (in scratched Roman letters, "fecit" in single-line script, opposite design):
F. Greenwood / fecit 1746

GOBLET H 205. **Bowl** round funnel, ⌀ 82. **Stem** small knop / baluster / teared ball knop / inverted baluster / base knop. **Foot** domed, ⌀ (86)

OWNERSHIP auction Mensing, Amsterdam, 6.X.1938 (Hfl. 300) / Huisman / W. J. H. Mulier, 's-Gravenhage / Gemeentemuseum, 's-Gravenhage (OG-5-1954 - W. J. H. Mulier legacy of 1954)

REMARK See note sub 46.2. Engraving and goblet virtually identical with that of 46.4 but the decoration on the latter not quite as well executed.

LITERATURE Auction Catalogue Mensing 1938: 29 (lot 344). van Gelder 1955: pl. XXX(3). Jansen 1962: 115, fig. 213. van Gelder & Jansen 1969: 77, fig. 213.

*   *   *

46.4 (Fig. 106)
A pendent full-blown rose with stalk and some leaves to the right. Background blank.

INSCRIBED (in scratched script, opposite design):
Nulle Roze sans épine [No rose without a thorn]

SIGNED (in scratched Roman letters, "fecit" in single-line script, below design):
F. Greenwood / fecit 1746

GOBLET H 200. **Bowl** round funnel, ⌀ (81). **Stem** small knop / baluster / teared ball knop / inverted baluster / base knop. **Foot** domed, ⌀ (84).

OWNERSHIP G. van der Schoot [in 1930] / ?

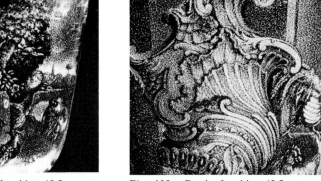

Fig. 107. Bowl of goblet 46.5   Fig. 108. Bowl of goblet 46.5

REMARK   See notes sub 46.2 and 46.3.

LITERATURE   Buckley 1930b: 13 (No. 16), pl. 20;   1930c: 14 (No. 16), pl. 20.
Haynes 1944: fig. VII. Berryer 1954: 41.

*   *   *

46.5 (Figs. 48, 107, 108)
A large rococo ornament to the left of a pastoral scene with nine different
birds such as guinea fowl, peacock, lapwing, which are all on the ground; a cock
standing on a stone and a columbine bird aflight.   Trees, bushes and the silhouetted church tower of a village in the background which is all in stipple.

SIGNED   (in scratched script letters, "fecit" in single-line script, some of the
letters with flourishes; opposite design on lower half of bowl):
F. Greenwood fecit / 1746

GOBLET   H 240. **Bowl** round funnel, ⌀ 90. **Stem** angular knop / inverted baluster
with tears in knop / base knop. **Foot** conical, ⌀ 102.

OWNERSHIP   A. Churchill Ltd (who obtained the goblet in 1947) / J. Strauss,
State College, Pennsylvania / The Corning Museum of Glass, Corning, N. Y.
(79.3.290 - J. Strauss bequest of 1979)

REMARK   The engraving on this glass may have been inspired by a picture
by Greenwood's friend Aart Schouman who is well-known as a painter of numerous
avian subjects.

LITERATURE   Anonymous 1947: 13, figs. V, Va. Strauss 1955: 99 (No. 246),
fig. 246. Buechner 1957: 46, fig. 12a. Lloyd 1969: fig. p. 142. Anonymous 1980:
109 (No. 35), fig. 35. Lanmon 1980: 314, pl. IX [part].

*   *   *

Fig. 109. Bowl of goblet *46.6   Fig. 110. Bowl of goblet *46.6

*46.6 (Figs. 109 - 111)
A nude Bacchus, face ¾ to dexter, wearing a crown of vine leaves, seated on a
barrel from which wine is flowing into a wide bowl. Bacchus is holding a bunch
of grapes with his right hand, resting it on the barrel. Naked Silenus, face ¾ to
sinister, is sitting behind Bacchus, holding him round the chest. To the left a
standing bare-bosomed female figure, a Maenad, who with both hands is holding
up a tambourine while turning her head to look at a Satyr behind her. To the
left of the Maenad the head and neck, in profile to dexter, of a donkey as well
as a nude Bacchante who is pouring wine from a bulbous vessel into a wide
shallow glass held by yet another Satyr seated, in back view, on the ground.
A large tree to the left of this scene. A grazing goat, symbolising Lust, facing
to sinister, to the right of the barrel. Background in stipple, with foliage and
trees in the distance. The design occupies the entire circumference of the bowl.

INSCRIBED (mostly in single-line script, some doubling of lines in capitals;
on a wall, opposite Bacchus):
Het druivenbloet, / Dat lieflyk zoet, / Noemt Salomon een spottir [recte: spot-
ter]. / Die 't gulzig drinkt, / En brast en klinkt, / Wort vroeg berooit en zotter.
Cf. Fig. 111. [The blood of grapes, / That lovely sweet, / Which Salomon calls
a mocker. / He who drinks it greedily, / And revels and clinks, / Soon becomes
indigent and more foolish.]

SIGNED (in single-line script with some slight scrolls from G, d and f; below
inscription):

F: Greenwood f:^t

GOBLET H 241. **Bowl** round funnel, ⌀ 106. **Stem** teared ball knop / weak
knop / single-teared inverted baluster / single-teared base knop. **Foot** domed,
folded, pontil mark fairly rough, ⌀ 104.

OWNERSHIP R. Bernal, London / auction Christie, London, 20.IV.1855 (£4) /
G. S. Nicholson, London / auction Christie, London, 19.II.1858 / Felix Slade,
London / British Museum, London (S.903 - F. Slade bequest of 1868)

EXHIBITED Masterpieces of Glass, British Museum, London, VIII - IX.1968.

EEN BAGCHENAAL.

H et druivenbloet,

Dat lieflyk zoet,

Noemt Salomon een fpotter.

Die 't gulzig drinkt,

En brast en klinkt,

Wordt vroeg berooit en zotter,

Fig. 111. Inscription on goblet *46.6. (Greenwood 1760: 76).

REMARKS   Cf. goblet 30.1. - Greenwood (1760) published the engraved poem, giving it the title "Een Bagchenaal" [A Bacchanal] (Fig. 111).

Red wine was sometimes called 'the blood of grapes' because of its colour and no doubt because it was a more agreeable drink than real blood which used to be imbibed at ceremonial sacrifices of yore. At certain religious services red wine is still being taken as representing the blood of Christ.

The phrase "Noemt Salomon een spotter" is based on the Old Testament, The Proverbs [of Solomon] 20 : 1 - "De wijn is een spotter, de drank luidruchtig; Onwijs is hij, die zich er aan te buiten gaat." [Wine is a mocker, strong drink is raging: And whosoever is deceived thereby is not wise.] - Willem Jacobszoon van Heemskerk calligraphically inscribed "De wyn is een spotter" on a green roemer in 1681.

LITERATURE   Greenwood 1760: 76. Auction Catalogue Christie 1855: 264 (lot 3244). Bohn 1857, 1862, 1876: 324 (No. 3244). Auction Catalogue Christie 1858: 5 (lot 46). Slade 1871: 158 (No. 903), fig. 258. de Castro 1883: 280. Dillon 1907: 297. Schmidt 1914: 14. Hudig 1926: xxvii. Buckley 1930b: 14 (No. 24), pl. 28; 1930c: 15 (No. 24), pl. 28. Honey 1946: 10, 132-133. Anonymous 1968: 169, fig. [5]. Tait 1968: 172, fig. 241a, b. Savage 1973, 1975: fig. p. 41. Coppen-Gardner 1975: fig. [6].

*   *   *

46.7 (Fig. 112)

A half-length full-face portrait of a wide-eyed, rather fearsome-looking man wearing a plumed cap and a breastplate and holding the hilt of a sword or a dagger in his right hand. Background stippled, to the left the pedestal of a column.

SIGNED   (in scratched Roman letters, "fecit" in single-line script, opposite design):

F. Greenwood fecit / 1746

GOBLET H 250. **Bowl** round funnel, ⌀ (91). **Stem** inverted baluster / central knop / baluster / prebasal knop. **Foot** conical, folded, ⌀ (103).

OWNERSHIP H. Brown, Aldbury nr Tring/ auction Sotheby, London, 14.XI.1947 (£350) / C. Davis, London / The Corning Museum of Glass, Corning, N. Y. (50.2.10)

REMARK Cf. goblet 43.5 which may have a similar, if not identical, engraving.

LITERATURE Auction Catalogue Sotheby 1947b: 6 (lot 228), pl. XII fig. 228. Winchester 1955: 62, fig. XI. Steenberg 1958: fig. 129. Davis, D. C. 1964: fig. 71. Burton 1969: fig. 54. Davis, D. C. 1973: fig. b p. 444. Anonymous 1974: fig. 90. Gardner 1979: fig. 42. Charleston 1980: 155, pl. 69.

Fig. 112. Bowl of goblet 46.7

* * *

46.8 (Fig. 113)
A half-length figure of a man, face $\frac{3}{4}$ to sinister, wearing a floppy cap, holding a clay-pipe with his right hand to the flame of a candle held in the left one. A dish candle-holder standing to the left. Background stippled. The scene within a simple frame, with some drapery to top left.

SIGNED (in scratched Roman letters, "fecit" in single-line script, a small scroll below the date; opposite design on base of bowl):
F. Greenwood / fecit 1746

GOBLET H 250. **Bowl** round funnel, ⌀ 95. **Stem** inverted baluster / central knop / baluster / ball base knop. **Foot** rather flat, folded broadly, pontil mark smooth, ⌀ 108.

OWNERSHIP J. A. Smits van Nieuwerkerk, Dordrecht / Museum für Kunst und Gewerbe, Hamburg [already in 1894]

EXHIBITED Tentoonstelling van voor Nederland belangrijke Oudheden en Merkwaardigheden, &c., Delft, VII - VIII.1863

REMARK See note sub goblet 47.1.

LITERATURE Anonymous 1863: 93 (No. 2271). Brinckmann 1894: 585. Pazaurek 1902: 26. Schmidt 1914: 14. Anonymous 1921: 32. Hudig 1926: xxvii. Buckley 1930b: 13 (No. 14), pl. 18; 1930c: 14 (No. 14), pl. 18. Kämpfer & Beyer 1966: 282, fig. 138. Weiss 1968: frontispiece, fig. 77; 1966, 1971, 1972: fig. p. 174; 1980: fig. 77.

* * *

47.1 (Figs. 114, 115)
A half-length figure of a man, face $\frac{3}{4}$ to sinister, wearing a floppy cap, holding a clay-pipe with his right hand to the flame of a candle held in the left one. Background stippled, with some drapery and, to the right, another man, wearing a hat.

Fig. 113. Bowl of goblet 46.8   Fig. 114. Bowl of goblet 47.1

INSCRIBED (in single-line script, except for the capitals, on the foot in two concentric lines):
Gelyk de rook in dunne lucht / Verdwynt en ylings heenen vlucht / Verlaat allengs de veege ziel / Haar zwakke en brooze levenskiel / F. G. - Cf. Fig. 115. [Just as smoke rarefies in the air / And vanishes rapidly, / So a doomed soul imperceptibly leaves / Its weak and frail vessel of life. / F. G.]

SIGNED (in single-line script, opposite design):
F. Greenwood fecit Anno 1747

GOBLET H 205. **Bowl** pointed round funnel, ϕ (86). **Stem** two knops / inverted baluster / base knop. **Foot** domed, ϕ (80).

OWNERSHIP J. A. Baron van der Heim van Duyvendijke, 's-Gravenhage [seen by J. van Lennep and J. ter Gouw in the 1860s] / Gemeentemuseum, 's-Gravenhage (OG-34-1930 - van der Heim legacy of 1930)

EXHIBITED Tentoonstelling van voor Nederland belangrijke Oudheden en Merkwaardigheden, &c., Delft, VII - VIII.1863

REMARKS Greenwood published the engraved poem in 1760 with the heading "Een tabakrooker" [A tobacco smoker] (Fig. 115).
Either this glass or 46.8, which shows exactly the same smoker, may be the "tabakrooker" [tobacco smoker] owned in the middle of the 18th century by bachelor Pauls Schepers. He bequeathed it (together with two other Greenwood glasses: 42.1 and 48.3) in his testaments of 27.II.1755, 31.VII.1755 and 7.III.1757 (Gemeentelijke Archiefdienst, Rotterdam: O.N.A. 2282:30, 2283:21, 2286:32) to his second cousin Gerard Schepers (Rotterdam 1720-1757; married Jacoba Prins 1746) who, however, died on 23.III.1757, shortly before the death of Pauls Schepers on 13.IV.1757. The goblet may thereafter have passed into the Gevaerts family who also belonged to Greenwood's circle of friends. Maria Arnoudina Gevaerts, a daughter of Paulus Gevaerts, married Jacob van der Heim, a burgomaster of Rotterdam, in Dordrecht on 27 July, 1749. Among their descendants are Barons van der Heim van Duyvendijke.
Van Lennep & ter Gouw (1869) commented that the rather gloomy sentiment expressed in the poem would make one hesitant either to light a pipe or to drink from this goblet.

EEN TABAKROOKER.

Gelyk de rook in dunne lucht
Verdwynt, en ylings heenen vlucht,
Verlaat allengs de veege ziel
Haar zwakke en brooze levenskiel.

Fig. 115. Inscription on goblet 47.1. (Greenwood 1760: 77).

LITERATURE Greenwood 1760: 77. Anonymous 1863: 158 (No. 3840). J. C. K. 1865: 299. van Lennep & ter Gouw 1869: 241. Buckley 1931: 49 (No. 31), pl. 29. van Gelder 1932: 264, fig. 11. Schlosser 1956: fig. 166. Braat 1962: 30. Jansen 1962: 115, fig. 215. Schlosser 1965, 1977: fig. 164.

* * *

47.2 (Fig. 116)
A floral decor composed of budding roses, chrysanthemums and a tulip, also a small unidentifiable Lepidopterous insect, a ringlet butterfly at rest and a damselfly. The design occupies the entire circumference of the bowl.

SIGNED (in scratched Roman letters, "fect" in single-line script, below rose buds):
F. Greenwood / fec^t 1747

GOBLET H 250. **Bowl** round funnel, ⌀ 95. **Stem** inverted baluster / central knop / weak baluster / prebasal knop. **Foot** rather flat, folded, ⌀ (105).

OWNERSHIP Musées Royaux d'Art et d'Histoire, Bruxelles (8855 - apparently obtained in the early 1950s)

REMARK A composition of flowers and insects was first very effectively engraved with a diamond, but in line-work, by Anna Roemers in 1621.

LITERATURE Berryer 1954: 37-41, figs. 6-8; 1957: 48-49, fig. 17, pl. XXVIII; 1958: 219 (No. 601), fig. 601. Fettweis 1965: 22 (No. 274); 1970: 42, fig. 36.

* * *

Fig. 116. Bowl of goblet 47.2

Fig. 117. Bowl of goblet 47.3   Fig. 118. Bowl of goblet 47.3

47.3 (Figs. 117, 118)
A palette with eight paint-brushes in the thumb-hole and a maulstick obliquely
behind it, encircled by a laurel crown. Background blank.
Stippling fairly coarse; brushes engraved in fine lines.

INSCRIBED (in script with thin lines in stipple but wider lines in scratches and
stipple, with large flourishes flowing from the first and last letter; opposite
design):
Pictúra

SIGNED (in rather roughly scratched Roman letters, "fect" in single-line script,
below design:
F. Greenwood / fec^t. 1747

GOBLET **H** 200. **Bowl** pointed round funnel, ϕ 90. **Stem** knop with two tiers
of tears / inverted baluster [repaired, the straight part being ensheathed in sil-
ver] / base knop. **Foot** conical, folded narrowly, pontil mark fairly smooth, ϕ 89.

OWNERSHIP Private museum of Repelaer van Spijkenisse, Haarlem / H. P. van
de Wall Repelaer, Dubbeldam / H. van de Wall Repelaer, Dubbeldam / Private
collection, The Netherlands

EXHIBITED Tentoonstelling Het Hollandsche interieur in de XVIIIe eeuw, Rijksmuseum, Amsterdam, 14.III - 3.V.1931 / Herdenkingstentoonstelling Aart Schouman,
Dordrecht's Museum, Dordrecht, 27.VIII - 2.X.1960.

REMARK In analogy with the comparable "Poësis" goblet (46.1), this glass was
probably engraved [rather hurriedly] as a present for a fellow-artist or for a
painters' brotherhood or guild. If the latter was the case, it could have concerned
the Pictura brotherhood in 's-Gravenhage.

LITERATURE Buckley 1930b: 13 (No. 18), pl. 22; 1930c: 14 (No. 18), pl. 22.
Anonymous 1931: 17-18 (No. 48). Bol 1960: 94 (No. 184).

*   *   *

Fig. 119. Bowl of goblet *47.4   Fig. 120. Bowl of goblet 47.5

*47.4 (Fig. 119)
An orange flanked by leaves between which two very small oranges just below
the rim of the bowl. Background blank.
   Some lines in leaf-nerves.

SIGNED (in scratched script, opposite design):

F. Greenwood fec[t]

GOBLET H 173. **Bowl** pointed round funnel, ∮ 80. **Stem** ball knop with oblique
tears / inverted baluster / base knop. **Foot** fairly high conical, ∮ 89.

OWNERSHIP E. Meurrens / auction Sotheby, London, 6.VI.1947 / A. Craig /
National Gallery of Victoria, Melbourne (171.5 - purchased from H. Phillips,
London, for £250 through the Felton bequest in 1959)

REMARK See notes sub goblet 47.5.

LITERATURE Auction Catalogue Sotheby 1947a: 8 (lot 72), frontispiece.
Charleston 1950: fig. 6. Anonymous 1962b: 148 (No. 44), fig. 44. Ebbott 1971:
23, fig. 16. Warren 1975: 1499, fig. 6. Edwards 1980: 45, pl. p. 44.

                    *   *   *

47.5 (Fig. 120)
An orange flanked by leaves between which two very small oranges just below
the rim of the bowl. Background blank.
   Some lines in leaf-nerves.

SIGNED (in scratched script, opposite design at base of bowl):
F. Greenwood / fecit 1747

GOBLET H 202. **Bowl** funnel, ∮ 87. **Stem** angular knop / single-teared ball
knop / knop / inverted baluster containing a tear extending into knop above /
base knop. **Foot** conical, ∮ 92.

OWNERSHIP Deutz van Lennep, Meerenberg estate, south of Heemstede /
J. Goudstikker, Amsterdam / auction Mensing, Amsterdam, 21.24.XI.1950 /
Historisch Museum, Rotterdam (25 [previously GL 144] - purchased in 1951)

EXHIBITED Tentoonstelling Oude Kunst, Rijksmuseum, Amsterdam, VII - IX.1936

REMARKS   The orange presumably represents stadholder Willem IV, Prince of Orange-Nassau (1711-1751) who married Anne (1709-1759) daughter of George II King of Great Britain and Ireland, Elector of Hannover, in 1734.   After a French invasion on 17.IV.1747, Willem IV - already stadholder of Friesland, Groningen and Gelderland - was soon elected stadholder of all Seven United Provinces. This was followed by a nomination to Captain-General and Admiral-General of the Dutch Republic; he was also appointed managing-director of both Dutch East and West India Companies.   On 30 April, 1747, the City Fathers of Dordrecht complyingly proclaimed Prince Willem IV to be stadholder.   When the Prince visited that town on Monday 5 June, 1747, he was given a glorious reception, culminating in a grand dinner, lasting all afternoon, which burgomaster Johan Gevaerts had organised in his honour at the Town Hall.   It is well possible that Greenwood, a good friend of the burgomaster, engraved some Orange-goblets for the occasion.   If the large orange on each goblet (*47.4, 47.5) represents the Prince, then the two small ones might symbolise his wife Princess Anna and their very young child Princess Wilhelmina Carolina (1743-1787) [there were no signs yet of the future stadholder Prince Willem V of Orange-Nassau (1748-1806)].

In the same year, 1747, Aart Schouman (still residing in Dordrecht) stipple= engraved a rather similar goblet with a rose [for Princess Anne ?] and two oranges while in the frame of his 1750 bust portrait of Prince Willem IV he also included two small oranges [the two children, then alive].

LITERATURE   Buckley 1931: 49 (No. 30), pl. 28.   Anonymous 1936a: 152 (No. 751);   1936b: 153 (No. 751).   Auction Catalogue Mensing 1950: 24 (lot 342). Beydals 1952: 4.

*   *   *

*47.6   (Fig. 121)
The half-length seated figures of a man and a woman, the latter on the right, face $\frac{3}{4}$ to sinister, wearing a head-cover and a low-cut dress, raising her right hand and with the left stroking a small dog which is resting in her lap.   By her side, to the left, a man wearing a cap, his grinning face $\frac{3}{4}$ to dexter, holding a cat against his chest with both hands.   Stippled background with some drapery left and right.

SIGNED   (in scratched script, opposite design):   F. Greenwood fecit

GOBLET   H 286.   **Bowl** ± round funnel, $\emptyset$ (131).   **Stem** teared inverted baluster with collaring each end / base knop [a massive stem].   **Foot** domed, $\emptyset$ (147) [broken in half but mended].

OWNERSHIP   Sir John Risley / Churchill Ltd, London (in 1947) /   ?

REMARK   The engraving is perhaps meant to be an allegory or persiflage of married life [cat and dog] or it simply intends to convey domestic bliss.   It is also possible that the dog in the woman's lap alludes to marital fidelity although dogs were often symbols of prostitutes.   The cat could be a symbol of female dominance or of concupiscence.

Fig. 121.   Bowl of goblet *47.6

Fig. 122. Bowl of goblet 47.7   Fig. 123. Bowl of goblet *47.8

LITERATURE   Risley 1922: 297, pl. III [part]. Bles 1924: 56, pl. 18 fig. 25.
Hudig 1926: xxvii.   Thorpe 1929: pl. XCIII fig. 1.   Buckley 1930b: 13 (No. 22),
pl. 26; 1930c: 14 (No. 22), pl. 26.   Anonymous 1947: 13.   Haynes 1970: pl. 40a.

*   *   *

47.7 (Fig. 122)
Two half-length smiling nude figures, partly covered by some drapery around them.
The young man on the left, face ¾ to dexter, with two roses in his hair.   His
left hand is resting on the woman's left shoulder while holding one end of a garland which hangs down along the woman's left breast below which it ends up in
the man's right hand.   The woman is resting her right hand on the right forearm
of the man.   A tree to the right with a foliate branch extending over the woman,
foliage to the left.   Behind the couple the pedestal of a pillar or a statue; a rectangular slab low down in the foreground.   Background all in stipple.

SIGNED (in scratched script, opposite design):
F. Greenwood fecit Anno 1747

GOBLET H 285. **Bowl** pointed round funnel, ⌀ 125. **Stem** inverted baluster /
central knop / baluster. **Foot** conical, ⌀ (137).

OWNERSHIP Deutz van Lennep, Meerenberg estate, south of Heemstede /
A. Vecht, Amsterdam / auction Sotheby, London, 10.XI.1938 (unsold) / A. Vecht,
Amsterdam / W. J. H. Mulier, 's-Gravenhage / Gemeentemuseum, 's-Gravenhage
(OG-4-1954 - W. J. H. Mulier legacy of 1954)

EXHIBITED Tentoonstelling Het Hollandsche interieur in de XVIIIe eeuw, Rijksmuseum, Amsterdam, 14.III - 3.V.1931 / Tentoonstelling van Oude Kunst, Rijksmuseum, Amsterdam, VII - IX.1936

REMARK Cf. goblet *47.8. - The engraving is quite a free adaptation of
Adriaen van der Werff's painting [1694] of a couple caressing in a park landscape
and being spied upon by a mythological godlike figure and children (Rijksmuseum,
Amsterdam, inv. C 265).   Snoep & Thiels (1973) suggested that the scene may
represent Paris (educated among shepherds) and his beloved Oenone (a nymph of
Mount Ida) being watched in the painting by her father the rivergod Cebrenus
who perhaps foresaw their forthcoming separation.

LITERATURE   Anonymous 1931: 17 (No. 47).   Buckley 1931: 49 (No. 29), pl. 27.
Anonymous 1936a: 155 (No. 766);   1936b: 156 (No. 766).   Auction Catalogue
Sotheby 1938: 47 (lot 136), frontispiece.   van Gelder 1954: 54, fig. 5.   Esmeyer
1957: No. 20, pl. 20.   Braat 1962: 30, fig. 33.   Jansen 1962: 115, fig. 214.
Snoep & Thiels 1973: fig. 11a.   Gateau 1974: fig. p. 70.

*   *   *

*47.8   (Fig. 123)
Two half-length smiling nude figures, partly covered by some drapery around
them.   The young man on the left, face $\frac{3}{4}$ to dexter, with two roses in his hair.
His left hand is resting on the woman's left shoulder while holding one end of
a garland which hangs down along the woman's left breast below which it ends
up in the man's right hand.   The woman is resting her right hand on the right
forearm of the man.   A tree to the right with a foliate branch extending over
the woman, foliage to the left.   Behind the couple the pedestal of a pillar or a
statue; an oblong slab low down in the foreground.   Background all in stipple.
The unframed design occupies nearly two-fifth of the circumference of the very
large bowl.
     Stipples mixed with quite a number of fine scratches.

SIGNED   (in stippled script with flourishes, opposite design):

F. Greenwood fec^t

GOBLET   H 317.   **Bowl** round funnel, ϕ 150.   **Stem** [repaired with a hallmarked
(tarnished) silver collar between bowl and stem] teared knop (within collar) /
teared inverted baluster / teared knop [remainder of stem missing].   **Foot** a replacement of hallmarked silver (quite tarnished) with five ostrich feathers and a
crowned N engraved on it, ϕ 136.

OWNERSHIP   Randolph Berens / auction Sotheby, London, [date ?] 1924 /
C. Davis, London / Victoria and Albert Museum, London (C.1378-1924   - bought
for £24 in 1924)

REMARK   This is exactly the same design as (but having the edge on) 47.7, q.v.
     The metal of both collar and foot (heavily tarnished silver) is hallmarked -
apparently: maker GHA London 1833-1854 = George Henry Allen, a goldworker
at 13, King Street, Soho, London.

LITERATURE   Bles 1924: 56.   Buckley 1930b: 14 (No. 25), pl. 29;   1930c: 15
(No. 25), pl. 29.   Rackham 1934: 318, fig. 23.   Honey 1946: 134.   Snoep & Thiels
1973: fig. 11a.   van Hall 1976: fig. 3.

*   *   *

48.1   (Fig. 124)
Seated in a monumental garden a nude shepherd and, lower down to his left,
a nude shepherdess leaning her left elbow in his lap whilst looking up at him;
drapery across their laps.   Looking down at the woman, the shepherd is holding
a flute in both hands.   On the ground, to the right, the top end of a crook.
Stippled background with trees and, behind the couple, a large socle [of a
pillar ?] partly covered with plants.   The design, occupying just over half the
circumference of the bowl, is framed left and right by a scratched vertical line.
     Almost entirely in stipple but here and there some fine lines.

SIGNED   (in scratched script with little spalling, opposite design):
F. Greenwood / fecit 1748.

GOBLET   H 248.   **Bowl** round funnel, ϕ 94.   **Stem** inverted baluster / central
knop / baluster / base knop.   **Foot** fairly high conical, folded, pontil mark fairly
smooth, ϕ 103.

Fig. 124. Bowl of goblet 48.1   Fig. 125. Bowl of goblet 48.3

OWNERSHIP D. Hudig, Rotterdam (purchased in 1893) / Mrs D. M. Hudig - Philippi, Rotterdam / Hudig collection [private], Rotterdam

REMARKS The engraving is based on Adriaen van der Werff's 'The shepherd in love', a painting owned in the middle of the 18th century by Adriaen Brouwer, now in the Staatliche Kunstsammlungen [erstwhile Königliche Gemäldegalerie], Kassel (Buckley 1930: pl. 23A). Greenwood perhaps copied an engraving of that painting or had a small-scale copy made by his friend Aart Schouman.
The flute is here obviously a phallic symbol.

LITERATURE Buckley 1930b: 13 (No. 19), pl. 23; 1930c: 14 (No. 19), pl. 23.

*   *   *

*48.2
A shepherd and a shepherdess, shown to knee-length.

SIGNED Neither signed, nor dated.

GOBLET H 180 [i.e., if not a lapsus, considerably smaller than the previous goblet (48.1) which carries a similar design].

OWNERSHIP H. A. Steengracht van Duivenvoorde, 's-Gravenhage / auction Muller, Amsterdam, 8.V.1913 (Hfl. 200) / auction Muller, Amsterdam, 28.XI.1913 / H. Schieffer, Amsterdam (in 1931) / ?

EXHIBITED Tentoonstelling Het Hollandsche interieur in de XVIIIe eeuw, Rijks-museum, Amsterdam, 14.III - 3.V.1931

REMARK The engraving has been attributed to Frans Greenwood in the Auction Catalogues of Muller (1913a, b): "La date du costume (vers 1730) [the couple are here not in the nude as on 48.1] ainsi que le procédé de la gravure ne nous font pas hésiter d'attribuer ce verre gravé à l'artiste F. Greenwood. Voir la repro-duction [which, unfortunately, was not published]". Anonymous (1931) also re-marked: "probably by Frans Greenwood."

LITERATURE Auction Catalogue Muller 1913a: 65 (lot 873); 1913b: 101, (lot 1588). Anonymous 1931: 17 (No. 46a).

*   *   *

48.3 (Fig. 125)
A half-length figure of a shepherdess with full breasts swelling from her low-cut
bodice [left mamilla rather off-centre], looking at spectator and wearing a broad=
brimmed hat with floral decoration while holding with her right hand a flowering
rose stalk as well as a crook which is resting on her right shoulder. Trees right
and left, also silhouetted ones in the stippled background. Sides and bottom
framed by a thin line, upper part of engraving reaching rim of bowl.

SIGNED (in single-line script, downstrokes scratched, opposite design on lower
half of bowl):
F. Greenwood fec^t. Dord^t. A^o 1748.

GOBLET H 251. **Bowl** round funnel, ⌀ 107. **Stem** angular knop / inverted
baluster, knop with two tiers of tears / base knop. **Foot** conical, pontil mark
fairly smooth, ⌀ 120.

OWNERSHIP A. van Hoboken van Cortgene, Rotterdam / Museum Boymans -
van Beuningen, Rotterdam (142 - presented by A. van Hoboken van Cortgene
in 1922)

REMARKS The engraving is a somewhat modified copy of one of the charming
portraits of a shepherdess painted by Paulus Moreelse (Utrecht 1571-1638), on
the whole agreeing well with the one illustrated in J. van Haeften, [1987], Dutch
and Flemish old master paintings: No. 15, col. pl.
    This is probably the glass with the stippled "herderin" [shepherdess] owned in
the middle of the 18th century by bachelor Pauls Schepers who bequeathed it
(together with two other Greenwood goblets: 42.1, 46.8 or 47.1) in his testaments
of 27.II.1755, 31.VII.1755 and 7.III.1757 (Gemeentelijke Archiefdienst, Rotterdam:
O.N.A. 2282:30, 2283:21, 2286:32) to his second cousin Gerard Schepers (Rotterdam 1720-1757, married Jacoba Prins 1746) who, however, died on 23.III.1757,
shortly before the death of Pauls Schepers on 13.IV.1757.

LITERATURE Hudig 1926: xxvii. Buckley 1930b: 13 (No. 20), pl. 24; 1930c:
14 (No. 20), pl. 24. van Gelder 1955: pl. XXX(2). Braat 1962: 48, fig. 68.
de Neeve 1967: 28, fig. 5. van Gelder & Jansen 1969: 76, fig. 212. Schrijver
1980: fig. 77.

*   *   *

49.1 (Figs. 49, 126)
A pendent full-blown rose, a bud and a leafstalk; to top left a small Lepido-
pterous insect [unidentifiable] and a damselfly. Background blank.

SIGNED (in single-line script but downstrokes and capitals scratched, opposite
design):
F. Greenwood fec^t / 1749

GOBLET H 207. **Bowl** pointed round funnel, slightly flared, ⌀ 96. **Stem** teared
ball knop / teared inverted baluster / base knop. **Foot** conical, pontil mark
smooth, ⌀ 95.

OWNERSHIP H. A. Steengracht van Duivenvoorde, 's-Gravenhage / auction
Muller, Amsterdam, 8.V.1913 (Hfl. 380) / H. Stibbe, Berlin / J. Mühsam, Berlin
(1913-1927) / The Art Institute, Chicago (1927-1321 - presented by J. and A. N.
Rosenwald in 1927)

EXHIBITED Sammlung Mühsam, Königliches Kunstgewerbemuseum, Berlin, 1914

REMARK Cf. goblets 46.2, 46.3, 46.4, 47.2, *49.2

Fig. 126. Bowl of goblet 49.1   Fig. 127. Bowl of goblet *49.2

LITERATURE   Auction Catalogue Muller 1913a: 65 (lot 874). Anonymous 1914: 59. Schmidt 1914: 14, 19 (No. 28), pl. 2 No. 28. Hudig 1926: xxvii. Bennett 1928: 53, fig. 8a. Buckley 1930b: 13 (No. 21), pl. 25; 1930c: 14 (No. 21), pl. 25. Berryer 1954: fig. 9.

*   *   *

*49.2   (Fig. 127)
A pendent full-blown rose on a short foliate stem. An unidentifiable Lepidopterous insect on the wing approaching the bloom from the left; to the right of the rose a damselfly resting on rose leaves. Background blank.
    Rose entirely in stipple, some lines in the insects.

SIGNED   Neither signed, nor dated.

GOBLET   H 206. **Bowl** cup, ∅ 78. **Stem** plain [?], only upper 27 mm visible, remainder of broken stem encased in a silver collar mounted on an 18th-century silver salt-cellar made in Haarlem in 1708 which serves as foot.

OWNERSHIP   A. J. Enschedé, Haarlem / Rijksmuseum, Amsterdam (NM 10754-95 - A. J. Enschedé legacy of 1896)

REMARKS   Cf. goblets 46.2, 46.3, 46.4, 47.2, 49.1. - The wine-glass belongs to a type which dates from the first half of the 18th century and is characterised by a cup bowl and a folded foot while the stem is either straight or has a knop [possibly annulated] in the middle and perhaps a base knop as well. In view of the fact that Greenwood appears to have used only knopped-stem goblets for his stipple-engravings, the missing greater part of the stem was presumably knopped.
    The glass doubtlessly broke just before the engraving was finished because Greenwood (as in several other instances of damage) did neither sign nor date the engraving [which is typically his hand]. Only after the engraving was quite finished will this cup bowl have been mounted on the Dutch silver salt-cellar -- a combination which is as odd as it will be unique among the multitude of preserved eighteenth-century goblets. An unadorned plain cup bowl with only a stumpy stem would surely not have deserved such a dainty 'foot'.

LITERATURE   Hudig 1926: xxviii.

Fig. 128. Bowl of goblet 55.1   Fig. 129. Bowl of goblet X.1

55.1 (Figs. 44, 50, 128)
To the left a half-length figure of a young voluptuous woman looking at viewer.
She is wearing a string of pearls in her hair which falls in ringlets over her bare
shoulder. With her right hand she is holding the top edge of her rather flimsy
dress to cover or uncover her left breast partially. To the right, behind her,
a smirking older man is ogling her. The scene flanked by a vase and drapery
and with trees in the stippled background.

SIGNED (in scratched script with flourishes flowing from F, G and d, opposite
design):
F. Greenwood Fecit / A^{0} 1755 / Etat. 75

GOBLET **H 247. Bowl** pointed round funnel, quite tall, ϕ (113). **Stem** ball
knop with two tiers of oblique tears / inverted baluster / base knop. **Foot**
conical, ϕ (116).

OWNERSHIP Baron Cornelius von Heyl zu Herrnsheim (in 1927) / Museum
Heylshof, Worms (821)

LITERATURE Swarzenski 1927: 147 (No. 821). Buckley, B. T. 1935: 41 (No. 33),
pl. 25.

*   *   *

X.1 (Fig. 129)
A seated bareheaded and barefooted woman, face in profile to sinister, dressed
in long flowing robes which leave the bosom quite uncovered; with her right hand
she is holding the top of the garment.
     Head, left shoulder, upper arm and left breast in finished stipple, the right
hand and breast only partially stippled. The garment, a foot and the greater part
of the left arm merely indicated in stippled outlines.

SIGNED Being quite unfinished, the engraving is neither signed nor dated.

GOBLET **H 231. Bowl** wide cup, ϕ 124. **Stem** hollow annular knop / hollow
inverted baluster. **Foot** domed, folded, pontil mark fairly smooth, ϕ 133.

OWNERSHIP A. J. Enschedé, Haarlem / Rijksmuseum, Amsterdam (NM 10754-96
- A. J. Enschedé legacy of 1896)

REMARKS   The attribution of this unfinished engraving to Frans Greenwood is based upon the following observations:

(a) The execution of the stippling is identical with that of Greenwood's.

(b) Greenwood tended to utilise virtually the full height of a bowl for an engraving - this is also the case in this instance.

(c) Engraving of hands was not quite Greenwood's forte and in some of his designs fingers have a tendency to resemble carrots - that trait is also noticeable in the present engraving.

(d) Greenwood's stippled primary outlines do not stand out as single dotted lines (as may be the case in Wolffian types of stippling); this goblet shows in fact soft outlines with a width of several stipples. Such lines would therefore merge successfully with engraved areas and this would presumably agree with Greenwood's method of marking out a design on glass.

(e) Greenwood had an appreciative painter's eye for the superbly simple but somehow appealing mammary form when at optimum of development. Therefore this unfinished design is a typical example of a bare-bosomed lady such as Frans obviously enjoyed portraying.

(f) Greenwood used knopped-stem goblets for his stipple work, preferably sturdy ones. This goblet - very likely made [possibly in Holland] in the first half of the 18th century - fits that category; it is unusual in being composed of a large wide bowl (ideal for embellishment), a hollow knopped rather short stem and a domed folded foot. The glass - which is markedly akin to goblet 28.3 (Fig. 53, p. 118) - is probably a one-off, just as some other heavy unusual goblets used by Greenwood (*47.6, *47.8).

The stippling on this goblet having as close an affinity with Greenwood's last known engraving of 1755 as with a number of his earlier engravings, dating is not feasible. However, it may not be unreasonable to suggest - if the above assumptions are at all correct - that this could be the last goblet that Frans Greenwood attempted to engrave and which for some reason or other could not be finished. Otherwise it would have been another excellent example of his portrayals of a feminine subject.

LITERATURE   Hudig 1926: xxvi, pl. G.

*   *   *

EEN BOOTSGEZEL.

't Is een ontuchtig dier , een zwyn,
Die al zyn wellust fchept in wyn;
Want hy , verr' van behoude reê,
Zwerft als een roerloos fchip in zee.

Fig. 130. Inscription on goblet X.2. (Greenwood 1760: 77). [He who derives all his pleasures from wine / Is a lewd animal, a swine; / Because, far from the shelter of a harbour / He will be roving the seas like a rudderless ship.]

X.2 (Fig. 130)

A goblet engraved with "Een bootsgezel" [a sailor].

INSCRIBED   (See Fig. 130).

OWNERSHIP   The fate of this goblet is unknown.   Is it still extant ?

LITERATURE   Greenwood 1760: 77.

*   *   *

X.3

A goblet, stipple-engraved with two reclining children, after Adriaen van der Werff.

OWNERSHIP   In the middle of the 18th century this goblet was owned by bachelor Pauls Schepers, Rotterdam, who bequeathed it in his testaments of 27.II.1755, 31.VII.1755 and 7.III.1757 (Gemeentelijke Archiefdienst, Rotterdam O.N.A. 2282:30, 2283:21, 2286:32) to his nephew Adriaan Prins (Rotterdam 1723 - ?) [his father Adriaan (1692-1780), a director of the United Dutch East India Company, was married (1720) to Elizabeth Schepers (1701-1756)] who became the new owner of the goblet after the death of Pauls Schepers on 13 April, 1757.   Of the five Greenwood goblets in the possession of Pauls Schepers this one was said to be the largest.

REMARK   A relevant painting by Adriaen van der Werff could not be traced.

*   *   *

X.4

A goblet, stipple-engraved with Venus and Satyr(s), after a painting by Adriaen van der Werff.

OWNERSHIP   Like the preceding item (X.3), this goblet was also once the property of Pauls Schepers who bequeathed it in the same testaments to his nephew Willem Prins (Rotterdam 1730 - [?]1807), a brother of Adriaan (see notes sub X.3).

REMARK   It is possible that Venus was depicted as surprised by Satyr(s) while asleep, or at her toilet; Cupid may be present.   A relevant painting by Adriaen van der Werff could not be traced.

*   *   *

X.5

A goblet with a portrait of Joost van den Vondel, presumably engraved between 1738 and 1753.

OWNERSHIP   Arnold Hoogvliet (mid-18th century).

REMARKS   An inscription by Arnold Hoogvliet on a mezzotint-engraved portrait of Frans Greenwood by Aart Schouman indicates that "He who with a diamond on my goblet gave life to Vondel, thus lives by Schouman's steel [graver]." (Fig. 24).   -   Presumably after Arnold Hoogvliet's death in 1763 the goblet became property of his son Johannes (born 1738) who was a member of the literary Society 'Kunst wordt door arbeid verkreegen' [Art is acquired through work] in Leiden (Anonymous 1794).   At various times Johannes declared that eventually he would present the Society with the goblet "on which Frans Greenwood has very nicely stippled the portrait of Vondel" and which had been dedicated by the great Arnold Hoogvliet to the "flourishing of Poetry".   However, Johannes Hoogvliet died suddenly without having put the promised donation in writing.   During the annual meeting of the Society on Wednesday 11 June, 1794, the members were informed that the Society had been able to purchase the goblet together with an accompanying album [with an introduction by the poet Pieter Verleus; this album has not been traced] at a public auction and the hope was expressed that the goblet would be used during dinner the same evening to toast with it 'The Flourishing of Poetry'.

The Society 'Kunst wordt door arbeid verkreegen' owned a large meeting-room on the Langebrug, Leiden. Placed in the middle of an end-wall was the famous Pan Poëticon Batavum cabinet (which included portraits of Frans Greenwood, see p. 37), flanked in one corner by a large stove, in the other corner by a sideboard . The collection of goblets, of various sizes, belonging to the Society was stored in and on this quadrantal corner sideboard (Backer 1789: 264); the Vondel goblet would have been stored there too. When, on 12 January, 1807, a ship laden with gunpowder exploded in nearby Rapenburg, the meeting-room suffered great damage and much of its contents was smashed to smithereens. There seems little doubt that Greenwood's Vondel goblet was among the numerous casualties.

Aart Schouman stippled a very good medallion portrait of Joost van den Vondel on a goblet in 1774 [Gemeentemuseum, 's-Gravenhage, OG-6-1954] which he then presented to the literary Society 'Konstliefde spaart geen vlijt' in 's-Gravenhage of which he was an honorary member. Schouman copied a 1674 portrait by Philips Koninck which had been presented to the circle in 1774.

LITERATURE Hoogvliet 1753: 198. Anonymous 1794: 5. J. C. K. 1865: 299. Hudig 1926: xxvii. Buckley 1930b, c: pl. 2 [Schouman's mezzotint portrait of Greenwood with Hoogvliet's poem].

* * *

ENGRAVINGS N O T ATTRIBUTABLE TO FRANS GREENWOOD

A

A standing boy ["Mars" (de Neeve 1964), "a putto" (Bolten 1969)], face slightly to sinister, wearing a plumed helmet. He is resting his right hand on a shield, bearing the coat of arms of Orange-Nassau, and is holding a lance topped by the Hat of Liberty with his left hand. Bushes to his right, an anchor and a caduceus on the ground. A sun in his splendour above.

SIGNED (in Roman letters, below design):
F. Greenwood fct 1734

GOBLET H 135. **Bowl** elongate ovoid, ∅ 57. **Stem** with a pair of white spiral threads around a white lace twist. **Foot** conical, pontil mark fairly rough, ∅ 74.

OWNERSHIP Snouck Hurgronje (according to Bolten, 1969; this goblet is not listed in the catalogue of the 1931 auction of the Snouck Hurgronje collection [Mensing]) / D. Katz, Dieren / Nijstad Antiquairs, Lochem / A. J. Guépin, Eindhoven / M. C. Guépin

EXHIBITED Tentoonstelling van Oude Kunst, Rijksmuseum, Amsterdam, VII - IX. 1936 / Herdenkingstentoonstelling Aart Schouman, Dordrecht's Museum, Dordrecht, 27.VIII - 2.X.1960 / Meisterwerke der Glaskunst, Kunstmuseum, Düsseldorf, 22.XI.1968 - 5.I.1969

REMARKS Neither design nor execution (very fine stipple, with marked highlights) are at all characteristic of Frans Greenwood.

The type of goblet, with opaque twists, came into use only after 1750 (as is generally understood). This particular glass is also very small; Greenwood really favoured tall goblets [average height 225 mm].

Greenwood used knopped-stem goblets for his stipple-engravings and none of his genuine glasses have a twist stem.
There are no other known Greenwood engravings dating from the period 1731 - 1737 and none are signed in scratched roman letters prior to 1741.
On none of the genuine Greenwood engravings is 'fecit' abbreviated as 'fct'.
The inclusion in glass engravings of the Hat of Liberty topping a lance occurred mainly in the last quarter of the eighteenth century.
de Neeve (1964) observed that Prince Willem IV married Princess Anne in 1734, the date on this glass. The engraving, however, does not seem to have a direct bearing upon that event.
The engraving is reminiscent of the workmanship of a certain late 18th= century stipple engraver.

LITERATURE   Anonymous 1936a: 159 (No. 791);   1936b: 160 (No. 791).   Bol 1960: 93 (No. 182).   de Neeve 1964: 382, 383 (Note 11).   von Saldern & Hilschenz 1968: 49 (No. 126), fig. 126.   von Saldern 1969: 301.   Bolten 1969: 45 (No. 150), fig. 44.

*   *   *

B
An unframed bust portrait of eight-year-old Prince Willem V of Orange-Nassau, face ¾ to dexter, with long hair and wearing a sash over his left shoulder and the star decoration of the Order of the Garter on the left lapel.

GOBLET   H 197.   **Bowl** round funnel, ⌀ 81.   **Stem** angular knop / knop / inverted baluster, teared / base knop.   **Foot** fairly high conical.

OWNERSHIP   Mme Lucien Sauphar / ?

REMARKS   This is perhaps the goblet "bearing a portrait of Prince Willem V very ingeniously stippled by A. Schouman" from which toasts were drunk when that Prince was installed as Patron of the 'Pictura' Brotherhood in 's-Gravenhage on 15.X.1766.   The portrait is a copy of a drawing in coloured crayon made in 1756 by Jean Etienne Liotard.   Aart Schouman copied that original as a drawing in 1759 and this was later engraved by J. Houbraken for publication in Wagenaar, J., XX: pl. facing p. 448.
Pelliot (1929) erroneously attributed the engraving to F. Greenwood instead of A. Schouman.

LITERATURE   Gram 1882: 71.   Pelliot 1929: pl. III.   Buckley 1931: 16, 20 (No. B).

*   *   *

C
A half-length figure of Bacchus, face ¾ to sinister, looking at a wine-glass held in his right hand.   Fruiting vines below.

INSCRIBED   (in Gothic letters, slanting, opposite design):
de Wyn Ncgotie

GOBLET   H 162.   **Bowl** pointed round funnel, ⌀ 66.   **Stem** straight, with a pair of white spiral threads around a white central rod.   **Foot** conical, ⌀ 81.

OWNERSHIP   V. [A.] von Lanna, Praha / Uměleckoprůmyslové muzeum, Praha (10350)

REMARK   Jiřík (1933a, b, 1934) attributed, without comment, the decoration to F. Greenwood - an assertion which cannot possibly be maintained.   One might be inclined to ascribe the engraving to G. H. Hoolaart.

LITERATURE   Jiřík 1933a: 33 (No. 1);   1933b: 36 (No. 1);   1934: 25 (No. 1).

*   *   *

INDEX OF ENGRAVED INSCRIPTIONS

B = on the bowl   F = on the foot

*   *   *

INDEX OF OBJECTS
SHOWN IN ENGRAVINGS

*   *   *

DEPOSITORIES OF ENGRAVED GOBLETS
in alphabetical order

AUSTRALIA

MELBOURNE
National Gallery of Victoria - *47.4

BELGIUM

BRUXELLES
Musées Royaux d'Art et d'Histoire - 47.2

ENGLAND

CAMBRIDGE
Fitzwilliam Museum - *41.2

LONDON
British Museum - 38.1 *46.6
Victoria and Albert Museum - 20.1 28.1 *28.4 *47.8

sine loco
Private collection - 45.1

GERMANY (WEST)

BERLIN
Kunstgewerbemuseum, Stiftung Preussischer Kulturbesitz - 22.5

HAMBURG
Museum für Kunst und Gewerbe - 46.8

KASSEL
Hessisches Landesmuseum - 22.3

NÜRNBERG
Bayerische Landesgewerbeanstalt - 46.2

WORMS
Museum Heylshof - 55.1

sine loco
Private collection - *44.1

NETHERLANDS

AMSTERDAM
Rijksmuseum - 22.1 24.1 43.3 *49.2 X.1
J. Six van Hillegom - 22.4
Vecht collection - 39.1 43.1 43.6

ARNHEM
Gemeentemuseum - 46.1

DORDRECHT
Museum Mr Simon van Gijn - 44.2

'S-GRAVENHAGE
Haags Gemeentemuseum - 46.3 47.1 47.7

ROTTERDAM
Historisch Museum van Rotterdam - 47.5
Hudig collection - 48.1
Museum Boymans - van Beuningen - 30.1 42.2 48.3

s i n e l o c o
A. C. R. Dreesmann - 42.1
Private collections - 22.2 *28.2 41.1 43.4 47.3

U N I T E D S T A T E S O F A M E R I C A

CHICAGO
The Art Institute - 49.1

CORNING
The Corning Museum of Glass - 46.5 46.7

NEW YORK
The Metropolitan Museum of Art - 28.3

U N L O C A T E D
*38.2 38.3 40.1 *43.2 43.5 46.4 *47.6 *48.2 X.2 X.3 X.4

* * *

L I S T O F F O R M E R O W N E R S
d e a l e r s e x c l u d e d

H. van Beeftingh (Rotterdam) - 40.1
R. Berens [England] - *47.8
R. Bernal (London) - *46.6
Earl of Bradford [formerly Viscount Newport] (Weston Park, Shifnal) - *44.1
H. Brown (Aldbury near Tring) - 46.7
W. Buckley (Basingstoke) - 20.1 28.1 *28.4

D. H. de Castro (Amsterdam) - 43.3
D. H. de Castro Dz. (Amsterdam) - 43.3
A. Craig [England] - *47.4

Deutz van Lennep (Meerenberg estate near Heemstede) - 39.1 43.1 47.5 47.7

A. J. Enschedé (Haarlem) - *49.2 X.1
W. A. Evill [England] - *41.2

P. Gevaerts (Dordrecht) - 39.1

J. A. Baron van der Heim van Duyvendijke ('s-Gravenhage) - 47.1
C. von Heyl zu Herrnsheim (Worms) - 55.1
A. van Hoboken van Cortgene (Rotterdam) - 30.1 48.3
van Hoëvell Sr [The Netherlands] - 43.5
van Hoëvell Jr [The Netherlands] - 43.5
A. Hoogvliet (Vlaardingen) - X.5
J. Hoogvliet (Leiden) - X.5
D. Hudig (Rotterdam) - 48.1
Mrs D. M. Hudig - Philippi (Rotterdam) - 48.1
Huisman [The Netherlands] - 46.3

R. Kneppelhout van Sterkenburg ('s-Gravenhage) - 22.1
Kunst wordt door arbeid verkreegen (Leiden) - X.5

E. Meurrens [England ?] - *47.4
A. von Minutoli (Liegnitz = Lignica) - 22.5
J. Mühsam (Berlin) - 28.3 49.1
W. J. H. Mulier ('s-Gravenhage) - 46.3 47.7

G. S. Nicholson (London) - *46.6

A. Prins (Rotterdam) - X.3
W. Prins (Rotterdam) - X.4

A. van Rechteren Limpurg [The Netherlands] - 43.6
Repelaer van Spijkenisse (Haarlem) - *28.2 43.4 47.3
E. van Rijckevorsel (Rotterdam) - 42.2
J. Risley [England] - *47.6

G. Schepers (Rotterdam) - 42.1 or *44.1 46.8 or 47.1 48.3
P. Schepers (Rotterdam) - 42.1 or *44.1 46.8 or 47.1 48.3 X.3 X.4
H. Schieffer (Amsterdam) - 38.3 *48.2
G. van der Schoot [The Netherlands] - 46.4
J. P. Six [The Netherlands] - 22.4
Mrs Six van Hillegom [The Netherlands] - 22.4
F. Slade (London) - 38.1 *46.6
J. A. Smits van Nieuwerkerk (Dordrecht) - 46.8
S. C. Snellen van Vollenhoven (Leiden) - 24.1
H. A. Steengracht van Duivenvoorde ('s-Gravenhage) - 28.3 *48.2 49.1
J. Strauss (State College, Pennsylvania) - 46.5

A. Vecht (Amsterdam) - 41.1 47.7
J. Vriesendorp van Renesse (Epe) - 44.2

H. P. van de Wall Repelaer van Puttershoek (Dubbeldam) - *28.2 43.4 47.3

*   *   *

LITERATURE REFERENCES
- part III -

A., J. - 1893 - Greenwood. -- Nederl. Leeuw 11: 4

ANONYMOUS - 1794 - Handelingen der jaerlijksche vergadering van het tael- en dichtlievend genootschap, ter spreuk voerende: Kunst wordt door arbeid verkreegen. -- Leyden, Woensdag 11 Wiedemaand [June] 1794. 19 pp. [X.5]

ANONYMOUS - 1863 - Catalogus der tentoonstelling van voor Nederland belangrijke oudheden en merkwaardigheden, in de provincie Zuid-Holland voorhanden, of met betrekking tot die provincie elders bewaard, gehouden te Delft, Julij - Augustus 1863. -- Delft (J. H. Molenbroek). [vi+]189 pp. [46.8 47.1]

ANONYMOUS - 1891 - Jaarverslag van het Koninklijk Oudheidkundig Genootschap, Amsterdam: 11 [43.3]

ANONYMOUS - 1907 - Führer durch die Sammlung des Kunstgewerbe-Museums, Berlin. -- Berlin (G. Reimer). (Ed. 14). 207 pp. [22.5]

ANONYMOUS - 1914 - Ausstellungen. -- Zschr. alte & neue Glasmalerei (1914): 59 [28.3 49.1]

ANONYMOUS - 1921 - Führer durch das Hamburgische Museum für Kunst und Gewerbe. Die Schausammlungen des Erdgeschosses. -- Hamburg. 59 pp. [46.8]

ANONYMOUS - 1928 - Nederlandsch en Duitsch glaswerk. -- Nwe Rotterd. Courant 15.II (avondblad): 2, 2 figs. [28.3]

ANONYMOUS - 1929a - Dutch Art. An illustrated souvenir of the exhibition of Dutch art at Burlington House, London. -- London (The Anglo-Batavian Soc. & Country Life Ltd). (Ed. 1) 128 pp., frontispiece, 166 figs. [20.1 28.1]

ANONYMOUS - 1929b - Dutch Art. An illustrated souvenir of the exhibition of Dutch art at Burlington House, London. -- London (Executive Committee of the Exhibition & Country Life Ltd). (Eds. 2, 3) 128 pp., frontispiece, 168 figs. [20.1 28.1]

ANONYMOUS - 1929c - Catalogus van de Tentoonstelling van Oude Kunst door de Vereeniging van Handelaren in Nederland in het Rijksmuseum te Amsterdam. -- Amsterdam (H. J. Koersen). (Eds. 1, 2 - identical). xiii+247 pp., 184 pls. [38.3]

ANONYMOUS - 1931 - Catalogus van de tentoonstelling "Het Hollandsche interieur in de XVIIIe eeuw" - georganiseerd door het Koninklijk Oudheidkundig Genootschap en de vereeniging "Het Kantsalet" - in de zalen van het K. O. G. in het Rijksmuseum te Amsterdam, 14.III - 3.V.1931. -- Amsterdam. 94 pp., 4 pls [43.4 47.3 47.7 *48.2]

ANONYMOUS - 1936a - Catalogus van de Tentoonstelling van Oude Kunst uit het bezit van den internationalen handel. Rijksmuseum Amsterdam. Ingericht door de Vereeniging van Handelaren in Oude Kunst in Nederland ter herdenking van haar 25-jarig bestaan. -- Amsterdam (Voorlopige catalogus). [xvi+]191 pp., 11 pls. [39.1 43.1 43.6 47.5 47.7 A]

ANONYMOUS - 1936b - Catalogus van de Tentoonstelling van Oude Kunst uit het bezit van den internationalen handel. Rijksmuseum Amsterdam. Ingericht door de Vereeniging van Handelaren in Oude Kunst in Nederland ter herdenking van haar 25-jarig bestaan. -- Amsterdam (Ed. 2). xx+224 pp., 145 pls. [39.1 43.1 43.6 47.5 47.7 A]

ANONYMOUS - 1947 - The art of Greenwood. Glass Notes (7). -- London (Arthur Churchill Ltd): 12-13, figs. V, Va [46.5 *47.6]

ANONYMOUS [D. C. Röell] - 1952 - Verslagen 's Rijks verzamelingen van geschiedenis en kunst (1951). -- 's-Gravenhage (Staatsdrukkerij- en Uitgeverijbedrijf). LXXIII. 222 pp., illus. [22.1]

ANONYMOUS - 1954 - VIe Oude Kunst- en Antiekbeurs der Vereeniging van Handelaren in Oude Kunst in Nederland. -- Delft. 104 pp., illus. [43.6]

ANONYMOUS - 1962a - Catalogue, Commemorative exhibition 1937 - 1962, Circle of Glass Collectors. -- London. 72 pp., 28 pls. [22.1 41.1 *41.2]

ANONYMOUS - 1962b - Recent important acquisitions made by public and private collections in the U. S. and abroad. -- Jl Glass Studies 4: 139-149, figs. 1-50. [*47.4]

ANONYMOUS - 1968 - A galaxy of glass. British and V. and A. Museum's display nation's finest glass treasures for International Glass Congress. -- Antique Coll. (Aug. - Sept.): 167-171, 11 figs. [*46.6]

ANONYMOUS - 1974 - Glass from the Corning Museum of Glass. A guide to the collections. -- Corning, N.Y. (The Corning Museum of Glass). (Ed. 4). 107 pp., 129 figs. [46.7]

ANONYMOUS - 1980 - Important acquisitions from the Strauss collection. -- Jl Glass Studies 22: 103-111, figs. 1-44. [46.5]

ANONYMOUS - 1985a - Een mooie aanwinst. -- Mededelingen Museum Simon van Gijn, Dordrecht. (Februari). 2 pp. [44.2]

ANONYMOUS - 1985b - 37e Oude Kunst- en Antiekbeurs der Vereeniging van Handelaren in Oude Kunst in Nederland. -- Delft. xix+120 pp., illus. [45.1]

ANONYMOUS - 1987a - (Advertisement F. Laméris). Tableau 10(1): 49, figs. p. 51, 58 [22.2]

ANONYMOUS - 1987b - (Advertisement F. Laméris). -- Antiek 22(3): fig. p. 191 [22.2]

ANONYMOUS - 1987c - 39th Delft Art and Antique Fair 1987. -- Apollo 126 (308, N.S.): fig. p. 38 [22.2]

ANONYMOUS - 1987d - (Advertisement F. Laméris). -- Apollo 126 (308, N.S.): fig. p. 41 [22.2]

ANONYMOUS - 1987e - 39e Oude Kunst- en Antiekbeurs der Vereeniging van Handelaren in Oude Kunst in Nederland. -- Delft. xxvii+115 pp., illus. [22.2]

ANONYMOUS - 1987f - Agenda 1988. -- Amsterdam (Vereeniging van Handelaren in Oude Kunst in Nederland). [130 pp.], illus. [22.2]

AUCTION CATALOGUE CHRISTIE - 1855 - Catalogue of the celebrated collection of works of art from the Byzantine period to that of Louis Seize, of that distinguished collector, Ralph Bernal, Esq., deceased; &c. 5.III - 30.IV.1855. -- London (Christie). 357 pp., frontispiece, pls. [*46.6]

AUCTION CATALOGUE CHRISTIE - 1858 - Catalogue of the very choice collection of fine old Venetian & German glass and porcelain, of that well-known amateur George Stewart Nicholson (decd) . . . comprising . . . some pieces signed by F. Greenwood [recte: one piece]. 19.II.1858. -- London (Christie). 8 pp. [*46.6]

AUCTION CATALOGUE CHRISTIE - 1985a - The Bradford collection of 18th century Dutch engraved glass. 4.VI.1985. -- London (Christie). 95 pp., illus. [*44.1]

AUCTION CATALOGUE CHRISTIE - 1985b - Fine Dutch glass. 24.IX.1985. -- Amsterdam (Christie). 91 pp., illus. [*28.2]

AUCTION CATALOGUE MENSING - 1938 - Tableaux anciens et modernes, antiquités, objets d'art, &c. 4-7.X.1938. -- Amsterdam (Mensing & Fils). 51 pp. [46.3]

AUCTION CATALOGUE MENSING - 1950 - Catalogue . . . Jacques Goudstikker, verrerie du XVIe au XVIIIe siècle. 21-24.XI.1950. -- Amsterdam (B. F. M. Mensing). 59 pp., 10 pls. [47.5]

AUCTION CATALOGUE MULLER - 1913a - Catalogue des antiquités et objets d'art . . . Les verres gravés de la collection du Jhr. H. A. Steengracht van Duivenvoorde. 8.V.1913. -- Amsterdam (F. Muller & Cie): 64-71, pls. (17-27) [28.3 *48.2 49.1]

AUCTION CATALOGUE MULLER - 1913b - Catalogue des antiquités et objets d'art . . . verrerie . . . 25-28.XI.1913. -- Amsterdam (F. Muller & Cie). 111 pp., 53 pls. [*48.2]

AUCTION CATALOGUE SOTHEBY - 1938 - Catalogue of a fine collection of rare Gothic, early Renaissance and later European glass, the property of an amateur . . . comprising . . . fine Netherlands engraved and stippled glasses . . . and four superb signed glasses by Frans Greenwood. 10.XI.1938. -- London (Sotheby). 53 pp., 20 pls. [39.1 43.1 43.6 47.7]

AUCTION CATALOGUE SOTHEBY - 1947a - Catalogue of fine English and Continental glass including . . . a fine stippled wine glass by Frans Greenwood. 6.VI.1947. -- London (Sotheby). 16 pp., 9 pls. [*47.4]

AUCTION CATALOGUE SOTHEBY - 1947b - Catalogue of the celebrated collection of old English glass, the third and last portion, the property of Henry Brown. 14.XI.1947. -- London (Sotheby). 23 pp., 13 pls. [46.7]

AUCTION CATALOGUE SOTHEBY - 1957 - Catalogue of English glass, fine Continental glass. 30.VII.1957. -- London (Sotheby). 26 pp. [*41.2]

AUCTION CATALOGUE SOTHEBY - 1974 - Catalogue of fine English and Continental glass comprising . . . two very rare unrecorded stippled goblets by Frans Greenwood, signed, one dated 1742. 3.VI.1974. -- London (Sotheby). 45 pp., 12 pls. [42.1 *44.1]

AUCTION CATALOGUE SOTHEBY - 1987 - English and Continental glass and paperweights. 13.VII.1987. -- London (Sotheby). 87 pp., illus. [45.1]

AUCTION CATALOGUE SOTHEBY MAK VAN WAAY - 1984 - Catalogus 386. Decorative arts. 1.X.1984. -- Amsterdam (Sotheby Mak van Waay B.V.). 56 pp., illus. [45.1]

AVERY, C. L. - 1928 - German and Dutch glass from the Mühsam collection. -- Bull. Metropol. Mus. Art, New York 23 (1): 3-15, figs. 1-13 [28.3]

AVERY, C. L. - 1936 - In: A special exhibition of glass from the museum collections. -- New York (The Metropolitan Museum of Art). 45 pp., 1 col. pl., 41 pls. [28.3]

BATE, P. - 1905 - English table glass. -- London (George Newnes Ltd) & New York (Charles Scribner's Sons). xiii+130 pp., 67 pls. (Re-issued by B. T. Batsford, London, 1913). [38.1]

BENNETT, B. - 1928 - The Mr. and Mrs. Julius Rosenwald collection of glass. -- Bull. Art Inst. Chicago 22 (4): 46-55, figs. 1-10 [49.1]

BERRYER, A.-M. - 1954 - Enrichissement du département de la verrerie. -- Bull. Mus. royaux Art Hist. (4) 26: 32-64, figs. 1-24 [43.6 46.2 46.4 47.2 49.1]

BERRYER, A.-M. - 1957 - La verrerie ancienne aux Musées Royaux d'Art et d'Histoire. -- Bruxelles. 131 pp., 29 figs., 46 pls. [47.2]

BERRYER, A.-M. - 1958 - La verrerie du moyen âge et des temps modernes. -- In: Trois millénaires d'art verrier à travers les collections publiques et privées de Belgique. Catalogue général de l'exposition. -- Liège (Musée Curtius): 105-260, illus. [47.2]

BEYDALS, P. - [1952] - Verslag omtrent de toestand en de aanwinsten van het Historisch Museum over het jaar 1951. -- Rotterdam. 5 pp. [47.5]

BLES, J. - 1924 - Rare English glasses of the XVII & XVIII centuries. -- London (Geoffrey Bles). 269 pp., frontispiece, 100 pls. [*47.6 *47.8]

BOHN, H. G. - 1857, 1862, 1876 - A guide to the knowledge of pottery, porcelain, and other objects of vertu. Comprising an illustrated catalogue of the Bernal collection of works of art, with the prices at which they were sold by auction, and the names of the present possessors. -- London (H. G. Bohn). (Ed. 2: 1862; Ed. 3 [G. Bell & Sons]: 1876). xxxviii+504 pp., illus. [*46.6]

BOL, L. J. - 1960 - Herdenkingstentoonstelling Aart Schouman 1710-1792. -- Dordrecht (Dordrecht's Museum). 96 pp., figs. 1-64 [*28.2 43.4 47.3 A]

BOLTEN, D. - 1957 - Breekbaar licht. Oud en nieuw glas. -- Delft (Museum Het Prinsenhof). [44] pp., 39 figs. [24.1]

BOLTEN, D. - 1969 - Een glasie van vrienschap. De glazen van de collectie Guépin. -- Delft (Museum Het Prinsenhof). 52 pp., 52 figs. [A]

BRAAT, W. C. - 1962 - Collections de verres des Pays-Bas. -- Bull. Journées int. Verre 1: 13-51, figs. 1-70 [22.1 24.1 41.1 42.2 43.3 46.1 47.1 47.7 48.3]

BRINCKMANN, J. - 1894 - Das Hamburgische Museum für Kunst und Gewerbe. Ein Führer durch die Sammlungen zugleich ein Handbuch der Geschichte des Kunstgewerbes. -- Hamburg. xviii+828 pp., illus. [46.8]

BUCKLEY, B. T. - 1935 - A further supplement to monograph on Frans Greenwood published in 1930. In: W. Buckley, D. Wolff and the glasses that he engraved. -- London (Methuen & Co. Ltd): 39, 41, pl. 25 [55.1]

BUCKLEY, W. - 1926 - European glass. A brief outline of the history of glass making, with notes on various methods of glass decoration, illustrated by examples in the collection of the author. -- London (Ernest Benn Ltd). xxxvi+96 pp., figs. A-L, 1-4, pls. 1-104 (in 35 copies one of the plates in printed in colour). [20.1 28.1]

BUCKLEY, W. - 1929 - Glass. In: Exhibition of Dutch Art 1450-1900. -- London (Royal Academy of Arts). (Eds. 1, 2, 3 - identical): 302-312 [20.1 28.1]

BUCKLEY, W. - 1930a - Glass. In: Commemorative catalogue of the exhibition of Dutch Art held in the galleries of the Royal Academy, Burlington House, London, January - March 1929. -- London (Oxford University Press): 285-295, pls. CXIX, CXX [20.1 28.1]

BUCKLEY, W. - 1930b - Notes on Franz Greenwood and the glasses that he engraved. -- London (Ernest Benn Ltd). (Ed. 1). 14 pp., 30 pls. (This edition of 250 copies was suppressed by the author soon after publication and most of the stock destroyed.) [20.1 22.3 22.4 22.5 24.1 28.1 *28.2 28.3 30.1 38.1 38.3 42.2 43.3 43.4 43.6 46.1 46.2 46.4 *46.6 46.8 47.3 *47.6 *47.8 48.1 48.3 49.1 X.5]

BUCKLEY, W. - 1930c - Notes on Frans Greenwood and the glasses that he engraved. -- London (Ernest Benn Ltd). (Ed. 2). 15 pp., 32 pls. [20.1 22.3 22.4 22.5 24.1 28.1 *28.2 28.3 *28.4 30.1 38.1 38.3 42.2 43.3 43.4 43.6 46.1 46.2 46.4 *46.6 46.8 47.3 *47.6 *47.8 48.1 48.3 49.1 X.5]

BUCKLEY, W. - 1931 - Aert Schouman and the glasses that he engraved. With a supplementary note on glasses engraved by Frans Greenwood. -- London (Ernest Benn Ltd). 50 pp., pl. 1-30 [39.1 43.1 47.1 47.5 47.7 B]

BUCKLEY, W. - 1939 - The art of glass. Illustrated from the Wilfred Buckley collection in the Victoria and Albert Museum, London. -- London (The Phaidon Press). 286 pp., 181 figs. [20.1 28.1 *28.4]

BUECHNER, T. S. - 1957 - Glass drinking vessels in the collection of Jerome Strauss. -- Connoisseur Year Book: 42-47, figs. 1-12 [46.5]

BURTON, J. - 1969 - Glass. Philosophy and methods. Hand-blown, sculptured, colored. -- London (Sir Isaac Pitman & Sons Ltd). 278 pp., 288 figs. [46.7]

CASTRO Dzn, D. H. DE - 1883 - Een en ander over glasgravure. -- Oud-Holland 1 (4): 274-291, 1 pl. [22.4 24.1 43.3 *46.6]

CHARLESTON, R. J. - 1950 - Cut and engraved glass - Part I. -- Pottery & Glass (October): 63-65, figs. 1-6 [*47.4]

CHARLESTON, R. J. - 1957 - Dutch decoration of English glass. -- Trans. Soc. Glass Technol. 41: 229-243, figs. 1-19 [20.1 22.4 28.1]

CHARLESTON, R. J. - 1980 - Masterpieces of glass. A world history from the Corning Museum of Glass. -- New York (Harry N. Abrams, Inc.). 239 pp., col. frontispiece, 2 b/w pls., 102 col. pls. [46.7]

COMSTOCK, H. - 1926 - The Mühsam collection of glass: Part I. -- Int. Studio 85 (355): 39-46, 14 figs. [28.3]

COPPEN-GARDNER, S. - 1975 - A background for glass collectors. -- London (Pelham Books). 172 pp., frontispiece, 19 figs. [*46.6]

DAVIS, D. C. - 1964 - English and Irish antique glass. -- London (A. Baker Ltd). 152 pp., frontispiece, 93 figs. [46.7]

DAVIS, D. C. - 1973 - English glass. In: P. Phillips (ed.), The collector's encyclopedia of antiques. -- London (The Connoisseur): 422-450, illus. [46.7]

DAVIS, F. - 1966 - The Country Life book of glass. -- London (Country Life Ltd). 96 pp., 129 figs. [28.1]

DAVIS, F. - 1974 - Talking about salerooms. Glass as an engraver's medium. -- Country Life 156 (4020): 142-143, figs. 1-6 [42.1]

DAVIS, F. - 1985 - Talking about salerooms. Pottery and potboiling. -- Country Life 178 (4588): 214-215, figs. 1-6 [*44.1]

DILLON, E. - 1907 - Glass. -- London (Methuen & Co.). xxviii+374 pp., 49 pls. [*46.6]

DOMELA NIEUWENHUIS, P. N. H. - 1986 - Kelkglas, Frans Greenwood, 1680 - 1763. -- Verslag 1985 Vereniging Rembrandt (Nat. Fonds Kunstbehoud): 30-31, 1 pl. [44.2]

DREIER, F. A. - 1981 - Die Kunstkammer im 19. Jahrhundert. In: J. Hildebrand & C. Theuerkauff, Die Brandenburgisch - Preussische Kunstkammer. Eine Auswahl aus den alten Beständen. -- Berlin (Staatliche Museen Preussischer Kulturbesitz): 35-44, illus. [22.5]

EBBOTT, R. - 1971 - British glass. -- Melbourne (Oxford University Press). 31 pp., 41 figs. [*47.4]

EDELSTEIN, A. (ed.) - 1974 - Art at auction. The year at Sotheby Parke Bernet. 1973-1974. Two hundred and fortieth season. -- London (Sotheby Parke Bernet Publications). 479 pp., illus. [42.1]

EDWARDS, G. - 1980 - Wine glass. In: A. Brody et al., Decorative arts from the collection of the National Gallery of Victoria. -- Melbourne (National Gallery of Victoria): 45, pl. [*47.4]

ELVILLE, E. M. - 1961 - The collector's dictionary of glass. -- London (Country Life Ltd). 194 pp., col. frontispiece, 275 figs. [20.1]

ESMEYER, A. - 1957 - Glas door de eeuwen. - Old glass. -- 's-Gravenhage (Gemeentemuseum). 55 pp., 24 figs. [47.7]

FALKE, O. VON - 1910 - Führer durch die Königlichen Museen zu Berlin. Das Kunstgewerbemuseum. (Ed. 15). 152 pp., 30 pls. [22.5]

FALKE, O. VON - n. d. - Führer durch das Schlossmuseum. -- Berlin (Reichsdruckerei). 88 pp., pls. I-XXXII [22.5]

FETTWEIS, H. - 1965 - Florilège de la verrerie ancienne. Musées Royaux d'Art et d'Histoire, Bruxelles. 28 pp., 13 col. pls. [47.2]

FETTWEIS, H. - 1970 - Collections de verres de Belgique. Bruxelles (Musées Royaux d'Art et d'Histoire). -- Bull. Assoc. int. Hist. Verre 5: 32-47, figs. 13-43 [47.2]

FLEMING, J. & HONOUR, H. - 1977 - The Penguin dictionary of decorative arts. -- London (Allen Lane, Penguin Books Ltd). 896 pp., illus. [20.1]

FOGG, G. (ed.) - 1987 - Sotheby's art at auction. -- London, New York (Sotheby's Publications). 448 pp., illus. [45.1]

FRIEDRICH, C. - 1884 - Die altdeutschen Gläser. Beitrag zur Terminologie und Geschichte des Glases. -- Nürnberg (G. P. J. Bieling [G. Dietz]). viii+264 pp., 40 figs. [46.2]

GARDNER, P. V. - 1979 - Glass. -- New York (Cooper-Hewitt Museum. The Smithsonian Institution's National Museum of Design). 128 pp., 99 figs., 30 col. pls. [46.7]

GARNIER, E. - 1886 - Histoire de la verrerie et de l'émaillerie. -- Tours (Alfred Mame et Fils). vii+573 pp., col. pls. I-IV, pls. A-D, figs. 1-119 [46.2]

GATEAU, J. C. - 1974 - Die Glaskunst. -- Genève (Bonvent). 127 pp., illus. (also a French edition: La Verrerie). [47.7]

GELDER, H. E. VAN - 1932 - Oud-Hollandsch versierd glas. -- Meded. Dienst Kunst Wetensch. 2 (8): 259-268, figs. 1-18 [47.1]

GELDER, H. E. VAN - 1954 - W. J. H. Mulier, glasverzamelaar. -- Meded. Dienst Schone Kunsten 9 (3-4): 52-54, 90, figs. 1-5 [47.7]

GELDER, H. E. VAN - 1955 - Glas en ceramiek. De kunsten van het vuur. -- Utrecht (W. de Haan N.V.). 125 pp., 32+79 pls. (Glass: 11-46, pls. I-XXXII). [24.1 46.3 48.3]

GELDER, H. E. VAN - 1959 - Glas. In: Th. H. Lunsingh Scheurleer, Sprekend verleden. Wegwijzer voor de verzamelaar van oude kunst en antiek. -- Amsterdam (Scheltema & Holkema N.V.): 71-82, pl. 2, figs. 50-65 [41.1]

GELDER, H. E. VAN & JANSEN, B. - 1969 - Glas in Nederlandse musea. -- Bussum (W. de Haan). 78 pp., 228 figs. [24.1 46.3 48.3]

GERSPACH, E. - 1885 - L'art de la verrerie. -- Paris (A. Quentin). 320 pp., 152 figs. [22.4 24.1]

GLERUM, H. - 1970 - Kunsthandelaar en verzamelaar. Art dealer and collector. Vierde int. Tentoonstelling C.I.N.O.A. -- Amsterdam (Historisch Museum). 316 pp., illus. [43.1]

GOOL, J. VAN - 1751 - De nieuwe schouburg der Nederlantsche Kunstschilders en schilderessen: Waer in de Levens- en Kunstbedryven der tans levende en reets overleedene Schilders, die van Houbraken, noch eenig ander Schryver, zyn aengeteekend, verhaelt worden. -- 's Gravenhage (gedrukt voor den autheur). II. xii+576 pp., pls. A-O

GRAM, J. - 1882 - De Schildersconfrerie Pictura en hare Academie van Beeldende Kunsten te 's-Gravenhage 1682-1882. -- Rotterdam (Elsevier). 136 pp. [B]

GREENWOOD, F. - 1719 - Gedichten van Frans Greenwood. -- Rotterdam (Arnold Willis). [xii+]126[+4] pp., title-pl. [pre-1719]

GREENWOOD, F. - 1760 - Vervolg van F: Greenwoods Gedichten, en Boere= Pinxtervreugt. -- Dordrecht (J: van Braam). [viii+]208[+4] pp., title-pl. & Boere= Pinxtervreugt (Ed. 2). 39 pp., 4 pls. [*38.2 40.1 *41.2 42.1 *43.2 *46.6 47.1 X.2]

HALL, M. VAN - 1976 - Drie glazen van Frans Greenwood. -- Spiegel hist. 11 (5): 308-309, figs. 1-3 [20.1 *28.4 47.8]

HAYNES, E. B. - 1944 - The Greenwood glasses. -- Connoisseur 113: 34-37, 60, figs. I-IX [22.4 22.5 24.1 *28.4 39.1 46.4]

HAYNES, E. B. - 1970 - Glass through the ages. -- Harmondsworth (Penguin Books). (Revised ed.). 310 pp., 96 pls. [*47.6]

HAYWARD, H. - 1960 - Stipple-engraving on glass. The Dutch artists. -- Antique Dealer Coll. Guide 14 (6): 24-26, figs. 1-4 [28.1]

HOËVELL, VAN - 1907 - Geëtste roemer van 1743. -- Navorscher 57: 114 [43.5]

HONEY, W. B. - 1946 - Glass. A handbook for the study of glass vessels of all periods and countries & a guide to the museum collection. -- London (Victoria & Albert Museum). xii+169 pp., 72 pls. [28.1 28.3 *28.4 *46.6 *47.8]

HOOGVLIET, A. - 1753 - Vervolg der mengeldichten van Arnold Hoogvliet. -- Rotterdam (Philippus & Jacobus Losel). [xxvi+]216 pp., 1 pl. [X.5]

HUDIG, C. J. - 1955 - Glas. In: H. E. van Gelder (ed.), Kunstgeschiedenis der Nederlanden van het einde van de zestiende eeuw tot onze tijd in Noord-Nederland. -- Utrecht (W. de Haan N.V.), Antwerpen (N.V. Standaard Boekhandel). (Ed. 3). II: 287-299, figs. 76-88 [43.3]

HUDIG, F. W. - 1926 - Diamond engraving. In: W. Buckley, European glass. -- London (Ernest Benn Ltd): xiv-xxxiv, pls. A-L. (also issued as a privately published reprint: An essay on Dutch glass engravers. -- Plymouth [The Mayflower Press, William Brendon & Son Ltd]. 23 pp., 20 pls.) [20.1 22.3 22.4 22.5 24.1 28.1 28.3 30.1 38.1 38.3 42.2 43.3 46.1 46.2 *46.6 46.8 *47.6 48.3 49.1 *49.2 X.1 X.5]

HUDIG, F. W. - 1929 - Glass at the exhibition of Dutch art. -- Old Furniture 6 (22): 133-140, figs. 1-11 [20.1]

ISINGS, C. - 1966a - Antiek glass. -- Amsterdam (J. H. de Bussy). 278 pp., VIII+129 figs. [30.1]

ISINGS, C. - 1966b - Schönes altes Glass. -- Hannover (Fackelträger-Verlag Schmidt - Küster GmbH). 123 pp., VIII+129 figs. [30.1]

JANSEN, B. - 1962 - Catalogus van Noord- en Zuidnederlands glas. -- Den Haag (Gemeentemuseum). 130 pp., 243 figs. [46.3 47.1 47.7]

JIŘÍK, F. X. - 1933a - Průvodce sbírkou skla. -- Praha (Uměleckoprůmyslové museum). 151 pp., 8 pls. [C]

JIŘÍK, F. X. - 1933b - Führer durch die Glassammlung. -- Prag (Kunstgewerbe-museum). 157 pp., 8 pls. [C]

JIŘÍK, F. X. - 1934 - Guide to the glass collection. -- Prague (Museum of Industrial Art). 127 pp., 8 pls. [C]

K., J. C. - 1865 - Frans Greenwood. -- Navorscher 15: 299 [47.1 X.5]

KÄMPFER, F. & BEYER, K. G. - 1966 - Glass. A world history. The story of 4000 years of fine glass-making. (Translated and revised by E. Launert). -- London (Studio Vista Ltd). 315 pp., 243 pls. [46.8]

LANMON, D. P. - 1980 - English glass from the Strauss collection at The Corning Museum of Glass. -- Apollo 111 (218, N.S.): 310-314, figs. 1-10 [46.5]

LAURENTIUS, TH., NIEMEIJER, J. W. & PLOOS VAN AMSTEL, G. - 1980 - Cornelis Ploos van Amstel. Kunstverzamelaar en prentuitgever. -- Assen (van Gorcum). ix+392 pp., illus.

LENNEP, J. VAN & GOUW, J. TER - 1869 - Het boek der opschriften. Een bijdrage tot de geschiedenis van het Nederlandsche volksleven. -- Amsterdam (Gebr. Kraay). xii+412 pp., illus. [47.1]

LIEFKES, J. R. - 1987 - Museum Mr. Simon van Gijn. Catalogus van de glasverzameling. -- Dordrecht (Museum Mr. Simon van Gijn). 132 pp., [2] col. & [211] b/w illus. [*28.2 44.2]

LLOYD, W. - 1969 - Investing in Georgian glass. -- London (The Cresset Press). 160 pp., illus. (1971 ed. by Barrie & Jenkins Ltd / Gorgi Books). [46.5]

MCNAB DENNIS, J. - 1972 - Dutch decorative arts of the eighteenth century in The Metropolitan Museum of Art. -- Apollo 96 (129, N.S.): 428-437, figs. 1-15 [28.3]

MATCHAM, J. & DREISER, P. - 1982 - The techniques of glass engraving. -- London (B. T. Batsford Ltd). 168 pp., frontispiece, b/w & col. illus. (Corrected reprint: 1983). [20.1]

NAPIER, I. - 1945 - Frans Greenwood and his glasses. -- Trans. Circle Glass Coll. (58): 3 pp. (mimeographed)

NEEVE, B. R. M. DE - 1964 - Dutch engraved glass in the A. J. Guépin collection. -- Apollo 80 (33 N.S.): 379-383, figs. 1-9 [A]

NEEVE, B. R. M. DE - 1967 - Decorative Arts Department at the Boymans - van Beuningen Museum. -- Apollo 86 (65 N.S.): 26-37, figs. 1-37 [48.3]

NEWMAN, H. - 1977 - An illustrated dictionary of glass. -- London (Thames and Hudson Ltd). 351 pp., 17 col. pls., 608 figs. [22.1]

PAREAU, A. M. - 1896 - Beschrijving legaat de Castro. Gegraveerd, geëtst en op andere wijzen versierd glaswerk. -- Jaarverslag Kon. Oudheidk. Gen., Amsterdam 38: 21-51 [43.3]

PAREAU, A. M. - 1900 - Nederlandsche glasgraveurs en glasëtsers en hun werk. -- Jaarverslag Kon. Oudheidk. Gen., Amsterdam 42: 1-72

PAZAUREK, G. E. - 1902 - Die Gläsersammlung des Nordböhmischen Gewerbe= Museums in Reichenberg. -- Leipzig (Karl W. Hiersemann). 27 pp., 18 text-figs., 40 pls. [22.5 43.3 46.2 46.8]

PELLIOT, M. - 1929 - Verres anciens. -- Paris & Bruxelles (G. van Oest). viii+155 pp., 48 pls. [B]

PELLIOT, M. - 1936 - Verres hollandais. -- Revue Art, Paris (3) 70 (373): 75-94, figs. 1-13 [43.6]

RACKHAM, B. - 1930 - [Review of] Notes on Frans Greenwood and the glasses that he engraved. By Wilfred Buckley. -- Burlington Mag. 57 (330): 148

RACKHAM, B. - 1934 - The glass collection of the Victoria and Albert Museum, London. -- Trans. Soc. Glass Technol. 18: 308-322, figs. 1-24 [*47.8]

RIEMSDIJK, B. W. F. VAN - 1897 - Het legaat van Mr. A. J. Enschedé. -- Woord en Beeld: 102-108, figs. I-III

RILEY, N. - 1975 - Highlights. Antique glass in Shropshire. -- Antique Dealer Coll. Guide (June): 147, figs. 5-8 [*44.1]

RISLEY, J. - 1922 - A Frans Greenwood goblet. -- Burlington Mag. 41 (237): 297-298, pl. III [*47.6]

RITSEMA VAN ECK, P. C. - 1980 - Nederlands glas 1600-1800. -- Algem. Geschiedenis Nederlanden 9: 283-288, 528-529, 9 figs. [22.1]

ROBERTSON, R. A. - 1954 - Chats on old glass. -- London (Ernest Benn Ltd). 180 pp., 46 pls. [28.1]

ROBERTSON, R. A. - 1969 - Chats on old glass. -- New York (Dover Publications Inc.) (Revised ed.). xiii+167 pp., 77 pls. [28.1]

ROOSENDAAL, C. J. VAN - 1967 - Een reeks notities bij de herontdekking van twee achttiende-eeuwse Dordtse glazen. -- Antiek 2 (5): 218-221, figs. 1-2 [44.2]

RUEMPOL, A. - 1967 - Flonkering van de wijn. Dordrecht 1300-1800. -- Dordrecht (Museum Mr. Simon van Gijn). 20 pp., 9 pls. [44.2]

SALDERN, A. VON - 1969 - Rare glass from private collections. -- Apollo 89 (86 N.S.): 300-303, illus. [A]

SALDERN, A. VON & HILSCHENZ, H. - 1968 - Meisterwerke der Glaskunst aus internationalem Privatbesitz. -- Düsseldorf (Kunstmuseum). 125 pp., illus. [A]

SAVAGE, G. - 1965a - Glass. -- London (Weidenfeld and Nicolson). 128 pp., 141 figs. (2nd impression: 1969) [20.1 28.1]

SAVAGE, G. - 1965b - Glas. -- Frankfurt am Main (Ariel Verlag). (German translation of 1965a by E. Schindel). 128 pp., 141 figs. [20.1 28.1]

SAVAGE, G. - 1968 - L'art du verre. -- Paris (Librairie Hachette). (French translation of 1965a by J. Carlander). 128 pp., 141 figs. [20.1 28.1]

SAVAGE, G. - 1972 - Glass. -- London, New York, Sydney, Hong Kong (Octopus Books). (New ed. of 1965a). 97 pp., 141 figs. [20.1 28.1]

SAVAGE, G. - 1973 - Glass and glassware. -- London (Octopus Books Ltd). 128 pp., illus. [*46.6]

SAVAGE, G. - 1975 - Glass of the world. -- New York (Galahad Books). 128 pp., frontispiece, illus. [*46.6]

SAVAGE, G. - 1978 - Glass and glassware. -- London (Cathay Books). 128 pp., illus. [*46.6]

SCHACK, C. - 1976 - Die Glaskunst. Ein Handbuch über Herstellung, Sammeln und Gebrauch des Hohlglases. -- München (Keysersche Verlagsbuchhandlung). 344 pp., frontispiece, 8 col. pls., 53 text-figs., 6 maps, 331 figs. [24.1]

SCHLOSSER, I. - 1956 - Das alte Glas. -- Braunschweig (Klinkhardt & Biermann). (Ed. 1). 302 pp., 229 figs., 6 pls. [47.1]

SCHLOSSER, I. - 1965 - Das alte Glas. -- Braunschweig (Klinkhardt & Biermann). (Ed. 2). 388 pp., 311 figs., 20 pls. [47.1]

SCHLOSSER, I. - 1977 - Das alte Glas. -- Braunschweig (Klinkhardt & Biermann). (Ed. 3). 452 pp., 362 figs., 24 pls. [47.1]

SCHMIDT, R. - 1911 - Die gerissenen und punktierten holländischen Gläser und verwandte deutsche Arbeiten. -- Cicerone 3 (21): 817-829, figs. 1-14 [22.5]

SCHMIDT, R. - 1912 - Das Glas. -- Berlin (Georg Reimer). viii+402 pp., 218 figs. [22.5]

SCHMIDT, R. - 1914 - Die Gläser der Sammlung Mühsam. Beschreibender Katalog mit kunstgeschichtlichen Einführungen. -- Berlin (Verlag für Kunstwissenschaft). 81 pp., text-figs., 36 pls. [22.3 22.4 22.5 24.1 28.3 43.3 46.2 *46.6 46.8 49.1]

SCHMIDT, R. - 1922 - Das Glas. -- Berlin & Leipzig (Walter de Gruyter & Co.). (Ed. 2). viii+419 pp., 233 figs. [22.5]

SCHMIDT, R. - 1927 - Europäisches Glas. Die Sammlung Wilfred Buckley. Mit einer Einleitung von Robert Schmidt. -- Berlin (Ernst Wasmuth AG). 48 pp., 104 pls. [20.1 28.1]

SCHNITZER, B. K. - 1978 - Glass at the Fitzwilliam Museum, Cambridge. -- Cambridge (Cambridge University Press). 127 pp., illus. [*41.2]

SCHOTEL, G. D. J. - 1841 - Letter- en oudheidkundige avondstonden. -- Dordrecht (Blussé en van Braam). viii+216 pp.

SCHRIJVER, E. - 1961 - Glas en kristal. Deel I. Van prehistorie tot midden 19e eeuw. -- Bussum (C. A. J. van Dishoeck). (Ed. 1). 120 pp., text-figs., 30 pls. [22.1]

SCHRIJVER, E. - 1963 - Glass and Crystal. I. From earliest times to 1850. -- London (Merlin Press). 134 pp., 32 pls. [22.1]

SCHRIJVER, E. - 1969 - Antiek glas en kristal. -- Bussum (C. A. J. van Dishoeck). (Ed. 4). 144 pp., 32 pls. (Ed. 5: 1972) [22.1]

SCHRIJVER, E. - 1980 - Glas en kristal. -- Haarlem (de Haan). (Ed. 7). 236 pp., frontispiece, 165 text-figs., 8 col. pls. (20 figs.) [48.3]

SLADE, F. - 1871 - Catalogue of the collection of glass formed by Felix Slade, Esq., F. S. A. With notes on the history of glass making, by Alexander Nesbitt, Esq., F. S. A., and an appendix containing a description of other works of art presented or bequeathed by Mr Slade to the nation. (Privately printed and published). [7+]L+184 pp., 259 figs., 22 col. pls. [*46.6]

SMIT, F. G. A. M. - 1982a - Punktierbilder auf Glas. Holländische Meister des gestippten Glases im 18. Jahrhundert. -- Weltkunst 52 (19): 2620-2624, figs. 1-9 [44.2]

SMIT, F. G. A. M. - 1982b - Uniquely Dutch. The story of glass stipple-engraving. -- Glass Engraver 29: 24-35, figs. 1-6 [44.2]

SMIT, F. G. A. M. - 1987 - Frans Greenwood. [Description of his 1722 Vrientschap goblet]. -- Amsterdam (F. Laméris). 4 pp., 6 figs. [22.2]

SNOEP, D. P. & THIELS, C. - 1973 - Adriaen van der Werff. -- Rotterdam (Historisch Museum). 64 pp., 59 figs. [47.7 *47.8]

STEENBERG, E. - 1958 - Glasets historie. In: E. Steenberg & B. Simmingsköld, Glas. -- Stockholm (Bokförlaget Natur och Kultur): 1-239, figs. 1-282 [46.7]

STONE, P. & STONE, J. - 1953 - The pleasure of glass. German and Dutch engraving. -- Antique Dealer Coll. Guide 7 (10): 17-19, 4 figs. [28.1]

STRAUSS, J. - 1955 - Glass drinking vessels from the collection of Jerome Strauss and the Ruth Bryan Strauss Memorial Foundation. A special exhibition. -- Corning, New York (The Corning Museum of Glass of the Corning Glass Center). 140 pp., illus. [46.5]

SWARZENSKI, G. - 1927 - Die Kunstsammlung im Heylshof zu Worms. Beschreibender Katalog. -- Frankfurt am Main (Joseph Baer & Co.). vii+158 pp., pls. I-CXI [55.1]

TAIT, H. - 1968 - Glass in Europe from the middle ages to 1862. In: D. B. Harden et al., Masterpieces of glass. -- London (British Museum): 127-192, figs. 170-269 [*46.6]

THORPE, W. A. - 1927 - The decoration of glasses. -- Apollo 5 (26): 75-82, 11 figs. [28.1]

THORPE, W. A. - 1929 - A history of English and Irish glass. -- London (The Medici Society), Boston (Hale, Cushman & Flint). I: xv+371 pp., 35 figs.; II: xii, pls. I-CLXVIII (A one-volume facsimile edition, also of 500 copies, was issued by Holland Press in 1969) [*47.6]

THORPE, W. A. - 1930 - Frans Greenwood [book review]. -- Connoisseur 86: 324-325, 2 figs. [28.3]

VÁVRA, J. R. - 1953 - Pět tisíc let sklárského díla. Čtení z dějin skla. -- Praha (Orbis). 202+xxxiv pp., 32 col. pls., 405 figs. on 160 pls., 146 text-figs. [28.3]

VÁVRA J. R. - 1954a - Das Glas und die Jahrtausende. -- Praha (Artia). (A translation of J. R. Vávra 1953 by C. & F. Kirschner and E. Stern). 199+xxxv pp., 32 col. pls., 430 figs. on 172 pls., 161 text-figs. [28.3]

VÁVRA, J. R. - 1954b - 5000 Years of glass-making. The history of glass. -- Praha (Artia). (A translation of J. R. Vávra 1953 by I. R. Gottheiner). 191+xxxv pp., 32 col. pls., 430 figs. on 172 pls., 155 text-figs. [28.3]

VOSE, R. H. - 1975 - Glass. The Connoisseur illustrated guides. -- London (The Connoisseur). 222 pp., 8 pls. (figs. 1-32), 390 text-figs. [28.1]

VRIESENDORP, J. - 1901 - Geslacht Vriesendorp. -- Navorscher 51: 547-552

WARREN, P. - 1975 - Engraved by Dutch masters. Glass at Melbourne, Australia. -- Country Life 157 (4066): 1499-1500, figs. 1-8 [*47.4]

WATTS, D. C. - 1986 - Glass. In: E. Drury (ed.), Antiques. -- London (MacMillan): 60-101, illus. [*44.1]

WEISS, G. - 1966 - Ullstein Gläserbuch. Eine Kultur- und Technikgeschichte des Glases. -- Berlin, Frankfurt/M, Wien (Ullstein). 336 pp., 25 text-figs., 271 figs., 16 col. pls., 10 maps (Ed. 1, 2). [46.8]

WEISS, G. - 1968 - Antiek glas. -- Amsterdam / Brussel (Elsevier). (Translation by G. Messelaar). 214 pp., frontispiece, 181 figs. [46.8]

WEISS, G. - 1971 - The book of glass. -- London (Barrie & Jenkins). (Translation by J. Seligman). 354 pp., 25 text-figs., 271 figs., 16 col. pls., 10 maps [46.8]

WEISS, G. - 1972 - Ullstein Gläserbuch. Eine Kultur- und Technikgeschichte des Glases. -- Berlin, Frankfurt/M, Wien (Ullstein). 336 pp., 25 text-figs., 271 figs., 16 col. pls., 10 maps (Ed. 3) [46.8]

WEISS, G. - 1980 - Antiek glas. -- Amsterdam / Brussel (Elsevier). 214 pp., frontispiece, 177 figs., maps [46.8]

WELLENSIEK, H. & KEYSZELITZ, R. - 1974 - Art-price annual 1973-1974. 29 (N.S.) -- Munich (Kunst & Technik Verlags GmbH). 580 pp., illus. [42.1]

WESSELY, J. E. - 1867 - Abraham Blooteling. Verzeichniss seiner Kupferstiche und Schabkunstblätter. -- Leipzig (Rudolph Weigel). 92 pp.

WILKINSON, O. N. - 1968 - Old glass. Manufacture - style - uses. -- London (Ernest Benn Ltd). 200 pp., 14 text-figs., 125 figs. [28.1]

WINCHESTER, A. - 1955 - Three centuries of European glass at the Corning Museum. -- Connoisseur Year Book: 58-65, figs. I-XX [46.7]

WINKWORTH, W. W. - 1923 - A Frans Greenwood goblet. -- Burlington Mag. 42 (239): 106

ZWARTENDIJK, J. - 1919 - Constich glaswerk te Rotterdam. -- Rotterdamsch Jb. (2) 7: 45-56, 3 pls. [42.2]

*   *   *

ILLUSTRATION CREDITS

For reasons of economy and uniformity, descriptions of goblets are illustrated by engraved bowls only; outlines of the entire goblets are shown in Figs. 53 - 56.

Photographs are reproduced by courtesy of:

Rijksmuseum, Amsterdam: Figs. 20, 22, 23, 45, 46, 60, 65-67, 93, 127, 129
Museum Boymans - van Beuningen, Rotterdam: Figs. 21, 74, 91, 125
Historisch Museum, Rotterdam: Figs. 81-83, 120
Gemeentemuseum, 's-Gravenhage: Figs. 105, 114, 122
Koninklijke Bibliotheek, 's-Gravenhage: Fig. 24
Gemeentelijke Archiefdienst, Dordrecht: Figs. 35-37
Mr M. Hudig, Rotterdam: Fig. 124
Fotostudio Roeland Koning, Amstelveen: Figs. 61, 85, 86
A. Molendijk (photographer), Dordrecht: Figs. 47, 51, 69, 98, 100

British Museum, London: Figs. 75, 109, 110
Victoria and Albert Museum, London: Figs. 68, 123
Fitzwilliam Museum, Cambridge: Fig. 87
Christie's (auctioneers), London: Fig. 99
Sotheby's (auctioneers), London: Figs. 90, 97, 101, 112

Stadtarchiv, Worms: Figs. 44, 50, 128

The Art Institute, Chicago: Figs. 49, 126

National Gallery of Victoria, Melbourne: Fig. 119

Illustrations copied from literature:

Anonymous [A. Churchill Ltd] 1947: Fig. 107
J. Bles 1924: Fig. 121
W. Buckley 1930: Figs. 25, 58, 59, 62-64, 70-73, 77, 95, 96, 102-104, 106, 113, 117, 118
W. Buckley 1931: Figs. 78, 79, 92
H. Fettweis 1970: Fig. 116
J. van Gool 1751: Fig. 26

Other illustrations are by the author.

*　　*　　*